Praise for

THE ARTIST'S SIDE HUSTLE

"Stacie Bloomfield has created a launch plan for artists, without calling it that. *The Artist's Side Hustle* gives creatives the tools, mindset, and structure they need to build something real, scalable, and profitable. If you're looking to turn your passion into a business, this book is your blueprint."

—**Jeff Walker**, #1 *New York Times* best-selling author of *Launch*

The ARTIST'S SIDE HUSTLE

The ARTIST'S SIDE HUSTLE

Grow Your Creative Business in Just 5 Hours a Week

STACIE BLOOMFIELD

BUSINESS

HAY HOUSE INDIA
New Delhi • London • Sydney
Carlsbad, California • New York City

Hay House Publishers (India) Pvt Ltd
Muskaan Complex, Plot No. 3, B-2, Vasant Kunj, New Delhi - 110070, India

Hay House LLC, P.O. Box 5100, Carlsbad, CA 92018-5100, USA
Hay House UK Ltd, 1st Floor, Crawford Corner, 91-93 Baker Street, London W1U 6QQ, UK
Hay House Australia Publishing Pty Ltd, 18/36 Ralph St., Alexandria NSW 2015, Australia

Email: contact@hayhouse.co.in
Website: www.hayhouse.co.in

Cover design: Laura Kaucher • *Interior design:* Nick C. Welch
Interior illustrations: Stacie Bloomfield

First published by Hay House India, 2026
10 9 8 7 6 5 4 3 2 1

ISBN 978-93-6611-814-7

Printed at Repro India Limited

MIX
Paper from responsible sources
FSC® C047271
FSC
www.fsc.org

Hay House is committed to a sustainable future for our business, our readers and our planet. This book is made from Forest Stewardship Council® certified paper.

To every artist reading this who's carving out time for creativity between day jobs and family responsibilities: This book is for you.

Your art matters—whether it's happening in the margins of your planner or the minutes between meetings.

Those dreams you've kept hidden? They're not just dreams. They're the first steps of your journey. Keep showing up.

Your creativity isn't optional—it's essential. This is your permission slip to begin.

CONTENTS

INTRODUCTION

Let's kick this off with some honesty: The world is not always kind to artists. And for too long, I internalized that unkindness, becoming my own harshest critic.

One morning, while I was getting ready to give a speech onstage, the unkind voices in my head really let loose. What is it about early mornings that invite a certain kind of gloomy introspection? You've probably been there before: those days when all the negativity you've ever felt or been told about yourself bubbles up and demands your immediate attention. The irony wasn't lost on me: I was simultaneously doubting my own artistic worth while preparing to give career advice to thousands of hopeful creatives, reassuring them that they could make it.

At this point in my life, I had been the owner, illustrator, and chief move-maker at Gingiber, my illustration company, for several years. As I was preparing to embody the best example of patient artistic wisdom I could muster, it felt as if every single hater, social media heckler, and harsh critic I'd ever met were gathered together for a fun brunch date in my brain. And they had *stories to share*, as my most uncomfortable memories came flooding back.

I remembered being six years old and excitedly showing my grandma a rooster I'd drawn in oil pastels—I was so *proud* of my creation. Her response? "You little shithead," she said, using her favorite nickname for me. "You're not very good."

I remembered my middle school art class when I had started to truly think of myself as an artist. After an assignment, I presented a portrait that I'd worked on for weeks in front of the class. My teacher's words stung: "There's a huge difference between being an artist and just copying other people. You should think about that." My people-pleasing muscles worked overtime to fight back tears without seeming rude, but all I said was, "Thank you for your feedback."

I remembered the e-mail I got from an old college friend and fellow art student after I started my Etsy shop. Instead of a hello or congratulations, I was handed an open-faced compliment sandwich: "Your drawings are—*cute*! But don't you kind of feel like a sellout? This isn't really art; it's just a bunch of doodles."

I remembered my new in-law asking to see samples of the baby clothing I was designing. She held up one of my creations (which were already selling well online, by the way) and said, "Stacie, I'd never pay twenty dollars for this." Cool. Thanks for your support and sharing your deep knowledge of the textile and online creative maker world. Love the constructive criticism.

The brunch crowd in my brain kept growing that morning as I was driving to give my presentation about how to make it as an artist. All those memories and doubts were coming along for the ride to ask the same question they always did: "Who on earth would listen to *you* for advice about being an artist? You're a *mess*!"

As I said, I'm my own worst critic. For a long time, every crummy comment thrown my way served only to validate my persistent sense of self-doubt. Eventually, I learned to turn minor cruelties and major setbacks into fuel. I wanted to prove to *myself*—not to anyone else—that I wasn't going to give up, even when quitting seemed easier. I wanted to build something beautiful that belonged only to me. I wanted to be an artist on my own, kinder terms.

I took my first step on my journey as an artist on a different gloomy morning, years earlier. (Like I said, there's something about early mornings.) My opening shift had just started, and I was already exhausted. The espresso machine hissed as I juggled three orders in my head: one venti caramel latte, one tall coffee with room, and one medium mocha with no whip. The drive-through line waits for no woman, and by the end of the day, I'd clock 14 hours on my feet managing a chronically understaffed coffee shop still reeling from the Great Recession.

My chest burned from the caffeine I didn't need but drank anyway, and my heart ached. (I prayed the two weren't related.) In a crib at home, my baby daughter, Violet, was fast asleep. I'd barely see her today—just like yesterday.

This was my life in 2009. Coffee shop manager by day, side hustler by night, and tired mom *all the time*. When it came to my art, all I could muster was scattered creative time in the quiet moments after the house settled into sleep. At that time, Gingiber was just a tiny Etsy shop I'd launched from my dining room table, but it was also my creative outlet—my lifeline. It wasn't much: just a jumble of hand-sewn aprons, simple little felt owls and foxes, and a creative voice that was still finding itself. But it was mine.

I was 24 years old, having spent the previous six years climbing from barista to manager. Alongside the coffee orders and employees, I was also managing my home life with my husband of four years, Nathan. While we loved each other deeply, I realized that our decision to marry relatively young came with some implicit expectations—at least on his family's side.

We got married at 20, while still in college, and afterward they made it clear that I would be personally held responsible for whether Nathan completed graduate school or not. Let that sink in—my husband's academic success (and by extension, his future career) was assigned to me by my new in-laws. (Who doesn't love a good wedding gift?)

So, I did what I always did at that point in my life: I followed the script laid out for me of being a good worker, student, wife. I took on extra shifts at the coffee shop, balanced a full course load, and made sure there was always enough money for tuition and textbooks. When I graduated in December 2007, I thought things might ease up—but a few months later, I was pregnant with Violet.

Nathan was still deep in grad school, so I kept up my heavy workload simply because there was no alternative. By the time Violet was born, it felt like I'd been running on fumes for years. Some days I'd wake up at 4 A.M. and not get home until midnight. I missed so many of Violet's firsts—moments I'll never get back. And yet, in those tiny pockets of time when the world slowed down, I turned to creativity to fill the cracks in my heart. I sketched a little deer, embroidered it onto a onesie, and thought, *What if someone else would buy this?*

Gingiber started small—just five hours a week, squeezed in after my daughter's bedtime or during a rare quiet moment at the dining room table. But unlike everything else in my life at the time, those hours were all mine. I stitched, sketched, and envisioned something bigger than myself, all while riding out a recession, raising a newborn, and managing an all-consuming job. It filled me with hope that my art could transcend being a hobby and become a path toward something new.

In hindsight, those years taught me everything I know about how to grow a side hustle: the grit required to show up for your dreams even when you're bone-tired, the dedication to make time for your creativity even when the world says there isn't any, and the determination to follow through when it feels like the odds are stacked against you.

The world is not always kind to artists. We're inundated with versions of the same message: Art is a pastime, not a profession, and while creativity is nice, it doesn't pay the bills. This message is everywhere—subtle, unrelenting, and demoralizing. It's in the well-meaning advice from family to "get a real job." It's in the stories about "starving artists," where creative success is directly tied to financial struggle. And it's in the absence of visible role models who've created stable, prosperous, fulfilling businesses from their art.

For years I believed this cultural message too. How could I not? My script said I must provide stability for my family, and art was the polar opposite of stability. Through years of late nights, countless rejections, and moments of utter exhaustion, I've learned that this narrative is misguided.

There *can* be stable, thriving businesses for artists. Art can be rewarding both emotionally *and* financially. It's not easy, but it's possible, and it begins with giving your art the care and kindness that the world never did. The simple fact is that many artists lack a blueprint—a collection of examples and principles that teach us not only how to make art, but how to make art *work*. We need a guide to finding a path that's sustainable and fulfilling even when we face doubt and adversity.

I didn't have anyone directing me when I began this process: I was playing it by ear, piecing together lessons from missteps, small wins, and whatever courage I could gather at the time. I wrote this book to be the map I wish I'd had during those early mornings when the house was quiet, but my mind was full of doubt. Throughout these pages, I share stories from my own journey, from artists I've had the privilege of mentoring through my courses and coaching programs, and from colleagues I've stood shoulder to shoulder with over the years—people who have built creative, sustainable businesses through grit, experimentation, and heart. You'll find encouragement, honest dos and don'ts, simple exercises, and clear Action Steps to help you move from planning and perfectionism into steady, confident motion.

Because here's the thing about art: It's versatile. It can grow and flourish in the most challenging conditions, because your art *wants to exist in the world*. It can survive (and thrive) as a side hustle, because slow and steady progress is how everything good gets rolling.

It's okay to not have everything figured out. You don't need to question whether your art can be significant and profitable. Trust that it can be. Know that right now, you're closer to that moment than you probably realize.

1

HOW ART BUSINESSES FAIL

Everywhere you look, someone's preaching about side hustles. You know the pitch: *Rise and grind! Turn your passion into profit! Build your empire while you sleep!* They make it sound so simple—just work harder and dream bigger, and success will follow.

If you're reading this book, you're probably currently making art as a side hustle or want to start doing so soon. You may even hope this could grow into a stable business that can support yourself and your family. (*Also,* you probably have great taste in books!)

Put simply, creating a side hustle means you're building a business on top of another job. Would you believe me if I said that it is not, in fact, all sunshine and daffodils? Every scrappy success story comes with long periods of doubt, anxiety, and frustration. At any moment, you might succumb to the temptation to give up, go grab your kid's stash of leftover Halloween candy, and trick-or-treat yourself to some self-pity. I've been there. I, too, have struggled with the pressure—oh, the *pressure*—to build something worthwhile in the margins of my day. It's freaking hard to not give in to thoughts of imminent, crushing failure, and the self-doubt that seeps into your mind in their wake.

The truth is side hustling takes much more than talent—it takes tenacity, grit, and *strategy*. When creative businesses fail, it's rarely because they aren't creative enough.

I've worked with thousands of artists who were starting from where you are right now. After two decades of doing this, I've come to recognize some common themes that make side hustles work. I've also seen the same handful of traps ensnare artists over and over again as they make the transition from dreaming to doing. By learning to recognize these pitfalls, we can conquer them.

Let's dive into four most common failure points I regularly see derailing art side hustles. The good news is that each of these is avoidable as long as you know what to look for. After each obstacle, I also describe simple action steps to overcome them and *live artfully* so you can focus on helping your side hustle kick butt and take names (in that order).

FAILURE POINT #1: NOT SHARING YOUR ARTWORK

Imagine that you have just completed your best work yet. Your pulse quickens at the prospect of posting it on social media—and then the doubt sets in. *What if no one likes it? What if they say it isn't good enough? What if they tell me* I'm *not enough?* You rally the courage to post it anyway. *Why is no one liking it? Maybe I need to give it longer than a minute...* You finally delete it, hoping nobody notices.

Sound familiar? Of course it does. It's a true story—about *me.*

It's exciting to be in the thick of creating something! But sharing it with the world? Holding up a little piece of yourself and hoping it connects with others? That takes vulnerability.

As side hustlers, the art we create feels deeply intimate because it emerges from precious moments carved from our busy schedules and because it often reflects our personal stories and dreams. We're staying up late or finding hidden pockets of time to try to do something meaningful with the beautiful mess of our mundane lives. Making art feels safe when it's just for us, but showing it to others takes real courage. That's when those inner doubts start creeping in: *What if I mess up? Can I even do this?* When those questions are swirling in your head, the last thing you want to do is draw attention to your work.

But here's the truth: Fear grows in silence. It flourishes when we allow the voices that criticize us—both internal and external—to dictate our decisions. To *live artfully* is to choose not to be deterred and to let your work speak for you.

I will never forget the first time I shared my art outside of my family or a classroom. It was during high school. I was a member of the student council, and our little crew was in charge of making banners for the homecoming basketball game. With craft paper and shoe-polish applicators, we wrote out supportive slogans, but eventually someone needed to draw our mascot on a banner, big and bold. I was sitting there, heart racing, thinking, *Stacie, you can draw this. You doodle that mascot all the time.*

So, I just began to draw—an enormous warrior's head straight onto the banner. I hoped nobody could tell my hands were shaking. As I finished and stepped back, one of my classmates looked at me and said, "Oh my gosh, *you can really draw*!"

That moment gave me a little bit of confidence. I was Stacie: The One Who Can Really Draw (his words, not mine). It was about more than proving to myself that I could do it; I also received immediate validation in the responses of my classmates. Our banners were a little more artful, in part, thanks to me.

Living artfully means giving each moment its due, however small or imperfect it may seem. If you create art, there will always be critics, and it's normal to want to avoid their scrutiny. But for every critic, there are dozens—perhaps hundreds—of people who will resonate with what you do and love your work. To find those people, you've gotta share your work!

Each time you share your art with the world, you're not just showing what you can do; you're choosing to live artfully, to embrace the joy in creating and connecting. You're not moving in fear of your critics but instead choosing to connect with your future fans. What you're creating is needed in the world. Take that first step.

Action Step:
Live Artfully by Sharing

Sharing your creations can be intimidating! This week, set a goal to share one piece, either on social media or in person. Make it manageable by taking small steps.

- **Select One Piece of Art:** The work doesn't need to be excellent—it just needs to be yours. Consider this act a reminder that your art is worth something.
- **Decide Who and How:** You can show your art in person to someone you trust, such as a friend, partner, or even a co-worker. Or you can post your art online through a personal social media account or one dedicated to your art.
- **Tell the Story:** When you share your work, tell its story! Why did you create it? What inspired your creativity? How did it make you feel?

FAILURE POINT #2: SELLING YOURSELF SHORT (LITERALLY)

Two mental blocks that often sabotage artists' growth are the fear or resistance of *selling* our work and *telling* people about it (marketing). I've seen the same story many times: Someone might have been making art for years, and they've got dozens or even hundreds of canvases painted or digital files of their designs. But ask them to put a price tag on their work? *Nope.* Ask them to share it on social media or tell people what they do? *Double nope.* The very thought makes them cringe, conjuring up images of pushy, sleazy salespeople, the kind who'll say anything to make a quick buck.

Before anyone can buy your art, they need to know it exists, and you need to be willing to sell it. While this may be a hard pill to swallow, here's some sugar to help that medicine go down: Selling your art doesn't have to feel icky. You can do it authentically and in a way that aligns with your values. The way you sell and market your work can be creative and personal—like your art itself.

When we hear the word *sales*, most of us picture something a little (or more than a little) manipulative. We resist the idea of selling our art because it feels like trying to trick people into buying things they don't need. But it isn't about manipulation; it's about connection. Your art tells a story, and somewhere out there is an audience who would love to hear it and pay you money for it. Selling and marketing art is about finding that audience.

Being your own salesperson is scary, but it can also be one of the most rewarding parts of your creative journey. You're not just selling a product; you're sharing a piece of yourself with the world. No one else can tell your story or articulate the nuance behind your "why" like you can.

Think about your favorite little knickknack you've ever purchased. Maybe it's a candle that smells like your grandmother's kitchen or a handmade mug that feels *just right* in your hands. Maybe it's a piece of jewelry that made you feel confident or a painting that brought warmth and coziness to your home. You love it because it delivers something meaningful to you.

That wasn't just a purchase; it was a connection. That's what your art can do for someone else.

Art carries meaning, and *people crave meaning*! Even something as simple as a sticker or a tote bag can enrich someone's everyday life in a tiny, tangible way. Your art is far from disposable; it brings real value to the world, and it's entirely appropriate to get paid for it.

When I started selling, both online and at local craft shows, I wrestled with these same fears. It felt really weird to ask a stranger to give me money for this handmade apron. *What if I'm selling too forcefully? What if they hate me and tell everyone how pushy I was?*

Those doubts crept in constantly. I kept reminding myself that the only way to find out was to try. I had to show up and sell, even though I had no idea how to do it. Because that's what I was there to do—sell my work. And people were there to buy. No one was being misled about the situation.

I started by just talking about what I had made. I talked about my daughter who inspired the owl pillow, because one of her first words was *owl*. I shared what was true and honest with anyone who would listen.

And every sale—every time someone chose to bring my art into their life—helped to quiet those fears just a little more.

Sophie Timms: From Legal Briefs to Embroidery

Sophie Timms, a member of The Creative Hive Mastermind that I run, is another artist whose side hustle journey began almost by accident. In late 2019, Sophie was leading what seemed like a sensible life, working full-time as a paralegal while pursuing her master's in law. During the COVID lockdowns of 2020, a casual Pinterest search for "fun DIY home decor" led her to discover embroidery. While friends dismissed it as just another "old lady craft" phase, Sophie found herself stitching at every possible moment—during lunch breaks, while dinner cooked, and into the evening hours.

Rather than keeping her work private, Sophie took a bold step: She created an Instagram account to share her projects. The response was overwhelming. Within six months, she had 10,000 followers. Her business evolved organically, starting with custom requests through Instagram messages, then setting up an online shop through Etsy.

Her first sale was a custom embroidery hoop for her cousin. "I know it was family," she reflected, "but it was in that moment I realized that people actually enjoyed my art and were willing to display it in their homes!" The real breakthrough came with her first digital pattern sale on Etsy. When she shared her "Choose Happy" design on Instagram, she made three sales on the first day, which were equivalent to half a day's wages from her office job. It was the moment she realized her side hustle could become something more.

Coming from an entrepreneurial family—both her grandfather and father had been their own bosses—Sophie knew running a business was possible and was already familiar

> with the basics. She developed a structured approach to task management, breaking down her goals into monthly, weekly, and daily lists, being careful never to overload any single day. This methodical approach grew her side hustle into a full-time business in less than two years.

I know you feel vulnerable and terrified, but if you want to turn your art into a business, you *must* learn to sell. You can't paint in private and expect people to magically appear at your door, asking to buy your work. You have to show up. You have to put your art where people can see it—and yes, where they can buy it.

Selling doesn't mean becoming someone you're not. You can sell your art with heart, honesty, and integrity. Start by sharing the story behind your work. Why did you create it? What does it mean to you? When you connect with people on a human level, the "ick factor" disappears.

Remember that selling your art isn't about tricking people into buying something they don't want; it's about helping them find something they'll love. It's not just about making money either; it's about giving your work the opportunity to reach the people who need it most. And if you're not putting your work out there, they won't have the chance to fall in love with it.

We have so many—perhaps even *too many*—ways to connect with people today, including social media, digital and physical newsletters, podcasts, word of mouth, referrals, online and physical marketplaces. Heck, once someone even went dumpster diving behind my studio and sold the misprinted calendars they found on their YouTube channel (accidental marketing, anyone?). But none of those platforms matter if you don't start sharing your art there.

Show up. Tell your story. Let people connect with your art in their own way. Live as your authentic self, and let your creativity connect with the world in a way that feels genuine and true to you.

Repeat this mantra until it sinks in: "I am a salesperson—with heart, integrity, and a gift to share."

Action Step:
Live Artfully by Selling

You don't need a fully stocked shop, a fancy display, or a perfect strategy–just start where you are. Right now, you're going to pick one piece of yours to focus on with the intention of selling it.

- **Take the First Small Step:** Consider the different ways to offer your art for sale and choose one simple action to take today. Could you post it in your Instagram stories? Look up local craft markets? Ask your favorite coffee shop if they display work from local artists?
- **Share the Why:** Whether you're posting about your art online or sharing it in person, tell the story behind it. What inspired you? What does this piece mean to you? Stories create connection–and connection often leads to a sale. If you're selling at a market, gallery, or even a local coffee shop, consider including a small card or sign that explains the story behind the piece. Help people see not just *what* you made, but *why* it matters.
- **Create a Simple CTA (Call to Action):** Make it easy for people to take the next step. Online, this might look like adding a link in your account profile or captions such as: "Check out my shop" or "This piece is available–DM me for details." In person, a small sign could say, "Interested in this piece? Just ask!" or "Available for purchase–tap me on the shoulder." Clear, kind invitations are powerful.

FAILURE POINT #3: SQUIRREL SYNDROME

When you cultivate creativity, you will inevitably reach a point where you have an abundance of ideas—more than you know what to do with. It's common for artists in this phase to struggle with maintaining focus and carrying their shiny new ideas to completion. Heck, as you read this section, your cheeks might already be burning because you feel called out. This is a place of healing, not judgment. But you know who you are, and you know exactly what I'm talking about.

You're in the middle of an exciting new creative project when an even more exciting and newer idea buries itself in your brain. One minute, you've said you'll launch a new print shop on Etsy. Suddenly, after listening to a podcast about art licensing, you've abandoned the idea of an Etsy shop and are researching licensing contracts. Maybe you've set aside time to apply to a local holiday craft show—but before you know it, you've got 47 browser tabs and a Pinterest board brimming with inspiration for using a Cricut machine to make decals for water bottles.

Here's the worst part: Ideas are good! Every success you have will start with an idea! The urge to hoard them and chase down every single one to see if it's worthwhile isn't just good for a dopamine rush; it's also good business sense (in theory).

This is Squirrel Syndrome—when every idea feels like a precious, perfect acorn for you to cram inside your skull for the winter.

Ideas are your superpower as a creative, but unless you can maintain the focus to see them through to the end, they'll quickly become your Achilles' heel. If you're constantly chasing new ideas, you're never giving any of them the chance to grow into something real. And for those of us with side hustles, the time we have to devote to our art is precious. When creativity pulls us in too many directions at once, it's easy to feel stuck and overwhelmed. Your side hustle deserves better than abandoned ideas and scattered energy.

I know this struggle too well, because I am the squirreliest squirrel who ever squirreled. (I checked with a zoologist and everything.) My sketchbooks are filled with children's book concepts, tea towel designs, and half-formed dreams of opening an art retreat center. Each of those ideas has a piece of my heart, and from time to time, they turn into real projects. But if I try to do everything at once, I end up finishing nothing. Over time and with great effort, I have learned to think up a zillion great ideas but also home in on the one idea that will move the needle forward for my immediate creative goals.

Now, you might be thinking: *But don't I need to try different things to find what works?* Absolutely! The key difference is between scattered attention and purposeful exploration. To show what that can look like, I spoke with my friend and fellow artist Genna Blackburn, whose creative journey I've followed and admired for years. I knew her story would be the perfect example of how intentional experimentation can lead to clarity and growth.

Genna Blackburn: Finding Purpose Through Structured Play

After eight years at a small design studio doing mostly file prep work, Genna Blackburn felt stuck. She was so frustrated that she nearly abandoned graphic design completely to become a massage therapist. Before making that drastic switch, she started exploring creative side projects during evenings and weekends.

Genna took a methodical approach, choosing projects where each built upon the last, helping her develop skills and discover what truly resonated with her. She designed logos to build her portfolio, taught herself calligraphy for wedding invitations, and worked on everything from business cards to book covers.

"Because these projects existed alongside my full-time job, there was no pressure—just room to play and experiment," Genna explained to me. This freedom allowed her to refine her craft and discover her true passion. Her structured exploration eventually led her to stationery and pattern design, where she found her sweet spot creating greeting cards, art prints, and wrapping paper. By building on each success, she found her calling and transformed from a frustrated graphic designer into a successful illustrator and surface pattern designer.

Genna's story shows us that the opposite of Squirrel Syndrome isn't rigid focus but purposeful exploration. She wasn't randomly chasing every new idea that crossed her path. She tried different things not because she was distracted, but because she was searching. And when she found what clicked, she was ready to commit to it fully.

That's where the Big Squirrel Brain Dump comes in. Here's what I want you to do now:

- **Write It All Down.** Grab a notebook, sticky notes, your notes app, or anything else you can write in. Jot down every shiny, fun, "someday" idea swirling in your head—no judgment, just acorns. Let them pour out, messy and unfiltered. This list is really just for you to capture your creativity at the moment.
- **Put It Away for a Day.** Allocate time to come back and evaluate your notes. So many great ideas—how do you choose? Which one feels the most exciting and practical right now? Which of them aligns with your current goals? (Don't know your current goals? We'll cover that soon!)
- **Pick One Idea.** Highlight or circle one idea. How do you decide which one? The truth is, there's no perfect choice. I'd rather see you committed to focusing on one idea for the next month than spin your wheels trying to pick the perfect idea to pursue. We're looking for direction, not perfection!

Repeat this Big Squirrel Brain Dump whenever you're bursting with ideas and lots of busy work, but not actually completing any projects. We can calm our inner squirrel by focusing on one goal. Make a plan, follow it, and stick with it long enough to see results. Quit too soon, and you'll never know what it could have been.

Eventually, with discipline and enough completed projects under your belt, you'll be able to say yes to inspiration when it strikes again. You can be confident that your brain will know what it takes to see an idea all the way through. Ideas come and go, but the real skill you're building is how to turn bright ideas into finished art.

I have seen way too many talented artists get trapped on the Squirrel Syndrome treadmill. They want to do it all—and so they do nothing. Seeing one idea through to the end generates momentum, and that momentum is what moves side hustles into full-blown businesses. Focus doesn't constrain your creativity; it amplifies your talent and lets your art thrive.

Action Step:
Live Artfully by Starting

You've done your first Big Squirrel Brain Dump and chosen your idea. Now it's time to begin, but without the overwhelm. You don't need a full plan–you just need a starting point.

- **Break It Down:** What's one tiny action you could take toward this idea in the next 24 hours? Maybe it's setting up a folder on your computer, sketching a rough draft, writing a working title, or pulling out supplies.
- **Lower the Stakes:** Don't wait until it's "the perfect time." Start messy. This isn't your final masterpiece–it's a spark.
- **Honor the Beginning:** Mark the start in some small way–light a candle, take a picture of your sketchbook, write the date in your notebook. Make this beginning feel real.

Starting is an act of bravery. You're not committing to the entire staircase–just the first step. Let it be enough.

FAILURE POINT #4: BUILDING WITHOUT A BLUEPRINT

Many artists struggle with something far simpler and more practical than they'd like to admit: They don't know what to *do* on a day-to-day basis, because they don't have a clear plan of action for their business. I have worked with artists who all carry a similar motto in their hearts: "If I just keep making, creating, just doing what feels right to me, everything will work out." Unfortunately, when your energy is undirected, it's more likely to dissipate than to do something useful.

I learned this lesson early with Gingiber. I spent my first year making whatever I felt like for my Etsy shop: felted animals one week, aprons the next, then jumping to art prints. Sure, I was creating, but I wasn't building anything solid. It wasn't until I stopped to map out what was actually selling (those animal illustrations!) and what my customers were asking for that I started seeing real growth.

Just creating is not a bad thing! But that initial momentum of creativity without strategy can take you only so far. Eventually, you'll need to choose a direction and commit. Otherwise, it's all too easy to burn time and energy—as well as confidence and morale—in an unfocused process of trial and error.

This does not mean you need to create a full-blown business plan right now (or even anytime in the near future). Your first attempt at creating a side hustle plan doesn't need to be flawless or complete. Think of it more like the first draft of a blueprint for a house—you need to know what you're building and get the basics right, even if you adjust the design details later.

How do you make a side hustle plan? That's what this whole book is about! But to get started and whet your appetite, I have a simple exercise to help identify your single best next step based on what you're doing now.

Action Step:
Live Artfully by Strategizing

- List everything you've created and shared in the past three months.
- Circle what got the most positive responses.
- Plan your next project based on that feedback, and set a specific date to complete it.
- Share your plan with someone who'll hold you accountable.

If this step seems overwhelming right now, start smaller. Set just one goal, specific and measurable, to accomplish this week. Perhaps it's making three new pieces, opening your Etsy shop, or sending one pitch e-mail. You can build on the momentum of what you started in the previous action step. Break down this week's goal into smaller, achievable tasks—then take the first step.

Your creative side hustle won't be an exact match with mine or anyone else's. And that's the point. Your journey is up to you. Your first step may not seem revolutionary, but it will mark the beginning of something bigger. Take it with courage, and trust that the road will be there as you walk it.

WHY DO WE RISK ALL THE FAILURE, ANYWAY?

Even before it becomes financially self-sustaining, your art side hustle can be a lifeline—not just as a possible source of income, but as a way to prioritize your creativity within an otherwise busy and demanding life. One of the artists I've mentored since 2023, Emily Johnson, offered a beautifully honest glimpse into what it really looks like to grow a creative side hustle while balancing motherhood, exhaustion, and the quiet hope that your art might someday become something more.

Emily Johnson: Painting Beyond the Midnight Hours

Each night, after coaxing her kids to sleep and scrubbing dinner plates, Emily Johnson would spread her watercolors across the kitchen table. Sometimes nights blurred into early mornings as she painted fine floral designs, dreaming that her art would become something more than a late-night hobby.

Her first sale—a set of hand-painted greeting cards—brought a review that called her work "breathtaking." That single piece of feedback ignited something in Emily. Each sale and glowing review provided objective proof that her work had value beyond her kitchen table. Progress wasn't always smooth. She had angry customers and lost sales when she forgot to order more matte black ink for her archival printer and couldn't keep up with growing demand. But even these setbacks showed her business was growing.

Those kitchen-table sessions evolved into a sustainable business that eventually allowed her to dedicate herself to art full-time. Most importantly, she proved that success doesn't require massive chunks of time—it can grow from consistent effort in the margins of a busy life.

Side hustles like Emily's aren't just about money. In a very real way, they're about possibility, about making space for your creativity and giving it room to grow.

Side hustles are testing grounds to experiment with all sorts of new mediums, crafts, and styles. And for many, they're also a safe space to sell art without the pressure of high-stakes leaps into full-time entrepreneurship. This last part, especially for those of us with families and loved ones to support, is a crucial factor in why side hustles are an effective tool for launching a business.

Side hustles let you claim your creativity. They can show you that your art really matters and you deserve your wildest dreams, but they're by no means the only way to do so. Let me be clear: Not every artist has to monetize every scrap of their creativity. Creation is deeply personal, and for many the excitement lies in creating without selling. You don't owe your art to anyone but yourself. But if you're reading this, my hunch is you have the same wild dream that I did years ago—you want to make beautiful art *and* have a sustainable career doing it.

Artists don't get a lot of positive messages about making money. If you manage to avoid the fate of the starving artist, you get branded a sellout instead. It's a real Catch-22. But wanting stability from your life as an artist is not selfish or naïve. It's the gas that will propel you to craft a life in line with your passions.

You want your art to go up on someone's wall and be part of their daily joy. You want to find your place in the world—not only artistically, but financially, showing that art can serve as the foundation for the life of your dreams.

Most of the time, the reason artist-run businesses fail is not because they aren't making beautiful, appealing art. They get stuck because fear, distraction, and a lack of direction paralyze the artists in charge of moving them forward. But those obstacles aren't insurmountable—and you've already started to plot your way around them.

Share your art bravely. Embrace the connection that comes when you share your art from an honest place. Focus on how you use your creative energy. And follow through on what you set out to do. Keep those truths in mind, and you're already far wiser than I was when I started out!

Whatever your next move looks like, take it boldly. Trust that every little step takes you closer to where you're supposed to be. The world needs what you have to share, and there's no better time than now to get started.

Before we dive into strategy, we have to start with what's going on inside our heads. A little trip down memory lane will help you uncover your limiting beliefs so you can adopt the mindset you need for success as an artist. In the next chapter, I'll take you back to a moment in my own story that shaped the way I thought about my worth as an artist.

Ready? Then let's plan your path forward—by looking backward!

2

THE ARTIST'S MINDSET

How old were you when you first realized you wanted to be an artist? For me it was when I was three years old, clutching a fat blue crayon in my tiny hand as I sat on the living room floor. I was doodling bulldogs—drawing dogs was kind of my thing back then. But I don't just view that moment as the birth of my life as an artist. It's also one of my formative memories with my dad.

From the time I could hold his giant woodgrain fountain pen in my little hand, drawing was how my dad kept me entertained. I was born with an immune system issue, which means that I couldn't go into the nursery with the other kids at church until I was about four years old. To keep his rambunctious daughter quiet during Sunday service, my dad would pull out the church bulletin, draw a little puppy dog in the margins, and hand me the pen. "Your turn," he'd say.

My job was to copy his drawing as best as I could. Every Sunday, without fail, it became our little game—and even when I wasn't at church, I'd find myself doodling dogs, trying to get them just right. Those moments spent sitting on the living room floor drawing dogs felt safe and secure, like home.

My little brain had it all figured out: *If I could draw puppy dogs and forest animals for the rest of my life, I'd be the happiest person on earth.* And it seemed completely possible to me back then; of *course* I'd grow up to be an artist! Why would I ever do anything else?

But then, I grew up. (Allegedly.) Somewhere along the way, that "anything is possible" mentality started to give way to self-doubt. Suddenly, there were rules and expectations in every corner of the world.

And living creatively? Well, it didn't quite feel as free and fearless as it did before. So, how can anyone find their way back to that magical, creative flow state that was so easy to tap into as a kid?

My journey to that state of mind started with a thought I never let go of, no matter how many setbacks and curveballs were thrown my way as I grew from puppy doodler to coffee shop store manager. It was something like a mantra or an affirmation that I told myself each day: "I am an artist. Even if I don't get to draw every single day. Making art makes me happy. Art lights up my soul. I am an artist." Through the power of repetition, I self-talked myself into an identity that felt true to who I really was. Without realizing it, I had developed the mindset of an artist, even if art was still just a tiny part of my daily life.

For side hustlers in particular—those of us who are building our creative dreams while juggling full-time jobs, raising kids, or managing countless other responsibilities—the right mindset isn't just a form of positive thinking. It is the narrative you use to define and support the actions you take on a daily basis. And the wrong narrative might be the very thing that's holding you back.

It's challenging enough to grow a thriving, side hustle creative business, but it's almost impossible to build anything new if you're clinging to the ancient myth of the "starving artist." That mindset needs to go, like, yesterday.

THE "NOT A REAL JOB" MYTH

Growing up, I learned that being an artist wasn't a "real" career path. I remember being in second grade and hearing adults talk about the mother of one of my classmates. "Oh, she's so *creative*," they'd say, their tone dripping with condescension. "How nice that she's pursuing her little hobby," they'd add, as if her choice to make art was an indulgence rather than a legitimate profession. Despite her success in selling her work, despite her ability to contribute to her family's income, her career wasn't taken seriously—simply because it involved art. I picked up their message loud and clear: Creativity wasn't a valid path to success. The script was already written for me—especially as a girl. Grow up, get married, be a supportive wife, and raise kids. Life outside that tidy little box was unimaginable. When I told people I wanted to grow up to be an artist, the response was almost always the same: "Oh, that's nice. But what's your real plan?" Art could be a cute hobby, but it wasn't something responsible adults pursued as a career.

My parents played into this mindset too, even while claiming to support my dreams. "You can be anything you want!" they'd say—as long as those dreams led to me graduating high school and attending a Christian university within 120 miles of my hometown, just like my sister before me. This condition seriously limited the paths I could see to becoming a professional artist on my terms. They saw my talent, and supported my love of drawing, but like many parents, they couldn't imagine a stable career for an artist. It didn't fit society's definition of a "real" job, so it didn't fit the future they wanted for me.

The stories we tell about famous artists reinforce this narrative. Take Vincent van Gogh. In the popular imagination we tend to focus on how he was misunderstood and unappreciated in his lifetime, as if suffering was the price of pursuing art. The message is clear: Choosing art means choosing struggle.

Even as an adult, this narrative was inescapable. When I opened my first Etsy shop, one family member—bless her heart—said, "If only you had gotten a degree in art education, then you could actually have a real career." *Ouch*. That stung. I had spent my whole life watching art bring joy to others: I loved the way children's faces lit up when they saw my animal drawings, how my high school friends treasured the portraits I made them, even how my coffee shop customers smiled at the chalk art I created for the menu board. Every day I saw evidence that art had real value, that it could touch hearts and transform spaces. To have someone close to me dismiss all of that as unmarketable—as somehow *fake*—felt like a slap in the face. Again, she couldn't imagine a future for an artist and assumed I shouldn't be able to either. Her comment lit a fire in me, because I finally recognized how damaging and limiting this mindset had become for myself and countless others.

The starving artist myth is more than just a cliché—it's a toxic narrative that sneaks into our minds and sets up camp. It tells us that art isn't worth pursuing, that creativity is frivolous, and that being an artist means choosing a life of struggle and sacrifice. It whispers:

"You'll never make it. No one will ever pay you for this." Over time, those words sink in and leave an impression.

It's a story that convinces us to dream small, doubt ourselves, give up before we ever really start. And for a long time, I believed it. I let it hold me back. But here's what I've learned: *It's not true.*

This idea that art isn't a valid career choice—that it's somehow less legitimate than other professions—is a trap that keeps too many talented artists from pursuing their true calling. But art isn't just a hobby or a "side thing." It's a career that requires skill, dedication, and business savvy, just like any other. And it's time we started treating it that way.

Liz Kohler Brown: From Service Desk to Artist Success

In 2016, Liz Kohler Brown found herself at a creative crossroads. She had spent years studying art in college, investing thousands of dollars in tuition, yet somehow ended up working a 40-hour-a-week customer service job that drained her energy and left her uninspired. At the end of each workday, she barely had the motivation to pick up a pencil, let alone pursue her artistic dreams.

Liz and I got to know each other in 2023 when we were in a mastermind together. She told me, "I knew I needed a drastic life change to get back into my creative work, so I quit my day job, packed everything I needed to survive into a backpack, and moved to Thailand, where I could 'press Reset' on the creative pulse of my life." She had $5,000 in savings, which afforded her a few months of living expenses. With this bold move, she finally had the time and space to focus on her art again, and for the first time in years, Liz started drawing and painting consistently. Everything shifted when she discovered the ease and mobility of creating patterns on her iPad. She uploaded a simple design to Spoonflower, an online shop where people can purchase designs from independent artists to be printed on fabrics. She wasn't expecting much to come of it. But then she received her first tiny sale—and a revelation.

"Until that moment, I never really believed that some unknown person on the Internet would actually buy my art and that I would get paid for it," she said. It was just five dollars, but it proved that making money from her art was possible.

From there, Liz kept going. At first, the earnings from her designs were barely enough to buy a cup of coffee while she worked. But after six months, she was bringing in $500 a month—enough to cover all her food—and that number kept climbing. Several years and hundreds of designs later, she surpassed her former desk job salary, making over $40,000 per year from her art.

Liz has since moved back to the United States and currently works from a tiny house art studio in her backyard, creating designs that make her excited to get out of bed each morning. Her journey wasn't instant or effortless, but it reinforced a lesson that every artist needs to hear: Success is a process, not a moment.

FROM STARVING TO STRIVING: THE MINDSET SHIFT

Art is valuable. Creativity is a powerful asset. And there are *so* many ways to make money as an artist. Once I started to see through the lie, I began to notice opportunities everywhere. And I had a new thought on repeat in my brain: "Don't tell me that I can't be an artist! That's not for you to decide."

I sold my first works of art to strangers at a Switchfoot concert when I was 15 years old. (Because really, what other type of concert would a wannabe emo Christian teen attend in the early 2000s? It was either that or a Relient K show.) I'd made custom T-shirts with hand-drawn portraits of the band for my friends and me to wear, officially crossing the line into "devoted superfan" in the process.

Mid-concert, someone tapped me on the shoulder, pointed to my shirt, and asked, "Where did you get that?" When I told them I'd made it myself, they enthusiastically said they'd pay me to make another one for them. One week later, I was swapping band shirts for cash at the mall. Forget dealing drugs—I was dealing art. I would draw portraits of my friends, and they paid me! As I made my way through high school, I realized that art wasn't just something I loved doing; it was a skill people valued enough to pay for.

I learned about defending the value of art the hard way in college, when I made a giant intaglio print of Albert Einstein for my printmaking class. A classmate loved it so much that they asked if they could have a copy for $100. I agreed to the price; they took the print—and conveniently forgot to pay me. So, naturally, a friend of mine snuck into their dorm room, "liberated" the print, and brought it back to me. I had gone from art dealer to (justified) art thief in just a few short years and learned that art—and boundaries—have value.

These experiences taught me something crucial: The starving artist myth only has power if you let it. Yes, society might undervalue art. Yes, rejection and doubt are part of the journey. But here's the truth: People want art. They're willing to pay for it. And your creativity has real, tangible worth.

The myth of the starving artist tells us to give up. To shrink. To believe we're not enough. But I'm here to tell you about a different path: The Striving Artist lifestyle. While the starving artist accepts limitations, the striving artist sees possibilities. While the starving artist struggles alone, the striving artist builds connections. While the starving artist suffers for their art, the striving artist strategizes for success.

There are countless myths and cultural narratives that are pushed on us that try to keep us in that starving artist mentality.

- Artists shouldn't "sell out" or focus on making money.
- True art is created purely for passion, not profit.
- Artists are scatterbrained, chaotic, and terrible at managing the "business" side of their craft.
- True art comes from pain, and you have to struggle emotionally, financially, or mentally to create anything worthwhile.

These beliefs are enough to make even the brightest of creative talents wither on the vine. This narrative of the struggling artist doesn't just limit those of us trying to make art—it gives everyone else permission to dismiss creative work as frivolous or unsustainable. It serves those who profit from creative voices by undervaluing their work, and it keeps talented artists from even trying to build something meaningful. Every time someone decides not to pursue their artistic dreams because "it's not practical," this limiting story claims another victim.

But the reality is that the world needs striving artists now more than ever. Art brings joy, meaning, and connection—and that is priceless. There is a place for your art in the world. You have something to say, and someone out there will be enriched by hearing it.

Once I let go of the starving artist narrative and embraced the striving artist mindset, everything changed. Barriers gave way to potentialities. I began to believe not just in the value of my art, but also in my ability to build a life around it.

When we change our way of thinking, that's when pieces begin to fall into place. A positive mindset promotes curiosity, openness, and a willingness to experiment. It helps us shrug off the sting of criticism and withstand the inevitable ups and downs of a creative life. With a resourceful mindset, we are able to recover from disappointments, learn from failure, and have the audacity to adapt. That's what being a striving artist is all about.

HOW A MINDSET CHANGES EVERYTHING

I used to think growing a creative business was a sprint—a mad dash to make money fast, build momentum, and "arrive" as an artist. I didn't want to waste any time, and I didn't want to prove anyone in my life "right" by not being successful as soon as possible.

When I first launched my Etsy store, I was convinced that success would come quickly if I just worked hard enough. While some weeks allowed for longer stretches of uninterrupted focus, I often found myself snatching what minutes I could after work, during my baby's naptime, and after bedtime. I'd stay up late, hand sewing aprons and pillows, drawing animals for new art print designs, and then listing them for sale online the next morning, obsessively refreshing my sales page as I waited for orders to flood in. (They didn't.)

Weeks passed, and I had yet to sell anything. I was exhausted, discouraged, and starting to wonder if the world had been right about art not being a reliable way to create any income. I was just throwing ideas against the wall to see what would stick. After another failed attempt to market my work, I broke down crying, feeling like a complete failure.

In that moment of self-loathing, I decided to distract myself by turning on one of my favorite comfort shows, *This American Life*. While looking it up online, I stumbled on a video clip of its host, Ira Glass, being interviewed on Current TV. In what has now become one of his most widely quoted reflections on creativity, he shared an idea that completely reframed my frustration. I'm paraphrasing, but the essence was this:

> *All of us who do creative work, we get into it because we have good taste. But there is this gap. For the first couple years you make stuff, it's just not that good. It's trying to be good, but it's not. But your taste is still killer. And your taste is why your work disappoints you.*

My frustration suddenly took on a new perspective. Did I just need to work at bridging the gap between the work I wanted to create and the skills I currently had? I was trying so many different things in that first Etsy store, not just sewing aprons and pillowcases but also using my new affinity for Adobe Illustrator to scan my pen-and-ink drawings and haphazardly color them. I was pouring every spare minute into my art and my business, but I was trying to skip over the learning phase. You don't become great without putting in the hours of work mastering your medium.

I thought about the countless artists I admired—including the famous artists I've adored since high school, like John Singer Sargent or Fairfield Porter, and the contemporary ones whose designs adorned products on Etsy and fabrics in my local craft stores—and realized their journeys weren't overnight success stories. Theirs were tales of persistent effort, continuous learning, and unwavering belief in their craft. My current struggle wasn't a sign of failure, but a normal part of the creative process.

I also realized that maybe I had some growth to do. Yes, I'd been able to sell portraits in high school, but now I was building something else.

I was trying to become an illustrator, complete with a different style of art making and a digital process that was relatively new to me. Maybe I just needed to keep showing up, learn more about the "market" I was diving into, and work diligently to improve my design skills.

Slowly I began to reframe my expectations. All the minutes I could dedicate to my side hustle didn't seem like much, but they added up to five hours a week—and those hours were stacking up into something meaningful. So what if it was taking me months to do what others could do in a weekend? What mattered was that I kept going. Building an art business isn't a quick, effortless process of instant success; it's all about consistent growth, learning, and adaptation. If I approached my own art side hustle with patience and resilience, I could weather the inevitable challenges. I had to adopt a "slow growth is good growth" mindset, or I was going to collapse in a pile of disappointment and misery.

Now, did I love the long haul of it all? Honestly, some (most) days, I hated it. There were countless times when I wished I could skip to the part where my dreams were fully realized. But success is a marathon, not a sprint. Slow growth meant steadily becoming stronger, more resilient, and more intentional with my identity as an artist over time. The pace may have been slower than I originally imagined, but every step brought me closer to the artist and business owner I wanted to be.

Having the right mindset is the same skill set that helps you handle criticism in the most productive way possible. Because let's be real: Criticism isn't about what other people are saying; it's about the stories we tell ourselves as we hear their words. Even harsh criticism only truly stings when it confirms something you already suspect may be true. By doing the work to shift our mindset, we can reframe those narratives, trust our own inherent value and skills, and maybe even tend to some of those lingering wounds we've been carrying around.

In case you're thinking that sounds like a lot of work—it is. Sometimes, instead of doing the deep work, it's easier to protect ourselves by shrinking the scope of our dreams and aiming lower in our goals. If we don't try too hard, we can't fail, right? If something doesn't go as planned, we've already given ourselves an emotional escape hatch. I know this game all too well, because I've played it for my whole life.

Growing up, I believed that if something didn't succeed after I gave it my all, that failure was also a reflection of my worth. I was raised on the idea that good people succeed and bad people fail, and when I didn't hit the mark, it felt like the universe—or worse, that *I myself*—had done something wrong. So, fast-forward to me trying to sell my art on Etsy, with no idea what I was doing and finding no success. I jumped to that old standby excuse that had become my knee-jerk reaction: I wasn't worthy of calling myself an artist because people weren't instantly in love with my illustrations.

I fell into a pattern. I'd keep my dreams at arm's length, not fully committing to the work I needed to do. I'd tell myself, *It's okay if it doesn't work out—I wasn't really trying that hard anyway. That doesn't count as a failure.* But by refusing to embrace my dreams, I was robbing myself of the joy of giving my art the respect and focus it needed to thrive.

Taking on the title of artist—saying, "This is who I am, and I'm putting myself out there"—is terrifyingly vulnerable. It means risking failure, but it also means giving yourself permission to actually try.

The shift for me happened when I started rewriting the narrative I was telling myself. Failures, setbacks, and slow growth were no longer signs that I wasn't good enough. They were simply proof that my timeline was mine. That's when I started embracing a new mantra: *Slow growth is good growth.* My progress, no matter how slow or "nontraditional," was valid. An artist's identity (much like a wizard) is never late, nor is she early. She arrives precisely when she means to.

The "artist's mindset" isn't about plastering on a fake smile and pretending everything is fine. It's about rethinking how we define success and failure. It's about trusting that every step—and every misstep—is part of your story, and that your story is worth telling.

RECLAIMING YOUR CREATIVE DREAMS

When you begin to dream about what your art can be, when you dare to imagine a life where your actions reflect the deepest parts of yourself, you will come to understand one thing: Honoring yourself and your own creative dreams isn't optional; it's a mandatory component of success. No one else is going to be able to nurture and cultivate your innermost desires. That's all on you.

But if you're anything like me, those moments of self-care and creative expression are the first to go when life gets busy. Trying to develop your true artistic calling and finding the "appropriate" path through life is a full-time job in and of itself. Taking care to prioritize your inner creator is not only crucial for your art, but it's the only way to reach the end of the marathon.

When I was growing up, my older sister was my idol. She was everything I felt I wasn't: confident, funny, effortlessly cool. I, by contrast, was the fidgety, buck-toothed little sister with a perpetually stuffy nose and an obsession with the animated film *101 Dalmatians*. I came up with a plan that was brilliant in its simplicity: I would just copy everything my sister did. Good sisters borrow; great sisters steal (their sibling's identity).

Some things my sister did, I was great at too. Take volleyball, for instance, where my tallness and gangly arms meant I was exceptional at blocking hits from the opposing team. I earned the nickname "The Windmill," and genuinely embraced this shared talent with my sister. Those same traits, however, did me *zero* favors on the cheer squad—and if the others had a nickname for me, I'm glad it never reached my ears.

This was when I started to wonder whether my theory of "If it worked for my sister, it would work for me" was making me happy. My entire sense of self was built on copying what others were doing and trying to win approval by fitting into their mold. But even when I did succeed—straight A's, valedictorian, leadership roles in every (non-cheerleading) club at school—I couldn't shake the feeling that I was playing a part in someone else's story.

I carried that mindset with me into adulthood. After high school, the "right" thing to do was clear: go to college, get married, start a family. So that's exactly what I did. I earned good grades and the bragging rights of "working myself ragged." I was married by 20, and we had a healthy baby girl. From the outside, I ticked every box of success that had been laid out for me since childhood—which didn't include art. I showed them all. I proved to myself I could handle it all. But it didn't feel like *my* life. It felt like a well-worn script that someone else had written for me. And through it all, the urge to create art never left me.

So, I started to make small changes. I drew when I could. I took risks that felt scary but thrilling, like opening my first Etsy store. That's when the mindset shift happened—not in an instant, but over time. I started to realize that building a life rooted in my own passions wasn't just a fleeting pie-in-the-sky dream; it was *necessary*.

Let me tell you, suppressing my creativity, even as an adult, was just like those years when my dad was trying to keep toddler Stacie sitting still during a Sunday service: absolutely impossible and guaranteed to end in total chaos—unless I could draw. When I went too long in between art-creation sessions, I was increasingly on edge, snapping at my poor husband over the tiniest things (sorry, babe!) and scrolling through social media with this weird mix of inspiration and soul-crushing envy.

My creativity wasn't just sitting quietly in the corner. No, it was basically throwing a tantrum, demanding to be heard. I'd find myself doodling on team meeting notes, daydreaming about new product ideas while folding laundry, feeling this constant low-grade creative itch that nothing—not my perfectly organized red planner nor my full-time job—could scratch. I couldn't silence the part of me that wanted to draw, paint, and daydream about a different type of life. A life where I was creating something worthwhile. Something lasting. I wanted to design wallpaper. I wanted to create products that could be sold in stores. I wanted to create book covers. I wanted to draw murals on my walls. I wanted to rip the carpet out of my daughter's nursery and paint the cement floor with a colorful design inspired by the latest issue of *Domino* magazine.

When I wasn't honoring my creative self, I wasn't just unhappy. My creativity wasn't some cute little hobby to be patted on the head and sent to sit in the corner. It was the very oxygen of my soul, and I was slowly suffocating myself by ignoring it. I was an artist. I had to make art. And I slowly came to the conclusion that walking my own path to happiness mattered more than following someone else's trail. Even if I had no idea what it would take to forge my own path, the match was lit. My passion was ignited. I was going to go all in, even if it took me a lifetime to get there.

How often do we shove our own dreams aside to make room for someone else's vision, only to leave them simmering on the back burner for years? And when do we decide it's *finally* time to bring them to the forefront? The longer you delay prioritizing those dreams and goals, the harder it becomes to remember what you wanted in the first place. Self-neglect leads to resentment, regret, and a whole bunch of emotional states that are *terrible* for creativity.

I never truly embraced an authentic, creative life—one rooted in my own passions and desires—until I had the courage to call myself an Artist. I longed to fully step into that identity, but the path wasn't clear. My husband was my biggest cheerleader from the start, but from well-meaning extended family, I heard the familiar concerns about financial stability. Those voices, combined with my own uncertainty, led me to make what felt like the "responsible" choice. So, like countless others, I built my college choices around what seemed practical. I stuffed my dreams into the shape of the socially acceptable creative, the one with a sensible career: I decided to study graphic design.

Graphic design did not excite me—not in the least. That's why it's so important to discover what lights you up. It's not about knowing it all right away; it's about allowing yourself the space to dream and allowing those dreams to change over time. It's about giving yourself permission to treat your own thoughts and goals with the same care and support that you give to *everyone else* in your life.

The rest of this chapter guides you through an exercise about building the unshakable foundation of your art business. Not by buying fancy art supplies or designing a killer Instagram grid (don't worry, we'll get to the tactical stuff later), but by doing the deep, personal work of cultivating self-belief and confidence. (Surprise! It's kind of like therapy!)

I'll walk you through key points to reflect on as you prepare to make real plans and take real steps forward, so you're not just thinking like an artist; you'll be acting like one too!

Sandra Mejia: Building Success Across Two Countries

Sandra Mejia, my friend and fellow illustrator, didn't start her career as a full-time artist. For years, she worked in project management, a job she was good at, but one that never quite felt like her. She longed for a more creative path, but in Colombia, opportunities in illustration and pattern design were scarce. Finding clients was an uphill battle, so she pivoted, designing and producing her own products to sell at craft fairs.

At first, her income was modest—the equivalent of less than $100 a month—but little by little, she built it into something more sustainable. When she finally left her corporate job to pursue art full-time, she sold her car to supplement her savings and give herself a small financial cushion. The transition was anything but smooth, filled with years of trial and error to gain traction. Then, just when she was beginning to see real momentum, she moved to Canada in 2014 and had to start over from scratch.

Reinvention became part of Sandra's journey. The challenges of starting fresh pushed her to explore new opportunities, leading her to licensing and online teaching—two things that ultimately gave her the creative freedom she had always craved. When she first started teaching online, her earnings were small, but by month six, she was making four times what she had in the beginning. Over time, she hit a milestone that once felt impossible: earning in a single month what she had previously made in an entire year.

Now, with over 130,000 students worldwide, Sandra has built a business that allows her to split her time between Colombia and Canada, create work she loves, and share her knowledge with others. Looking back, she realizes that success didn't come from one big breakthrough—it came from showing up, adapting, focusing on what she loved, and being patient in building the business she has today, one step at a time.

"If you're in that messy, uncertain stage right now, keep going; you never know where your art might take you," she said. The best part? She didn't have to follow anyone else's blueprints; she built her own.

EXERCISE:
REFLECTING ON YOUR PERSONAL ROADBLOCKS

Reflection isn't a way of giving yourself a pat on the back; it's a source of fuel for the journey ahead. You can't repair what you can't see, and intentional reflection helps you recognize the challenges that have been holding you back. It's a powerful tool for uncovering and clearing those hidden roadblocks on your creative path, so I've created a guided journaling exercise to help you do exactly that.

You might be thinking: *Can't I just think about this in my head?* Trust me, I've wondered the same—I prefer action to writing! But a groundbreaking neuroscience study from UCLA reveals why writing is a powerful tool for processing emotions. Researchers found that when we put our feelings into words—whether talking with a therapist, writing in a journal, or labeling our emotions—we actually decrease activity in the brain's emotional alarm center (the amygdala).

Lead author Dr. Matthew Lieberman says it like this: "When you put feelings into words, you're essentially hitting the brakes on your emotional responses." Most of us want to skip this step, believing that thinking about something is the same as working through it—but science proves otherwise. Writing creates a tangible map of your inner landscape that thinking alone can't replicate.

Let's get journaling! You won't need much: just paper and something to write with—if you choose to type on a computer, you'll need to print out the pages later—and enough silence and solitude to reflect in peace. I also suggest grabbing your beverage of choice.

This guided journaling activity invites you to pause, dig deep, and get curious about your inner narrative. Through these prompts, you'll uncover the beliefs, patterns, and opportunities that shape your creative journey—and build clarity for what comes next. Plan to spend between 30 and 60 minutes for each step.

As a running example, I will go back in time and complete this exercise as I would have when I first started Gingiber. Picture me in 2009: 22-year-old barista Stacie with more unfinished creative dreams than completed projects. I don't have a lot to visually mark that season of my life. I remember cracking open a watercolor set, only for it to collect dust on my side table, not touched again for months. I recall half-baked ideas for a kids book that never materialized and countless blank pages in notebooks that whispered of potential.

Step 1: Reflecting on the Past Year

What did you accomplish this year? Let's start with the fun stuff of your recent past. Scroll through your camera roll, your Instagram feed, or your planner—wherever you'd find evidence of everything you did over the past 12 months. Did you sell your first product? Open an Etsy shop? Ask a local coffee shop to sell your handmade mugs? Maybe you simply made time to draw consistently while juggling your day job and family. Write down a list of achievements.

2009 Stacie's accomplishments looked something like this:

- I drew during my lunch breaks (sometimes just for 10 minutes)
- I finally organized my art supplies that had been collecting dust
- I hearted three new artists on Etsy who inspired me
- I bought a sketchbook—and actually opened it (progress!)

Some of you will be seasoned artists and others will be just starting out. This isn't about reaching a certain number of items or measuring up to anyone else's standards. Write it all down—no win is too small!

What disappointed you this year? This part is less fun, but it's just as important. Maybe you never got around to attending that pottery class at the community college, or you bought a new sketchbook that went untouched for the whole year. (I'm guilty on both counts, so you're not alone!)

2009 Stacie's disappointments would have looked something like this:

- I did not get the admin job I applied for at the local university art department, for which I wasn't qualified on paper.

- The realization that we couldn't even afford childcare for our daughter and had to ask relatives for a loan, just so I could keep working round the clock, which kept me from spending time with my daughter during her first year. I will never get that time back.
- My sudden diagnosis with an autoimmune disease, probably brought on by the extreme stress of trying to "do it all" for everyone else while never making space to take care of myself.

Write these down in neutral, nonjudgmental words. Remember that these are all disappointments, not "mistakes." You didn't do anything wrong, and these aren't failures; they are clues to what needs your attention going forward.

What did you learn this year? Growth isn't always obvious, but it's always there. Think about where you invested your time and energy. Did you learn a new skill? Take a course? Did you figure out how to set boundaries or streamline your process?

2009 Stacie's lessons looked like this:

- **January:** I learned that I'm most creative in the morning.
- **March:** Comparison is the thief of joy (especially on social media).
- **June:** It's okay to start small—15 minutes of creativity counts.

Try to write one lesson for each month of the year. And remember: If you're just starting, your lessons might be about showing up, being curious, or simply giving yourself permission to try.

Step 2: Uncovering Limiting Beliefs

Not all roadblocks can be willed away with a different mindset. There are extremely valid external blockers—like not having enough hours in the day for your own pursuits, dealing with mental health struggles, or trying to figure out how to afford the next step in your business—that will understandably make it difficult for your business to move forward. But in my experience, the most pervasive roadblocks aren't external; they're the ones we build in our own minds. They show up as limiting beliefs—sneaky saboteurs that whisper things, like *I'm not talented enough to sell my art*, or *I'll never be as successful as [insert former bully who somehow became a lifestyle influencer HERE].*

Limiting beliefs feel like truth, but they're really just fear dressed up in a convincing disguise, like a reverse clown. Fear loves nothing more than to keep us stuck in place.

Let's call them out. Write down three limiting beliefs you've been holding on to. Then, rewrite each one as a liberating truth. Here's an example:

- **Limiting belief:** I'm bad at running an art business.
- **Liberating truth:** I'm *new* at running an art business, and my goals for myself may not have been realistic or fair. I'm learning and growing.

Once I opened my own Etsy store and decided to really *go for it* with my own art business, I struggled with my own collection of limiting beliefs, based on what I assumed it would take for me to become successful. Past Stacie thought, *If I quickly copy everything that every other "successful" artist is doing, I'll get there too.* I was all about speed and quantity and making money. Quality? Who had time for that? My plan was to hustle my way to the finish line, running myself completely ragged until I magically arrived. It had to work!

In a twist that surprised nobody, it didn't work. (Did I learn *nothing* from cheer squad?)

What I didn't realize at the time is that the mindset wasn't just exhausting and unsustainable, it was limiting. I was sprinting down someone else's path to success, and it left no room for my own voice, my own creativity, or my own pace.

The liberating truth I discovered was that success doesn't come from copying someone else's journey. It requires leaning in to what makes you unique. It's about slowing down, focusing on quality over quantity, and building something intentional and sustainable. Once I let go of the belief that I had to "get there" as fast as possible and started creating work that felt true to me, success felt both possible and authentic.

Take your time with this. Use your written words to paint a vivid picture of the future artist you want to embody. Think of this as rewriting the story you tell yourself into one where you're no longer stuck in doubt but moving forward with clarity and confidence.

Step 3: Giving Your Year a Closer Look

Now that we've identified our limiting beliefs, let's do a more expansive dive into the past year of your life. Reflect on these questions to get specific about where you are right now.

How many pieces of art did you make this year? Dig through your sketchbooks, iPad files, or Adobe Illustrator projects. Put it all on paper—even the half-finished stuff. Yes, even the stuff you thought shouldn't count as an "accomplishment" in step 1. You may be shocked by how much you've created—or you find yourself needing to devote time to creation again.

2009 Stacie's creative journey was all over the place:

- 3 half-filled Moleskine journals
- 12 digital doodles on my husband's computer (I didn't yet have one of my own)
- 1 completely abandoned self-portrait that was more "experimental mess" than masterpiece
- Countless screenshots of inspiration designs I'd someday "get around to"

If you're only dreaming of starting, that's fine too. Jot down some dream projects—ideas that spark the most excitement in you. What would you make if time, money, or skill weren't considered?

2009 Stacie's dream projects included the following:

- Reupholstering a hand-me-down sofa with special Japanese fabric I saved up for
- Selling my handmade pillows and art illustrations at a local arts and crafts show
- Decorating my daughter's nursery *so twee and so cute* that it could be featured on the *Apartment Therapy* blog

Your list doesn't have to be perfect. Just acknowledge what you've created, no matter how small or flawed or incomplete.

How did you grow as an artist? I like to make a distinction between growth and lessons. While lessons are insights about your process or mindset, growth is about tangible development in your creative skills.

2009 Stacie's artistic growth looked like:

- Finally getting comfortable with digital illustration tools I'd been intimidated by
- Developing a more consistent drawing style
- Learning to see my "mistakes" as part of the creative process, not failures
- Experimenting with color palettes that felt more authentically "me"

Think about skills you've developed, challenges you've faced, and new techniques you've experimented with. Identify where you've become more confident and intentional in your creative practice. Were you braver with your art this year? Did you try something that scared you? Did you start to trust your creative instincts more?

What are you most proud of? Remember, pride can be small: Maybe you drew consistently for a month or finally shared a piece of art publicly or simply sat down to create when your inner critic was screaming the loudest.

Growth is rarely linear. It's messy, sometimes invisible, but always happening—even when you can't see it.

What is one thing you learned from sharing or selling your art? If you shared your work publicly, what did you learn from the experience? There's always something to learn, whether it's the business side of pricing and marketing or interpersonal skills like how to deal with rejection.

It might be helpful to reinterpret challenges as insights. Instead of "No one wants to buy my art," reframe it to "I'm learning how to communicate the unique value of my work." What surprised you about sharing your art? What felt empowering? What would you do differently next time?

In 2009, my first art sales taught me valuable lessons about more than just making money. I learned that pricing isn't just about covering materials, it's about valuing my time and creative energy. The goal is to turn potential disappointments into stepping stones for growth. It's not about judging yourself; it's about understanding yourself.

In a single sentence, how would you describe this year? If you had to sum up this past year in a single sentence, what would it be? Let this be a reflection of your growth, challenges, and triumphs.

2009 Stacie would've described that year as the year I learned to "Trust the Process."

It was a year of uncertainty—balancing my creative dreams with the reality of a full-time job, a growing family, and the fear that I wasn't doing enough. But instead of forcing everything to happen at once, I focused on small, consistent steps. I created art in the margins of my life, carved out time late at night and early in the mornings, and trusted that steady effort would lead somewhere meaningful. And it did. Looking back, that was the year I proved to myself that slow growth is still growth—and that persistence, even in small doses, can change everything.

Step 4: Your Signposts for the Year Ahead

Now that you've reflected deeply on the past year—your accomplishments, disappointments, limiting beliefs, lessons, and creative growth—it's time to draw out what really matters most. Look back over everything you've written, and choose three key takeaways that feel like they could guide you going forward.

These can be lessons learned, mindset shifts, or reminders that kept surfacing as you worked through the earlier steps. Think of them as *signposts*—the kind you can return to when you're feeling lost or unsure about your next step.

Write down these three signposts and put them somewhere you'll see them often. Stick them to your bathroom mirror, write them on the inside cover of your sketchbook, or do what I do and tape them to your nightstand so they greet you each morning. These simple reminders can keep you moving in the right direction as you continue to navigate your side hustle. Here's what that looked like for me:

2009 Stacie's Signposts:

1. You don't need a perfect plan to begin—just start with what you have.
2. Rest is not laziness. You're allowed to care for yourself.
3. Stop waiting for someone to "discover" you. Show your work.

2024 Stacie's Signposts:

1. Focus on one idea at a time—everything doesn't have to happen this quarter.
2. Let it be fun. Play is a business strategy.
3. Trust your own voice—it's what built this whole thing.

Reflection is incredibly powerful—but only if we use it. Your signposts can become small anchors of clarity when self-doubt or overwhelm starts to creep back in. Don't just read them once—live with them. Let them remind you of who you are and what you're becoming.

I have some bad news. As you build your art business, it will be necessary to experience some fear from time to time. The only way to never feel fear is to never take any risk—and without risk, there is no growth.

In the next chapter, we're going to talk about the many ways fear shows up in your creative journey—and how to stop it from running the show. You'll hear real stories (mine and others'), learn how to quiet your inner critic, and complete two practical exercises to turn self-doubt into action and momentum.

3

HARNESSING FEAR, THE CHAOS GOBLIN

I probably seem confident. People tell me all the time, "Stacie, you're so put together!" or "You're so brave to have built this business." But here's the thing: Confidence didn't get me here—fear did.

Fear manifests differently for all of us. Sometimes you'll freeze and collapse in a heap of imposter syndrome and self-loathing. Sometimes you'll fight by barreling ahead in a situation where better judgment might advise stepping back. Sometimes you'll fawn, saying yes to more than you should in case the opportunities stop coming. Despite their differences, all these response modes have this in common: Left unchecked, they threaten to take away your agency, making you reactive instead of proactive.

To be dominated by fear is to let the Chaos Goblin take over. It means to experience life as something done to you, instead of something you build with purpose.

Although fear will never go away entirely, it can become a tool instead of a roadblock. It is possible to trap the Chaos Goblin on a treadmill and use it as an energy source. That requires first building awareness and naming your challenges clearly so you can start showing up for your creative work with more clarity, courage, and energy. In this chapter, I'll show you how I've encountered fear—and how I've learned to redirect it into something useful. You'll also learn how to harness that same energy as you face your own impostor syndrome, self-doubt, and the creative challenges ahead.

FACING FEAR AND GOING FOR IT ANYWAY—LIVING UNDER IMPOSTOR SYNDROME

It might be strange to hear that fear has been a driver in my career, but hear me out. Fear taught me something crucial about myself—I'm stubborn. Like, really stubborn. When fear whispers, "You can't," my immediate response is, "Watch me try anyway."

That determination, that refusal to let fear have the final say, is the same stubborn drive that kept me practicing in batting cages as a child when I played softball until my dad had to physically drag me home because I knew I could become a slugger; that had me staying up all night drawing that first paid portrait during high school, redrawing those base proportions until they were just right; that wouldn't let me quit even when my first Etsy shop sat empty for weeks. It's not about being fearless—it's about being relentless, and, perhaps, being a little idealistic.

There are a lot of reasons why the projects I've pursued since 2009 shouldn't have worked out, including the bare facts about how often and quickly small businesses go under. But at my core, I might just be naïve enough to believe that maybe I'll be the exception—the one who avoids all the pitfalls. And, if it doesn't work out perfectly, I'm certainly going to learn something along the way (and have a few good stories to share because of my efforts).

I am a fearful, naïve, peppy pessimist who lacks natural self-confidence. So, I try to tune out the negative noise, the innate self-deprecating inner monologue, and *choose* to become laser-focused on my current problem to solve, because I know that I can inch toward my goals as long as I just keep moving forward. One tiny step forward, and sometimes, 100 steps backward.

I wasn't a confident teenager, new mother, or emerging artist. Even after I started selling regularly, every sale felt like a fragile miracle. If a day passed without an order, I panicked. Maybe my art wasn't good enough. Maybe this whole thing was a fluke. I lived in a constant state of hypervigilance, waiting for it all to crumble.

My husband watched as I ripped out pages from my sketchbook, crumpling them into balls and tossing them in the trash. Nothing was ever good enough. I wasn't good enough. There would always be someone more talented, more professional, more savvy, less emotional. Someone who "deserved" success more than I did.

And that, right there, is the cruel voice of imposter syndrome, whispering, *"Who do you think you are?"* It finds a way to twist even your successes into something fleeting, something undeserved. Just like when I copied my sister's path growing up, my imposter syndrome convinced me that the only way to be worthy was to be someone else entirely—someone who had it all figured out, someone who never doubted or struggled. It took years to realize that those doubts weren't proof that I didn't belong; they were just proof that I was growing into something new.

What I didn't understand back then—and what I've learned through years of growth—is that imposter syndrome isn't really about your abilities. It's about fear. And fear, while powerful, isn't the truth. Yes, fear drove me to stay up until 2 A.M. perfecting my drawings, to obsessively check every detail of a product listing three times before publishing, to take every single custom order that came my way even when I was already overwhelmed. That fear-driven determination helped me build something real but also had me spending years feeling like I was running from a shadow, destroying my sketchbooks instead of learning from them, saying yes to everything instead of choosing what was right for me. I was succeeding, but I was exhausted—and worse, I couldn't even enjoy the success because I was terrified it would disappear the moment I stopped sprinting.

It wasn't until I found myself crying over yet another "perfect" piece of art that I realized: Fear could build an empire, but it couldn't build a life I actually wanted to live in. And fear of missing an opportunity also means that we aren't always making decisions from the strongest, most secure, or even most rational place. Case in point: my accidental boob bear licensing project.

THE BOOB BEAR, OR LESSONS FROM FOMO

By 2017, Gingiber had blossomed from a scrappy side hustle into a thriving career. I'd diversified my income streams—selling on Etsy, managing my own website (hello, real domain!), and breaking into wholesale markets thanks to my sister's hard work. My products were featured by big names like Martha Stewart Online, and I'd scored a licensing deal with Crate & Kids. From the outside it might have seemed like I had it all together, and I would have thought so too. Little did I know that a sinus surgery would become the backdrop for one of my most humbling and hilarious professional mistakes, one that could have been avoided had I addressed my fears of missing out on an opportunity.

Picture me less than 24 hours out of surgery, sitting in bed, watching *Anne with an E* on Netflix, fighting off a haze of medication-induced exhaustion. Should I have been resting? Yes. But instead, I was getting downright twitchy sitting still. With three kids—Violet, Lucy, and Dexter—I had very little time for myself, since I was still perpetuating the "do it all or else everything will fall apart" mentality. I didn't know how to let go and *allow* my body to rest.

Then, my phone buzzed with an e-mail from a client asking if I had time to take on a new project—a children's play mat shaped like a polar bear. Excited to jump on the opportunity, and with a heaping serving of FOMO (fear of missing out), I grabbed my sketchbook, cranked out a few thumbnail sketches, and sent them off. A few days later I received a reply from my client that will live in infamy:

> Stacie . . . I don't know how to say this, but what you've drawn looks like a bear with *very saggy boobs.* I'm not sure how this would work as a children's play mat. . . . Is this what you intended to submit?

Mortified, I opened the sketches I'd sent and gasped. Sure enough, what I intended to be a charming front-facing bear with long legs and round paws looked . . . anatomically inappropriate. My fear-driven ambition that led me to say yes to every project—along with the painkillers—had betrayed me.

I could've let this sink me. I could've let it validate all my lingering doubts about being a "real" professional artist. Instead, I decided to own it. I replied to the client, explaining the situation with honesty and a dose of self-deprecating humor. Thankfully, they laughed it off and gave me a second chance. In the end, the product turned out beautiful and became part of one of their future collections.

This experience, embarrassing as it is, taught me some invaluable lessons. The first is to not, under any circumstances, respond to client e-mails 24 hours post-surgery while on painkillers. Most importantly, I learned that mistakes are inevitable, but how we respond to them matters far more than the mistake itself. I could've let the fear of messing up paralyze me. I could've spiraled into imposter syndrome and wondered if I even deserved to have this career. Instead, I chose to acknowledge it, learn from it, and keep going.

Mistakes don't define you; they shape you. Sometimes they even make you laugh years later when you realize how far you've come.

TURNING THE TABLES ON SELF-DOUBT

Imposter syndrome doesn't go away just because you hit a milestone or even build a business that can fully pay your bills. Every new level of success brings a new set of "what-ifs." And that's okay.

When you try something new—whether it's sharing your first piece of art or launching your hundredth product—that flutter of uncertainty is natural. It's your inner artist saying *this matters to me*. But there's a crucial difference between productive self-doubt and paralyzing fear. Self-doubt asks, "How can I make this better?" while fear declares "This will never be good enough." Self-doubt motivates you to double-check your work; fear convinces you to hide it entirely. It's imperative that we recognize when that helpful flutter of uncertainty transforms into a limiting belief—when "I hope people like this new design" becomes "I'll never be able to succeed at this."

Self-doubt is a natural byproduct of growth, and a signal that you're stepping out of your comfort zone. Acknowledging its presence is great—but you can't let it freeze you. You can't let it convince you that one flop means failure or that you're unworthy of the room you've walked into. Self-doubt makes that jump from "stomach butterflies" to "paralyzing fear" when you allow yourself to think (and act) as if the worst outcome has *already happened*.

For most of us, it takes an active effort to stop this transformation from taking place. When you create, whether it's an art piece or a business plan, you are taking a risk. *What if I fail? What if I never succeed again?* The reality is that, yes, sometimes we take a risk, and it doesn't work out. *That's what makes it risky!*

But creative risk isn't like playing the lottery. If you're intentionally learning from your own experience and from that of others, you can bring that risk down and find a path to consistent success. Fear brings this cycle to a halt when we let it stop us from trying again. No one learns, no one grows. When you harness the Chaos Goblin, you can continue your creative pursuits even through the doubts, challenges, and mistakes. (Even the most successful artists—the ones you admire—have had their own *saggy bear* moments.) Take beloved artist, Oana Befort, member of my Creative Hive Mastermind and owner of Botanica Paper Co.

Oana Befort: Turning Fear into Creative Fuel

Oana Befort's creative journey began at a crossroads. She was expecting her first child, and the "safe" path was obvious: stay at her design job at a large ad agency, collect her steady paycheck, and prepare for maternity leave. But she was burnt out, and every day spent creating other people's visions left her feeling hollower. "The fear of staying stuck was eventually greater than the fear of leaving," she recalled.

She made the bold decision to quit, even though she worried about stability. Yet there was something refreshing about charting a new creative path, free from the confines of what others called a "real job." She started small, taking on logo design projects while learning to navigate motherhood. As she sketched during precious naptime hours or in the evening's calm, she could see that her creative path was right—she simply needed to trust it more fully.

Moments of doubt arose again when she began sharing her work. Friends who had once supported her creative dreams now questioned her choices. "You're ruining your career," they warned. "You're wasting six years of college by not having a real job." Even strangers online debated whether her work qualified as art. Though criticism weighed on her heart, an inner peace remained steadfast, eventually drowning out all those doubtful voices.

Instead of letting those voices paralyze her, she began to see them differently. "Nastiness is often bred from jealousy," she realized. "People who are secure in their own choices rarely feel the need to tear down others' dreams." This insight became a turning point. Each criticism transformed from a weight into fuel, pushing her to prove what was possible.

Her first art print sale on Etsy in August 2012 marked a crucial shift. It wasn't about the money; it was proof that someone connected with her vision enough to pay for it. Two major milestones followed: moving from Romania to the United States in 2016 and launching her Shopify store, which gave her business a more unified, professional image. The first time a wholesale representative approached her in 2019, she faced a new fear: Was she ready to scale? Instead of letting that fear hold her back, she used it to push herself to create products she herself would want to use.

Looking back, Oana sees how fear shaped her early decisions. "At first, I said yes to every project because I was afraid the opportunities would stop coming. I wish I'd taken more time to figure out my direction." Her early lack of confidence, amplified by negative voices around her, was her biggest roadblock. But through faith and determination, she learned to distinguish between the fear that holds you back and the fear that pushes you forward.

Her husband remained her strongest supporter through it all, believing in her dream from the moment he encouraged her to quit her job. His unwavering support helped her see that she didn't need everyone to believe in her; she just needed to believe in herself enough to keep going.

Today, Oana works more hours than she ever did at the agency, but it feels entirely different. "When you're working hard on someone else's dream, it drains you," she explained. "When you're working hard on your own dream, it fills you up." She's learned to give herself grace, to rest properly, to find joy in the process rather than just the outcome. Most importantly, she's learned that fear doesn't have to be an enemy—it can be a compass, pointing you toward what matters most.

That compass has led her to create Botanica Paper Co., an acclaimed stationery company where she blends her Romanian roots with botanical inspiration. It's a perfect full-circle moment for someone who grew up collecting greeting cards from far-away family members and hand-painting cards for loved ones. Her childhood passion, once shadowed by fear and doubt, has bloomed into a thriving business that allows her to collaborate with prestigious companies while staying true to her artistic vision.

FEELINGS ARE SIGNPOSTS, NOT EVIDENCE

Feelings can be positive or negative, but they do not have the last word on the truth. I think of feelings as indicators toward a deeper truth, like signposts along a hiking trail. It's entirely rational to fear failure and can even be helpful if that feeling spurs you to constructive action. But fearing failure is not the same as *experiencing* failure.

Instead of allowing a feeling to lead you down a path of worst-case scenarios, force yourself to consider: *What if everything works out?* To be clear, I am not saying that we should be militantly optimistic and pretend nothing bad can happen. (I am *not* an optimistic person by nature!) I'm simply suggesting that in new, emotionally risky situations, most of us are naturally inclined to focus on the negative. And, if left unchecked, this turns into a limiting belief, which is why we're working to actively interrupt that thought process.

So, if you feel like an imposter when you pitch your portfolio or open an online store to sell your custom works of art, here's what I want you to know: You're exactly where you need to be. That mix of uncertainty and determination you're feeling is not a sign that you're doing something wrong; it's a sign that you're doing something that matters to you.

You have a unique narrative of your artistic journey, and here's what I've learned from mine. Self-doubt can either paralyze you or propel you forward—the difference lies in what you do next. In my early days, that nervous energy of "Am I good enough?" pushed me to double-check every detail, to learn everything I could about my craft, to keep improving. But I had to pair that drive with actual steps forward: sending that first pitch e-mail, listing that first product, sharing that first piece of art.

This is why I say the cure for self-doubt isn't confidence—it's action. Not because action eliminates doubt, but because each step you take transforms that doubt from a wall into a catalyst. Every time you take action in spite of your uncertainty, you're not just moving forward—you're turning that self-doubt into fuel for growth. The following exercises will help you do just that.

EXERCISE 1:
BUILDING YOUR EVIDENCE LIST AGAINST MPOSTER SYNDROME

When the Chaos Goblin starts whispering that you're not enough, it tries to turn normal creative uncertainty into paralyzing fear. Our first line of defense is going to be a concrete list of successes, achievements, and positive feedback we can use as evidence to fight the lies. That's why you need an **Evidence List**.

You might be saying, "But Stacie, I'm new to this—I don't have evidence yet that I can do it!" Did you do the exercises in Chapter 2? If so, surprise! You've already started gathering your evidence. Every accomplishment you listed, every lesson you learned, every challenge you faced—that's all evidence of your capability and commitment.

If you haven't done those exercises yet, I really encourage you to go back and do them now. They're not just helpful for this chapter—they're foundational for the rest of the book. Don't skip the groundwork. It matters. Once you've completed them, come back here and use your responses to create your personalized Evidence List—or use the prompts below to start fresh.

Here's how to build your Evidence List. Imagine you're preparing for the ultimate Technical Challenge in *The Great British Baking Show*, but instead of Paul Hollywood scrutinizing your soggy pie bottoms, it's your inner critic questioning your talent—and they're being far more dramatic than necessary. We're going to collect every bit of evidence that proves you're not just capable; you're **Star Baker** material.

First, grab your journal, a notebook, your phone, your computer, or anything else you'd like to use to write. Then reflect on the following questions and write your answers down.

What skills are you proud of that you've already proven?
Every accomplishment there, from your first sketch to your latest creation, is proof of your capabilities. Maybe you're a natural at color composition, or you've mastered the art of precise line work. These aren't just skills you learned, they're part of who you are. Add these to your evidence list.

I'm encouraging you to look beyond just sales or awards to add to your list. Your evidence can be found in every small step you've taken: that time you shared your art with a friend, the skills you've been quietly developing, even the fact that you're reading this book right now. I want you to recognize your current strengths and the actions you've already taken, even if it feels like you're starting at square one. What challenges have you already overcome?

Think back to those "disappointments" we identified earlier. If you completed the exercises in Chapter 2, now's a good time to revisit them and look for moments where you adapted, learned, or bounced back. Each of those moments is evidence of resilience—and that's something worth celebrating. If you didn't do the earlier exercises, no worries. You can still reflect on these questions right now:

- What obstacles have you pushed through in your art journey or life in general?
- When was a time you wanted to give up, but didn't?
- What setbacks taught you something useful about yourself or your creative work?

Maybe you tweaked your pricing after a slow sales month. Maybe you paused a launch that wasn't ready and gave yourself more time to refine. Maybe you picked your art back up after years of putting it down.

These aren't failures—they're signs of growth. Every time you pivoted, restarted, or faced disappointment and kept going, you proved to yourself that you can navigate difficulty with creativity and strength. Remind yourself of that history. It affirms your ability to keep showing up, even when things don't go perfectly.

What makes you excited to keep creating?
Evidence isn't only about what you've done; it's also about what keeps you moving forward. Your enthusiasm for learning new techniques or exploring different mediums is more than just excitement; it's proof of your commitment to growth. Every new skill you're curious about is a sign that you're thinking like a professional artist.

Maybe you're daydreaming about illustrating a children's book, experimenting with a new digital painting tool like Procreate, joining a local printmaking class, or finally selling at that craft market you've been stalking on Instagram. These sparks of interest are part of your evidence. They show where your creative energy naturally wants to go.

Some of your answers here might echo the signposts you identified in the last chapter. That's great! This is about paying attention to where your motivation is pointing you so you can keep following that energy with intention.

This Evidence List isn't just positive thinking. It's your concrete proof that you can do this—even when imposter syndrome tries to convince you otherwise. Like a perfect pie crust, it's all about building strong layers of support. It's designed to serve as a reminder that, even if you're just in the starting stages, you already have the curiosity, commitment, and creative spark to make this happen.

EXERCISE 2:
CONFRONTING HINDRANCES AND CONSTRAINTS

Fear has a way of allowing problems to feel specific enough to be threatening, but vague enough to prevent us from solving them. Before we can overcome our roadblocks, we need to shine a light on them. This exercise is about naming your obstacles clearly, understanding how they affect you, and developing strategies to move past them. Just like a doctor can't treat an illness without a diagnosis, we can't address our creative roadblocks until we identify exactly what they are.

What single problem do you wish you could put behind you once and for all?
For me, it's my habit of expecting the worst from something good. I've been trying to unlearn this mindset for years, and while I have improved, I would love to completely silence this fear. Instead of thinking, "What if I hit rock bottom?" I'm learning to ask, "What if it all works out?"

What are the three biggest obstacles to your success and happiness at this moment?
Be honest with yourself. Perhaps it's work in progress, lack of time, or self-doubt. If you're side hustling, your roadblocks might be related to limited time, energy, or resources.

Once you've named your challenges, it's time to turn them from abstract fears into actionable problems. For each roadblock you've identified, ask yourself these questions:

- **Is this obstacle temporary or permanent?**

  Often what feels like a permanent limitation (like lack of time) can be addressed with new systems or approaches.

- **What's one small step you can take to chip away at this challenge?**

  For example, if your roadblock is "no time to create," could you start with just 15 minutes of sketching during your lunch break?

- **Who else might have faced this same challenge?**

  Look for artists you admire who've overcome similar obstacles; their solutions might work for you too.

A FOUNDATION TO DREAM UPON

It's not always easy to take the time to reflect, but it's hard work that's always worth doing. Few good things happen by chance. They happen because you've intentionally planned for them and aligned your actions with your goals and values.

Reflection helps you understand what's working, what's not, and where you'd like to go. By conducting an honest and continual evaluation of your life, you'll discover the insights within you to proceed with intention and focus.

Having taken a good, hard look at where you are—your values, your roles, what you are winning at, what you are struggling with—it's time to shift the focus. Reflection allows you to know exactly where you are in the present, so you can dream about where you'll go next. When you get clear about where you are and release yourself to dream big, *that* is when the magic happens. It's time to think big, be a little bold, and paint a vision for the life you want to build and the artist you want to become.

Let's dream a little bigger, shall we?

4

ALLOW YOURSELF TO DREAM BIG

Have you ever had a dream that felt so big, you didn't even know how to start bringing it to life? For me, that dream was writing and illustrating a children's book. For as long as I could remember, I had created my own little illustrated books and stories, but I hadn't seriously considered professionally creating children's books. That was, until Gingiber had really started to gain traction and grow a social media audience, and more and more people started asking me when I would release a children's book. I was six years into my career as an artist (three of those side hustling), making a living designing nursery art. By all accounts, I had everything I needed to make that leap.

Instead of pursuing my dream boldly, I let doubt and arbitrary rules box me in. I told myself: *If it hadn't happened by now, it probably never will.* At the same time, I was receiving a lot of outside advice—and most of it was contradictory. Some people told me, "If it isn't easy, it wasn't meant to be." Others said, "If you really want it, you have to push through no matter what." All those voices got in my head, and the confusion only multiplied my existing self-doubt.

It all came to a head when I put a timeline on my dream, essentially giving the universe an ultimatum: *Make this happen now, or I'm moving on.* Looking back, I can see how flawed (and unfair) that mindset truly was. I wasn't open to the possibility that my ideal timeline wasn't the right one. It was classic all-or-nothing thinking.

Bit by bit, I built walls around my dream out of assumptions that it could be accomplished only in a very specific way. After all, I had yet to attend a prestigious children's publishing conference to network with the "right" people. If I wasn't a part of the proper crowd, surely my dream wouldn't be achievable. I needed to meet the right literary agent for children's books. Also, I believed I needed a new portfolio filled exclusively with whimsical storybook-style art. Even though my nursery art was successful, I convinced myself it wasn't good enough for the children's book world—which really meant that I needed to *reinvent my entire artistic style* rather than trusting my established, authentic creative voice.

My limiting thoughts shifted over time, but the end result was the same: By being dogmatic about how I thought things *should* happen, I was stifling all the other ways they *could* happen. Dreams can't grow and flourish when they're crowded from all sides.

This idea of making a book featuring my art never went away, kept safe in a tiny little part of my mind. I was frustrated and unsure how to move forward. I could see the shape of my dream but couldn't move from recognition to action.

The answer would come to me in the form of *vision boards.*

VISION BOARDS: HOW TO DREAM BIG WITH PICTURES

One day, I suddenly remembered the "goal boards" I used to make at the beginning of every school year. It was analog and tactile—lots of cutting out of pictures and words that represented my ambitions, and gluing them to a poster board—but that's what made the ritual so meaningful and effective for me. Once it was finished, I'd hang it on the back of my closet door to keep me on track every day.

Years later, when the idea of creating vision boards to manifest your dreams and desires burst into the popular culture, I connected the dots. All this time, I had essentially been making vision boards, albeit by another name, for so long. (Before they were cool!) Why had I stopped that practice? And would it still feel satisfying to make again, years later?

I'm a believer in the power of vision boards. I see them as a tangible reminder that you've allowed yourself to envision, plan, and dream big. (And I do love putting pictures on poster board. So satisfying!) A vision board is where you give your dream space to exist without judgment or barriers as it crystallizes. It also serves as a gentle, positive, physical reminder of what you're working toward, and it keeps you oriented even as your path forward shifts and changes. (If you're not super familiar with the process, that's okay—the exercise in this chapter will guide you through how it all works and why.)

Creating a vision board for my dream felt like giving myself permission to *want* something again. As I put "writing a book" on my board, I started thinking about what I could do in my career to bring myself closer to this goal.

One day, a literary agent reached out to me. I sent her some of my art samples, but nothing came of it in the end. I hit a dead end. Then, I started creating and sharing artwork online that I thought was perfect for a children's book. No traction—another dead end. It felt like it was time to move on, so I made a simple Instagram post stating that someday, I would write and illustrate a book. Then I went about my life and business and honestly sort of forgot about this dream for a while.

Eventually, I started seeing signs that it was time for me to change direction as an artist. I realized that my kids had gotten a little bit older, and designing art for their rooms wasn't really lighting me up anymore. I had to be honest with myself about the art I *actually* wanted to create.

So, I started creating art for myself again. I was no longer restricted to nursery décor and drawings of animals. Heck, I could illustrate whatever popped into my head! While watching *Little Women* for the umpteenth time, I decided to illustrate one of my favorite Louisa May Alcott quotes. On a particularly dark mental health day, I created an art print about what I wanted to be true in my life, drawing "brilliant things happen in calm minds" on the silhouette of a young woman's profile.

I'd freed myself, and this phase of my creative journey was one of the happiest I had ever experienced. My art became almost like a journal of what I was thinking, processing, and feeling. The more my own thoughts inspired my art, the more I loved it.

As I started sharing this new type of honest creativity with my followers, people took notice. My newer, truer artwork caught the attention of one of the agents I had previously spoken to. They e-mailed me that they wanted to make a real, illustrated book with me. But this wasn't the illustrated children's book of my dreams—it was a gift book for creatives, just like me.

My vision board delivered the right project for me. The rejection I faced shaped the decisions I made going forward. When I got the offer to create a gift book for creatives, it didn't match the form of what I'd originally envisioned, but it matched the *energy.* It felt exactly how I thought achieving my dream would feel—joyful, fulfilling, and deeply personal.

That's the magic of vision boards: They let you name a big dream while remaining open to how it unfolds. Details may change, but the core of what you want remains the same. I realized that my goal of writing a children's book wasn't entirely my own. Designing nursery art had been fulfilling, but it was also something I had stumbled into because others encouraged me to pursue it. Writing a children's book seemed like the logical next step—but was it *my* step?

Vision boarding forced me to examine not just what I wanted, but *why* I wanted it. That rejection taught me an invaluable lesson: Dreams aren't fragile things. They can adapt and evolve as you do. My vision board didn't fail me—it redirected me toward something even better. The rejection helped me let go of my rigid ideas about how my dream would happen, freeing me to embrace new opportunities.

Vision boards allow you to dream big, but they also challenge you to do the work. They don't simply manifest things in your life; they prepare you to meet the opportunity when it arrives. By the time that agent reached out with the gift book idea, I was ready. I had been refining my art, exploring my voice, and trusting the process. In a way, my vision board knew what I needed better than I did.

Sarah May: Teaching by Day, Creating Always

For Sarah May, creativity was never just a hobby, it was part of who she was. From selling friendship bracelets at age nine to printing linocut tees for markets, she was always chasing creative fulfillment. But for 26 years, she had balanced her art with a full-time job as a middle school teacher, squeezing her business, Block21Prints, into the margins of her life. She carved out time early in the mornings, juggling family responsibilities, pets, and the daily chaos of life, because, as she put it, "You make and find time for what you love. Sacrifices are inevitable if you're serious about your goals."

For years, she saw her art as a side gig, something small. But in 2020, after joining my business course Leverage Your Art as well as a yearlong mastermind that I facilitate called The Creative Hive Mastermind, she realized something powerful: "Just because it's a 'side hustle' does not mean it is unimportant, small, or insignificant. This business is my heart and soul." That shift in mindset changed everything. She stopped treating Block21Prints as an afterthought and started treating it like the real business it was.

The results followed. Her designs landed in an REI store and a stationery shop she had admired for years. But success wasn't just about big wins—it was about persistence. Not every sale came easy, and she had to learn to stand firm when customers tried to haggle at markets. She also had to let go of doing everything alone, recognizing that burnout wasn't a badge of honor.

Looking back, Sarah wishes she had learned the business side of art earlier, but she knows that waiting for the "right time" is a trap. Her advice? "Go for it! It's never too late, and it doesn't matter your age." Most importantly, she encourages artists to define success on their own terms: "Be your own kind of brave—your wins are yours, and be proud of where you succeed."

EXERCISE:
MANIFEST YOUR DREAMS WITH A VISION BOARD

Vision boards can help you take your side hustle more seriously by thinking in the long term. They help you recognize and name your dreams and desires while remaining open to how they might appear.

You start to examine not just what you want, but *why* you want it. They also challenge you to do the work, so you're ready to meet the opportunity when it arrives.

Turning your dreams into something tangible is one of the greatest gifts you can give yourself. Every great journey begins with a clear destination in mind, and I'm here to equip you with the tools to dream boldly and take confident steps toward making it a reality.

Now let's make a dang vision board!

Step 1: Categorize Your Goals

The first step in creating your vision board is categorizing your dreams. For side hustlers, this structure helps ensure you're working toward your dreams in a well-rounded way, not just chipping away at your creative life.

These are the six categories that I personally like to use, along with what I used to represent them and why.

1. **Personal/Health Goals:** Because a thriving creative business starts with a thriving you.

   On my vision board: A photo of a woman meditating with the words *calm mind, happy heart.* I was juggling so much at the time that mental clarity and self-care became nonnegotiable.

2. **Relationship Goals:** Connection is important, even in the hustle of life.

   On my vision board: A picture of a date night setup with a small bistro table and candles. My goal was to carve out more intentional time with my husband, even amid the chaos of life.

3. **Financial Goals:** Money matters, whether you're saving for art supplies or paying off debt.

   On my vision board: A giant dollar sign paired with "debt-free" written in bold letters. I was determined to pay off our family's credit card debt so I could reinvest in my art business guilt-free.

4. **Business Goals:** This is your sweet spot, side hustlers—dream big here.

    On my vision board: A mock book cover with my name on it. I wanted to write and illustrate a book and putting it on my board was a way of saying "This is possible."

5. **Home Improvement:** Because your space impacts your creativity.

    On my vision board: An illustration of a cozy art studio setup. My dream was to turn a spare bedroom into my creative sanctuary, complete with a standing desk and an inspiration wall.

6. **Travel Goals:** Let's stoke your wanderlust, even if it's a staycation.

    On my vision board: A picture of Edinburgh, Scotland. I couldn't plan a trip right then, but seeing it on my board kept the dream alive.

Feel free to use my categories as a guide or come up with your own! The important thing is to focus on what genuinely excites you. The categories, pictures, and words should reflect what truly matters to you, not what you think you're "supposed" to care about.

A useful category is one that sets your heart racing or feels like a missing puzzle piece in your life. For instance, if home improvement doesn't excite you, skip it! Add a category like "Creative Exploration" or "Community Building" if that feels more aligned with your goals.

At the same time, avoid categories that feel too vague or obligatory, like "Be a better person" or "Make people proud." The goals need to be concrete, and your vision board isn't about living up to anyone else's standards; it's about honoring your unique dreams.

Step 2: Brainstorm Boldly

Now, let's dream big. In each category, be as creative as you can to develop as many goals as you can imagine. Don't worry about scale, practicality, or feasibility. For now, you're giving yourself permission to imagine what's possible. For artists who do their art as a side hustle, it might look something like this:

- **Personal/Health:** Begin a 10-minute morning stretching routine.
- **Relationships:** Find an online network of artists to exchange advice and support with.
- **Money:** Save enough to buy a new printer.
- **Business:** Launch a print collection inspired by my most memorable childhood experiences.
- **Home:** Carve out a corner of my living space for art making.
- **Travel:** Exhibit at my first out-of-town art fair as a vendor.

Once you've recorded your dreams in the categories you laid out earlier, it's time to get more specific with your focus.

Step 3: Identify Your "Personal Why"

This is where we connect your goals to their deeper purpose—your **Personal Why**. This is where we give your goals an origin story. Your "Personal Why" is the foundation of your creative journey, the deeper reason that drives you to pursue your art business. It's more than just making money; it's about what this journey means for you and your life.

For each dream, ask yourself the following questions.

- *What makes this meaningful to me?*
- *What impact could this have on my life?*
- *How would it feel to achieve it?*

Here's how that could look for a side hustle:

- **Goal:** Sell my first print on Etsy.
- **Why:** To reaffirm that my art has value and can contribute to supporting my family.
- **Goal:** Save $500 for a Cricut machine.
- **Why:** To expand my product line and create more stickers and cards.

This step ties your goals back to your Personal Why, creating motivation that lasts beyond fleeting excitement. When each goal is grounded in your Personal Why, it becomes more than just an item on a to-do list—it turns into a meaningful step toward the life you're building.

Step 4: Gather Visual Prompts

This is my favorite part of vision boarding. Look for any images, words, and colors that represent the goals you'll be bringing to life. Search online, in magazines, or even in your own camera roll for images that reflect what you're dreaming about. While the final materials you use for your actual board will depend on whether you decide to make a physical or a digital one, it's helpful not to limit yourself to a single medium while you're in the "searching for inspiration" stage.

For a side hustler, these visual cues could take many different forms, depending on what you want to accomplish.

- **Sell your art?** Search for images of colorful Etsy storefronts or booths at a local art fair.
- **Create more?** Clip pictures of sketchbooks and iPads or artists working in studios.
- **Save for tools?** Get ready for some dream setups—a Cricut machine, the Procreate app on an iPad, or a neat home office.
- **Travel for inspiration?** Print a photo of a city or art museum you want to visit.

Visual prompts are more than just pictures; they're neural blueprints of your potential future. Visualization is a powerful technique that can activate brain regions associated with goal achievement, decision-making, and emotional regulation. Neuroscientist Tor Wager has noted that imagination itself is a neurological reality—one that can shape our brains and bodies in meaningful ways.

Research reveals that visualization is most effective when you engage multiple senses. Dr. Colleen Hacker, a leader in mental skills coaching, emphasizes activating at least three senses when visualizing your goals.

This multisensory approach is a one-two punch of motivation—imagery has been found to be five times more effective than simple goal contemplation.

Look for images that represent your goals in vivid detail, capture the emotion you want to feel when achieving your goals, and spark a visceral response of excitement or possibility. Find images you can look at digitally or print out and store them in a folder or bag until you're ready to create your board.

Step 5: Assemble Your Vision Board

There's no right or wrong way to do this—what truly matters is creating a vision board that clicks with your own style and preferences.

- **Digital Vision Board:** Organize your images by category using a tool like Canva or Adobe Illustrator. Keep it as a PDF or JPEG file for quick reference on your phone or computer.
- **Physical Vision Board:** Get a poster board, scissors, and some glue. Go through your printed images and organize them in a way that inspires you. I like to group my images together by goal category, such as financial, health, artistic, relationship, etc.

When your board is done, display it prominently where you will see it every day, such as your bathroom mirror, closet door, or, like me, on the wall of your art studio. If you made a digital board, consider having it printed so you can hang it up, or making it the wallpaper of your phone, computer, or other electronic device. It should be nearby and ready to inspire you each time you sit down to create.

Keep a copy on your phone so you have a portable dose of motivation whenever you need a boost. (If you made a physical board, take a picture of it to keep on your phone.) Let this board serve as a daily reminder of where you're headed and why your dreams matter. Every time you look at it is a chance to reconnect with your vision and keep moving forward, one inspired step at a time.

Congratulations! You've created a powerful tool to guide your creative journey. Always remember that a vision board is only as impactful as the actions it inspires—its true power lies in encouraging you to take bold, decisive moves toward turning your dreams into reality.

For now, take a moment to celebrate what you have accomplished. You just took the first step toward something extraordinary. Those dreams aren't abstract anymore; they're in focus, prepared for action. Take a moment with your vision board every day. Use it as a reminder of your greatness and potential, and keep moving forward, step by step.

You've named the dream. You've built the vision. Now it's time to roll up your sleeves and bring it to life—one hour at a time. In the next chapter, I'll show you how to make real progress with just five hours a week. Because dreaming big is only half the story—the rest is showing up in the margins and making it real.

5

TURNING THE MARGINS INTO MOMENTUM WITH THE S.T.A.R. CYCLE

One of the most common myths I've seen repeated by artists goes something like this: *If I just had more time, I'd finally be able to grow my art business.*

We've all been there. I know I have. But my approach to business (and life) radically changed once I realized something: It's much harder to find more time than it is to make the most of the time you already have. Growing your art business is not a matter of having enough time; it's a matter of intentional focus.

Even if you found an extra 20 hours a week, without a plan for how to use them, those hours would vanish into laundry, e-mails, or any of several other equally compelling obligations and opportunities. If you're reading this book, you probably aren't struggling with a *lack* of things to do every day. What you're missing is a clear strategy to prioritize and make room for the goals you care about. What if, instead of dreaming about a perfect future full of free time, you could actually make progress—now?

That's where the **S.T.A.R. Five-Hour Monthly Cycle** comes in.

I developed the S.T.A.R. Cycle based on years of trial, error, and research into productivity, creativity, and time management. This method is designed specifically for artists looking to build a sustainable business with limited time.

This isn't about hustling harder or working until you're burned out. (Been there, done that, 0/10 do not recommend!) It's about working *smarter* and putting your energy into the right tasks at the right time. It's about aligning your efforts with your goals so even with just five hours a week, you can make real progress toward your creative dreams.

Let's do the math: Five hours of focused effort each week adds up to 260 hours a year. That's a month and a half of a full-time job, dedicated purely to your art. It's 260 hours to build a portfolio, launch a shop, or create an entire product collection, without sacrificing your creativity or your quality of life.

I've read more than enough books that promise an almost-magical solution to time management, motivation, and the other factors that keep us stuck in place. That's not what I'm doing here, because you're going to be using a resource you already know and use every day: the Margins of Life.

In this chapter, we'll identify those Margins, and then I'll show you exactly how to use the S.T.A.R. Cycle to grow your art business whether you're starting from scratch or leveling up. We'll uncover hidden hours, eliminate distractions, and create a framework where the reflections and insights you made in the previous chapters can be put into action!

FINDING TIME FOR YOUR ART BUSINESS IN THE MARGINS

The funny thing about self-care is that we often instinctively create moments of care for ourselves without even realizing it. Maybe it's an early morning cup of coffee during the half hour of quiet time you have before your kids wake up. Or it's brain dumping your to-do list during a 10-minute break during an evening shift. It could be when you've brought a packed lunch to the office instead of going out. These moments are all too easily swallowed by scrolling social media or streaming television online—but they are your margins, and we're going to put them to work.

The margins of life are individually small but collectively powerful. Once you learn how to harness these unnoticed pockets of time, they can become the bedrock to building and maintaining your side hustle in the long run. They're not mere gaps in your day—they're the places where dreams are sown and cultivated.

If you're waiting for the "perfect time" to build your art business, you'll be waiting forever. Life doesn't deliver neatly wrapped schedules tied with bows and bundled with instruction manuals—not for me, not for you, not for anyone. You won't always have ideal circumstances, but that's not a failing on your end. All the successful artists you admire make progress the same way you do: one step at a time. Your art career is a garden; just like tomatoes and squash don't emerge from the ground all at once, what look like big successes are really the culmination of persistent effort over time.

A sustainable art business isn't created through abrupt changes, nor is it found in immediate success. It's built through incremental, methodical progress—beginning where you are with what is available to you, with the goal of making a sustainable change that sticks. Sometimes, five hours a week is enough to start making progress, but I realize that for many of you, even five hours can feel unattainable.

If this is where you are right now, let's fix that by giving you tools and strategies to take your time back, spend it more purposefully, and free up headspace for your dreams. In order to reclaim the time you've lost in the margins, you first need to recognize the distractions that are stealing this precious commodity.

DISTRACTIONS AND COMMON TIME TRAPS

When I decided to audit the time I spent on my art, I noticed three recurring habits that consistently made my work sessions less effective. You might recognize these in your own daily life.

- **Multitasking:** Nothing kills efficiency (and the quality of our work) like trying to do too much at once. Rubinstein, Meyer, and Evans's 2001 study in the *Journal of Experimental Psychology* found that multitasking can reduce productivity by up to 40 percent. You can't create a masterpiece while also fielding e-mails and cooking dinner—believe me, I've tried! Your art deserves focused, intentional effort.

- **Constant Interruption:** The problem of fractured focus isn't limited to big, obvious types of multitasking; it's just as true for the small constant distractions of modern living. Notifications from social media, texts, and e-mails yank us out of our flow more quickly than a toddler asking for a snack. (And in my experience, toddlers have better manners than your average social media commenter.)
- **Perfectionism:** An hour spent creating is always more valuable than an hour spent thinking about creating. Too much pondering keeps you stuck in place, unable to finish a project. Teresa Amabile and Steven Kramer's book *The Progress Principle* shows how small steps forward can drive motivation and creativity. Imperfect work out in the world is better than a masterpiece that no one sees.

These distractions manifest in different ways, and I've experienced all of them firsthand. Early in my Gingiber journey, perfectionism cost me what could have been a life-changing opportunity. When I was invited to submit my portfolio by a friend in charge of finding local artists to paint wall murals at a new museum, my first thought was *Oh my gosh! What an opportunity!* This was followed immediately by *Oh no . . . I don't have a portfolio to share!*

Instead of simply sharing my existing work through my Etsy store link and letting them decide if it was a fit, I spent weeks agonizing over creating the "perfect" portfolio. I tinkered and tweaked until I did the worst thing possible: I never replied to the e-mail at all. That museum, Crystal Bridges in Arkansas, now hosts 785,000 visitors annually. Every time I visit, I think about my art not being on those walls, all because I let perfectionism paralyze me.

I learned my lesson. The next time an opportunity came up to share my portfolio, I kept it simple and didn't miss a beat. I realized that the discomfort of sharing something "imperfect" was nothing compared to the regret of missing an opportunity entirely.

And perfectionism wasn't my only challenge. According to Microsoft's 2023 *Work Trend Index*, the top 25 percent of business software users spend an average of 8.8 hours a week on e-mail. Smart Insights' 2025 report on global social media use found the average user spends more than two hours a day scrolling—equivalent to a part-time job. Imagine what you could accomplish if even half of that time was spent on your creative work.

My hope is that with the help of this book, you'll be able to recognize these time traps in your own life for what they are. Then you can make small adjustments, like setting limits on social media scrolling or batching e-mails into designated time blocks, to reclaim lost time for your art.

EXERCISE:
RECOGNIZING (AND RECLAIMING) THE TIME YOU'VE LOST IN THE MARGINS

Step 1: Conduct an Honest Assessment of Your Schedule

Write down all the things you do in a week. Work, family commitments, chores, Netflix binges, scrolling—all of it. Next, look for patterns: Are there moments that you could reclaim? For instance, if you spend an hour on Netflix every night, spend half of that sketching or brainstorming instead.

Action Step:
Audit Your Week

Track how you spend your time over the course of a week, then identify one recurring activity you can modify—whether by reducing, shifting, or eliminating it—to create a dedicated block of time for your art.

Step 2: Reclaim "Lost" Time

I've found that on a typical day, I end up having to spend a good chunk of time waiting. In the old days, we would just be bored in those moments, but now (for better or worse), it's easy to pull out the phone and scroll through social media. With some preparation, that's time that can be reclaimed for less passive tasks. Here are some examples of ways you can reclaim your waiting time:

- **Commute:** If you're fortunate enough to be able to use public transit, that travel time is great for sketching and jotting down ideas. If you drive, try listening to art business podcasts or audiobooks.
- **Lunch Breaks:** Take a few minutes of your break and get a little task done, such as posting on social media or organizing files.
- **Waiting Time:** School pickup lines and doctor's offices are two places where I end up waiting for half an hour or more on a regular basis. Carry a sketchbook, and it's possible to use that time making art or planning what to do during larger chunks of dedicated time.

Action Step:
Reclaim Lost Moments

Identify one "lost time" habit this week (like scrolling your phone while waiting) and swap it out for a small creative act, such as jotting down ideas or sketching for a few minutes.

Myra Romano: Turning Lost Time into Creative Gold

My student Myra Romano had already built a successful career, working her way up to creative director at major companies like American Greetings and Smucker's. But life took an unexpected turn when, after struggling with infertility for seven years, she found herself with three children in just 19 months. Her first baby was welcomed through IVF, then she unexpectedly became pregnant with twins. Her high-risk twin pregnancy required immediate bed rest, and with her husband frequently traveling, she stepped away from her career to focus on her family.

Myra mastered the art of reclaiming lost time through necessity. With three young children to care for, she learned to work in the smallest margins of life. She discovered creative ways to use even 15-minute windows—once even creating family placemats during Thanksgiving dinner prep that are still used today.

When she got her first iPad and Apple pencil, it transformed how she could use waiting time. "That was a huge game changer as we spent a ton of time in doctor's offices. It's how I illustrated three books during their middle school years." What others might view as lost time—waiting rooms, appointments, small gaps between activities—became her creative windows.

Through this experience, Myra discovered something profound: "What I uncovered was that when I'm not making art, it's not good for myself, my kids, my husband—or anyone, really. Making art is what fills my soul." This realization made finding and using these small pockets of time not just practical but essential. As she put it, "I came to understand the deep truth about myself: my life is most fulfilled when I'm creating and sharing art."

Myra's journey wasn't always smooth. Early in her career, an ad agency president told her she was "just a dime-a-dozen graphic designer." She didn't let those words defeat her. As she described it, "The next day, something shifted. I scoured the classifieds and discovered a new and growing field: web design. A few months later, I left that agency and joined my first dot-com startup." This resilience would serve her well in finding creative solutions to time management later in her journey.

Her most important lesson? "You don't have to do it all on your own." Finding ways to reclaim time sometimes means accepting help and building a support system that allows you to focus on what matters most.

Step 3: Reduce Distractions with a Focus Zone

Managing your distractions is truly an exercise in setting boundaries with *yourself.* If you don't draw a line and intentionally choose to ignore them as they appear, distractions will take your best creative hours. Here's how to regain your focus and be fully present with each task.

- **Turn off notifications:** Silence your phone or leave it in another room. If you work on a tablet, enable do-not-disturb mode.
- **Use sound-canceling tools if you can:** Play instrumental music or the sound of white noise, and consider using noise-canceling headphones. Even earplugs can do the job; anything to stop or mitigate audible distractions.
- **Clear your space:** Whether it's your kitchen table or a corner of your studio; clear off your space and have it ready for action.

Action Step: Set Up Your Distraction-Free Zone Today

Clear your workspace and pick a focus playlist. If your workspace has a door, make a sign to put up so your family knows when it's time to let you focus. You want to have the work, and only the work, front and center.

Step 4: Use Technology to Help Keep You on Track

Technology can steal your focus, but it can also support you. Consider these areas for leveraging it purposefully to use your time effectively and remain on task.

- **To-do lists:** There's no way I could keep track of everything I need to do just in my head. There are plenty of apps designed for managing to-do lists—just remember not to get caught up in finding the *perfect* one. The best system is the one you'll actually use. I've tried specialized to-do apps in the past, but the method that has worked for me (and that I've stuck with for years) is surprisingly simple: a draft e-mail. I keep an ongoing draft with my to-do list, and when I complete a task, I delete *just that item* from the e-mail. It's easy, syncs across all my devices, and doesn't require me to remember to open yet another app.
- **Task and project management:** For bigger or long-term tasks, you might find a project management app useful. For example, I use a Trello board to manage my fabric licensing work. Other apps in this category that colleagues have used include Asana and Notion. These apps are like beefed-up to-do lists for breaking down big tasks into smaller ones, and some include special features for working collaboratively on projects.

- **Time management:** I use Google Calendar extensively—everything I do is on my calendar, and if it's not on my calendar, it's not happening. I put a 15-minute reminder on every scheduled item to help me shift to a new mindset if needed. I also put personal events and appointments on the calendar; this gives me the confidence to plan without worrying about double booking. At the end of the week, if there are tasks on my to-do list that I didn't get done (and there always are!), I look at the next week and see if I can schedule blocks of time to knock them out.

There are other kinds of productivity apps that you might find useful, like time-trackers that can show you where you're spending your time and website blockers that can help you stay off social media. Just beware the siren song of the Perfect Toolkit. It's much better to start getting value out of an imperfect tool now than to dabble in a bunch of different ones, agonizing over which one to pick—the tool should support your productivity, not hurt it.

Action Step:
Stop Carrying It All in Your Brain

Identify an area where you would benefit from offloading some mental effort into a productivity tool, like a calendar or Trello board. Implement the tool in your daily practice and commit to using it.

STEP 5: PUT A LIMIT ON KNOWN TIME SPONGES

Not all tasks are created equally. Some bring you closer to your goals, like making art and researching potential licensing partners; just about any amount of time you put into them is well spent. Other tasks, like checking social media or reading e-mails, probably only need to happen a certain amount of time per day. But they can easily eat up way too much if we're not careful, soaking up time like a sponge that never gets saturated. Note that these aren't "complete waste of time" tasks! Instagram is a great tool for keeping up with trends, but it's also specifically designed to keep you scrolling for as long as possible. The way to deal with time sponges is to put limits on them.

Take a moment to come up with a list of your known time sponges. For example, here are some I've dealt with in my own career: checking e-mails every 45 minutes in case an important message comes, even though nobody expects a response that quickly. Reading through Instagram lists for "inspiration" but never executing on all of that inspiration. Tidying my art supplies when that time would be much better spent *using* them. (Some of these might sound familiar.)

Next, brainstorm a concrete strategy for taming your time sponges. These are some techniques that have worked for me and my students.

- **Scheduling:** If it's a task you need to do on a regular basis, put a recurring event on your calendar and only do the task at that time. Check and respond to e-mail only twice a day, for instance, at 10 A.M. and 4 P.M.
- **Timeboxing:** Put a specific time limit on a task and commit to stopping when time is up. For example, set a 15-minute timer before opening up social media, and quit the app when it runs out.
- **Mindfulness:** Ask yourself: "Is this directly aligned with my goals?" Observe yourself. It is much easier to focus on the right thing when you are aware of your time sponges, and more natural to act with intention rather than give in to knee-jerk reactions.

Not getting absorbed into time sponges is about not putting your time into the wrong work at the wrong time. If you want to pitch potential licensing clients, yes, it is true that putting research into trends is helpful. But ultimately, you need to pitch to potential licensing clients! I see many artists get stuck in research or observation mode instead of action mode. Send the pitch! Make the portfolio! Teach the class!

Action Step: Work with Intention, Not Just Motion

Write down your top three goals for the week. Each work session, prioritize one task that moves you closer to those goals. Identify the time sponges related to the goals and write down the limits you will put on them.

When you make time for your art—even in the middle of everyday chaos—you send yourself a bold, beautiful message: My art matters. My dreams are worth pursuing.

We all have 168 hours a week. It's the way that we put them to use that matters—and now that you've wrested those five hours a week from your margins, you have everything you need to use that time intentionally and effectively. The margins are your canvas, and you hold the paint.

THE S.T.A.R. CYCLE OF FOCUS

Building an art business alongside other commitments can feel overwhelming, like trying to juggle flaming swords while painting a self-portrait. I've been there (I'm still there!), and I've got the metaphorical burn marks to show for it. That's why I created the S.T.A.R. Five-Hour Cycle to help artists work smarter, not harder, starting with just five focused hours a week. My system divides your month into four themed weeks:

- Week 1: Strategize
- Week 2: Think and Create
- Week 3: Adapt
- Week 4: Reach Out

And don't worry, I didn't forget the necessary-but-not-so-fun stuff: Administrative Tasks. These are the less glamorous parts of your side hustle that separate a hobbyist from a professional. (We can call them Administr-YAY-tive Tasks, if that helps. I won't force you, but I highly recommend adopting the phrase, because a little silliness always helps.)

Each week, you'll dedicate *four hours to a Big Task* and *one hour to Admin.* By following this monthly rhythm, you'll strike a balance between structure and variety, keeping you inspired, focused, and steadily and purposefully moving toward your goals.

Week 1: Strategize—Plan and Dream

Strategize Week is all about laying the groundwork for what's ahead. We're going to do some focused thinking and learning this week; this is your permission slip to chase rabbits, dream big, and make plans. This kind of strategizing might not feel directly related to making art, but making a plan is how we get clarity. Think of it as planting seeds for future opportunities.

Your **Big Task** for this week is to spend four hours learning about something related to one of your big goals. If licensing is one of your goals, this might mean researching potential clients on LinkedIn and looking for trends on social media. If your goal is to start an online shop or integrate with a shipping partner, it might mean familiarizing yourself with a new platform.

For example, you might find some licensing companies and explore their submission guidelines or learn how to set up a shop on Etsy or create a list of art fairs you'd like to apply to. Take notes to capture what you learn, the resources you find, and any scraps of half-baked ideas that come to you.

Your **Admin Task** for this week is to spend an hour tending to the parts of your business that support your art. Examples of what I mean by this include organizing your digital files and research notes or tracking your expenses and income for the previous month or adding important deadlines to your calendar. These are the tasks that you would hand off to a business manager, but in this case, the business manager is you!

Research can get messy, but putting a little structure around it will help you get the most out of this time. I use a few simple strategies to bring order to chaos.

- **Use a simple spreadsheet:** Google Sheets is my best friend! (Note to my actual best friends—this is a joke). I create separate tabs for licensing, stores, and events, and keep track of contacts and potential leads. But there's no right way to do this; organize your notes in a way that works best for you.
- **Set a time limit:** Research can be a rabbit hole, so stick to your five-hour limit. (Remember the time sponges!) If you have more ideas than time to chase them down, add them to your notes to explore later.
- **Batch your tasks:** Spend one session finding leads, another recording them to your spreadsheet, and another reviewing submission guidelines. Batching is a great way to avoid the context-switching penalty.

Some folks love the research phase like a pig in mud, to the point of sometimes needing a kick in the pants to switch to action mode. Others might find research and strategy to be mostly "boring admin work" and try to avoid it. I'm here to tell you that properly harnessed, it's a vital creative tool, and it has become a crucial part of my own process.

For me, I know that the best way to grow my art business, outside of making art, is building a solid foundation for my business and creating real relationships with my ideal customers—the people who look at my art and feel an emotional connection to it.

If I can nail the administrative and research part of my side hustle, that means I have more time to devote to the relationship-building part of my journey. For me, for instance, my very first big pitch e-mail for art licensing resulted in not just an art licensing contract, but also industry relationships that have far outlasted the length of that initial contract. Ten years after that initial pitch, the former creative director contracted me to produce custom tea towels for her new company; I was top of her mind for this design opportunity, all because I did the seemingly "boring work" of sending a well-researched pitch e-mail. Each contact you add, each opportunity you uncover, is one step closer to turning your dreams into reality. Making a strategy is a prerequisite to working smarter.

Week 2: Think and Create—Art Without Limits

Think and Create Week is the time for your creativity to take center stage. No e-mails, no spreadsheets—just you, your art supplies, and the space to create. It doesn't matter if you're starting a new 30-day project, finishing up the last bits of last month's art project, or experimenting with fresh ideas and challenging mediums; this week is all about making art.

Your **Big Task** for this week is to spend four hours producing artwork or improving your technique. You might create three new designs for a collection or complete one or two larger pieces or do studies of a subject you want to improve on. You might even try making a piece in a new medium. The important thing is to make something. This work does not need to be perfect by the end of the week; it just needs to be created.

Your **Admin Task** for this week is to spend an hour on art maintenance. If producing art is like being a Formula One driver, art maintenance is like being on the pit crew. These are tasks like inventorying your art supplies and making a shopping list, backing up your digital files to cloud storage, or updating your portfolio with newly created pieces.

You've probably had moments when you were so immersed in your work that time seemed to disappear. Psychologist Mihaly Csikszentmihalyi coined the term *flow state* in his 1990 book, *Flow: The Psychology of Optimal Experience*, describing that zone where creativity thrives. Entering this state doesn't just improve the quality of your work; it makes the process more fulfilling.

One way to cultivate deep work is by setting up dedicated, distraction-free work sessions. (Refer to the "focus zones" I describe earlier in this chapter.) Turn off notifications, put your phone in another room, and give yourself uninterrupted time to create. The more you practice focusing deeply, the easier it becomes to tap into that creative flow.

Think and Create week is not only about finishing pieces; just as importantly, it is about mastering your craft. I've worked with so many aspiring artists who dream of making a living from their art but often skip over this crucial step. They see the goal of earning money from their work and dive into the business side without fully developing the skills that make their art truly stand out.

But when you take the time to deeply learn your medium, you're also learning how to optimize your approach to every part of your art. You create faster, with more confidence, and your work begins to reflect the unique qualities that only you can offer the world.

Mastery doesn't come from playing it safe or avoiding challenges. It comes from diving in, facing those creative roadblocks, and working to move past them for good. It might sound impossible now, but a day will come when creating art becomes the *easiest* part of your career. But first, you have to put in time to build a foundation that sets you apart.

Week 3: Adapt—Polish and Prepare

Adapt Week is all about setting up your work for success. Maybe that means formatting your designs for submission, organizing your portfolio, or preparing a product for launch. This week is when you'll polish your work and get it ready for the world.

Your **Big Task** for this week is to spend four hours polishing and editing your work for sharing. Last week we created some pieces; this week is about *completing* them, getting them into a final state, ready for sale or publication to the world. If your medium is physical, this might mean scanning or photographing a piece. If your design is meant for a product, it might mean making mock-ups. Having slept on the piece for a few days, you might be tempted to make design changes, and that's okay—but think of this phase as tweaking rather than making big edits.

Your **Admin Task** for this week is to tackle the boring but important steps required to publish a completed piece. Whatever your process looks like, I guarantee there are tedious parts you'd really rather not do when you've just finished a beautiful new piece of art. Maybe you need to format and optimize files for Etsy or a print-on-demand (POD) platform. Maybe you need to write and edit product descriptions or check your website and online shop for outdated info and broken links. Maybe you register the copyright on your design. Now is the time to take care of that business. These steps tend to be both repetitive and boring, so I like to use checklists to remember what needs to be done and keep myself on track.

Researchers Teresa Amabile and Steven Kramer analyzed nearly 12,000 diary entries from 238 employees to uncover what truly drives motivation. In their book, *The Progress Principle: Using Small Wins to Ignite Joy, Engagement, and Creativity at Work*, they revealed a fascinating insight: Even small steps forward can be among the most powerful motivators. By preparing and polishing your work, you create tangible results that build momentum and encourage you to keep going. Each piece you complete is one step closer to your long-term goals.

This step isn't just busy work; it helps to create opportunities and establish a professional mindset. When your work is polished and ready to go, you're saying to the world (and to yourself): *I take my art seriously.* Louis Pasteur famously said, "Chance favors the prepared mind," and this has definitely been my experience. By consistently producing work and bringing it to a complete, publishable state, you'll always be ready for that unexpected shop feature or opportunity to pitch to a dream client.

Week 3 is where preparation meets possibility. By polishing, formatting, and organizing your art, you're setting the stage for success and opening the door to new opportunities. You've done the work to create something amazing, and you took the time to refine and finalize it for a wider audience. Now you need to present your work to the world so you can actually reap the rewards!

Week 4: Reach Out—Shine and Share

Reach Out Week is all about stepping into the spotlight. Sharing your work can make you feel vulnerable, but it's also exhilarating to see your creations shine. Exactly what this looks like depends on you, your art, and your business, but however you share your work, the feedback can be both useful and gratifying.

Your **Big Task** for this week is to spend four hours getting a completed piece out into the world. This might mean publishing a new product listing, scheduling a week's worth of Instagram posts, writing a newsletter, or pitching your portfolio to three new clients.

Your **Admin Task** for this week is to review the effectiveness of your sharing. Respond to customer e-mails and social media messages, review analytics for your website traffic or e-mail open rates, or track pitches and follow up on leads. This is actually really important! Hitting Send on that pitch e-mail or publishing that social media post is just step one. Following up on the results is how you find things to improve for the next time. How many shares did this post get compared to that one? What feedback did this product photography get? Pitching is a skill, and like any skill, the way to improve is to practice and pay attention to the results.

Sharing your journey has another important side effect: Letting your audience cheer you on not only motivates you but also builds trust and connection. When the time comes to pitch a sale, you won't be talking to a cold audience, and fans who like and trust you are more likely to share about you to their own audience.

Not sure where to start? It doesn't have to be complicated; start simple and try different things as you gain confidence. To begin, pick one way to share your journey and execute it. There are many ways to do this; here are a few ideas that have worked for me.

- **A look behind the scenes:** People love to see artists at work! Try sharing a page from your sketchbook or a photo of your workspace. In-progress and before-and-after shots of a project give the audience a chance to follow along as a piece comes together. If you have a smartphone, it likely has the ability to record time-lapse videos; try making a condensed video of a work session. Use a tripod or table-clamped selfie stick to hold the phone and avoid moving the camera or the workpiece to get a clean video.
- **Write to your mailing list:** Your list is a great place for longer-form updates about what you're working on and why it matters to you. This can be scary, because every e-mail will be followed by some unsubscribes, but that's okay. A weekly e-mail to update your followers is totally appropriate.
- **Celebrate a small win:** It's easy to celebrate big wins, but it's just as important to celebrate the small ones too—like finishing a painting, sending a pitch, or creating a new design. This gives your audience a chance to celebrate with you.

However, you share, keep it real. Keep it you. Your audience doesn't need perfection; they just want to see *you* doing what you love. Every time you share, you're inspiring someone else to take a step toward their own dream. That's the power of connection.

MY STORY: HOW I USED THE S.T.A.R. CYCLE TO GAIN 100 HOURS A YEAR

When I started Gingiber, I did everything myself, trying to cut expenses wherever I could. I didn't realize that my frugality was costing me precious time that I could've used to make art—and art is where the real value in the business comes from.

I hand wrote the labels for every package. I'd drive them to the post office to have the postage applied. I felt so accomplished rolling up to the post office with bags of packages in tow. *Look at me, being so resourceful,* I thought. But something had to give. I was spending more time on shipping than creating, and I knew this wasn't sustainable. Here's how I used the S.T.A.R. Cycle to transform my shipping process and reclaim my creative time.

Week 1: Strategize

During my Strategy week, I sat down and really analyzed where my time was going. I tracked every minute I spent on shipping for a full week, including writing labels, preparing packages, driving to the post office, waiting in line. The numbers were shocking: I spent 17 hours a year just writing labels, and 86 hours driving back and forth to the post office. That's 103 hours—gone! Two and a half weeks of full-time work vanished into tasks that weren't moving my business forward.

I spent four strategy hours researching shipping solutions. I looked into shipping software options, label printers, and USPS pickup services. I made a spreadsheet comparing costs and features of different shipping platforms. During my one-hour Admin Task, I calculated exactly how much time and money I was spending on my current process versus what these new solutions would cost.

Week 2: Think and Create

This week wasn't about creating art directly, but about creating systems. I used my four focused hours to design my ideal shipping workflow. I mapped out exactly how I wanted packages to move from order to delivery, eliminating as many manual touch points as possible. I created templates for shipping labels and packing slips that would work with the new system.

For my Admin hour, I organized my shipping supplies and created an inventory system, so I'd always know when to reorder supplies before running out.

Week 3: Adapt

Implementation week was crucial. I used my four hours to integrate the shipping platform with my Etsy shop and learn how to use my new label printer. I created test labels and ran through my new workflow multiple times, tweaking it until it felt smooth and natural. What used to take 20 minutes now took 5.

My admin hour was spent creating a checklist for my new shipping process, ensuring I wouldn't miss any steps as I adapted to the new system.

Week 4: Reach Out

The final week was about making this change official. I updated my shop policies to reflect my new shipping schedule and communicated the changes to my customers through my newsletter. I explained that orders would now ship twice a week with tracking automatically e-mailed to them—actually an improvement in service!

During my admin hour, I created a simple spreadsheet to track shipping metrics: time spent, packages shipped, and any issues that came up. This would help me monitor the success of my new system.

The Results

Using the S.T.A.R. Cycle helped me see where my time was really going and create a plan to reclaim it. By taking four weeks to strategize, create new systems, adapt my workflow, and communicate changes, I transformed a major time sink into a smooth, efficient process.

With these new systems in place, I gained back 100 hours a year, which I could now pour into creating. That time translated directly into new products: I completed a fabric design, created a dozen new prints, and designed a calendar, all of which generated income over many months.

But the benefits went beyond just saving time. My customers were happier because they got tracking numbers automatically. I was less stressed because I wasn't racing to the post office every day. And most importantly, I had more mental space for creativity because shipping was no longer consuming my thoughts. I was able to teach this process to the first class of Leverage Your Art students that I served in 2020. One of my students, Rebecca Woolbright, used this method to grow a flourishing art product and manufacturing education career.

Rebecca Woolbright: Turning Naptime into Business Time

Rebecca Woolbright's creative journey began with a new baby at home and a surge of creativity seeking an outlet. Unlike many artists who transition from hobby to business, Rebecca started with clear business intentions, inspired by a honeymoon trip to Japan. "I was so inspired by their cultural attention to detail and the abundance of washi tape everywhere, I knew that was where I needed to start," she recalled. She wanted to contribute to her household while staying home with her child but wasn't sure how to make it work.

Rebecca was one of the first creatives that I mentored in my signature course, Leverage Your Art. Her background in bookkeeping for a Maui snorkel shop gave her valuable insights into wholesale and direct-to-customer sales. But the real challenge was time management—juggling a new business with a baby required strategic planning and focus. "Thank goodness for naptime!" Rebecca said. "I really put my head down and got to work whenever I had a sleeping baby!"

Using what she learned from my Leverage Your Art course, she made incredible progress toward her business goals. In those early days, she devoted 10 to 15 hours weekly to her business, but what made her progress remarkable was how she structured those hours. She worked in concentrated 90-minute blocks during naps, treating each session as sacred creative time. "Each day I knew I had at least one-and-a-half hours of work time and would have one focus for that time, and then when naptime ended, so did work," she explained. "It was never enough time, but also probably some of the best focus time I have ever had."

She maximized those precious hours by dividing them between learning Adobe Illustrator, researching manufacturers, and identifying potential retail shops. "I was so motivated to make it work that I had a ton of focus during this time," she reflected. While she wasn't following the common advice to "sleep when they sleep," the motivation and focus outside of baby life felt essential to her well-being.

Rebecca still has her first $5 bill from selling washi tape to a neighbor on Maui stuck to her vision board. "It was overwhelming and exciting and made me so nervous," she remembered. "Selling doesn't come naturally to me—I have had to work on this over the years."

The business grew steadily through these focused time blocks. Reaching 100 wholesale shops marked a significant milestone, as did receiving orders from strangers. Recently, she signed up with a licensing agent to help distribute her artwork more widely, a goal she'd set after learning such partnerships existed.

Her journey wasn't without challenges. "My biggest roadblock was time. I wanted more of it, and there just wasn't enough in the beginning," she admitted. Now, with both children in school for the first time in 10 years of running her business, she finally feels she has space to think. She also learned hard lessons along the way, like when she didn't order samples for her first washi tape production. "The quality was awful and didn't stick. I learned a lot with that investment that flopped! Total loss!"

Time is your most valuable resource. The point of the S.T.A.R. Cycle isn't to hustle harder with your reclaimed time, but to honor your creative dreams and give yourself a systematic path to success. Above all, the Cycle is *flexible*. Side hustlers aren't always bound by a strict schedule. If a weekly cycle doesn't work for you, adjust it to whatever serves you better! The aim isn't perfection; it's consistent and intentional movement without the burnout.

Your art business should be an extension of your passion, not a grind. Rotating your focus from one area to another each week will keep you productive, inspired, and creative—and keep your joy alive and well.

The most challenging element of this journey isn't doing the work; it's showing up consistently. Getting started can be daunting, and it's easy to tell yourself that it won't matter. But I can tell you: It matters more than you know.

Now that you've started reclaiming your time and putting a simple, sustainable system in place with the S.T.A.R. Cycle, it's time to look at what you're actually doing with those precious hours. Because not all work is created equal—and not all opportunities are the right fit for this season of your life.

In the next chapter, we'll explore what I call the Goldilocks Zone: that sweet spot where your time, your energy, and your creative dreams align. Let's make sure you're not just working harder—but working smarter on the right things, at the right time, for the right reasons.

6

LIVING IN THE GOLDILOCKS ZONE

When you're working alone, it's very easy to feel like the problems you face are unique just because you can't see what others are dealing with behind the scenes. One of the benefits of coaching as many budding art business owners as I have is that I get to see common patterns, and there are two patterns in particular that I see holding artists back *all the time*. In this chapter you'll learn how to recognize as well as how to break out of the following two habits to unleash your growth.

- **Overthinking** happens when you hold back from acting because things are just not quite good enough yet. "If only this was a little better. . . Just a few more edits . . ." If you find yourself tossing out piece after piece or tweaking that marketing plan to death trying to get it just right, you may be overthinking.
- **Underthinking** happens when, after taking action, you move on to the next project without looking back to see and *learn from* the results of the first one. If you find yourself doing the same thing over and over again and getting the same outcome, particularly if it's an outcome that disappoints you—you may be underthinking.

You might see parts of yourself in those lines. In fact, I would be surprised if you didn't—I mean it when I say I see these all the time, and I'd even say that part of maturing as a working artist is learning to fight both. By the way, both over- and underthinking are really just extreme forms of what are normally very healthy impulses. Having high standards for yourself is good! Being able to put a piece down and move on is good! But for some reason, many people find themselves taking these habits far enough that they start to hurt growth more than they help. I don't think this happens on purpose; more likely they are behaviors we tend to fall into unless we've made a conscious effort to avoid them.

When you are avoiding the traps of over- and underthinking I call it being in your **Goldilocks Zone**, and staying there as much as possible is an important engine for growth. Like porridge that is neither too hot nor too cold, the Goldilocks Zone strikes a balance between action and planning. If you do find yourself falling out of the Goldilocks Zone, don't worry! What I want you to take from this chapter is that *you are not alone*, and that *these patterns can be overcome.*

Before we get into the details of finding your Goldilocks Zone, I think it's important to be explicit about why it is so important.

THE GROWTH RATCHET: TWO SIMPLE STEPS TO SALES

When you strip away all the details about tools and media and technology and marketing and e-commerce (and on and on and on . . .), running an art business is actually very simple. In fact, there are only two steps.

- **Step 1:** Make art that people want to buy.
- **Step 2:** Sell the art to those people.

Piece of cake! Of course, it's not actually that simple. First of all, nobody is born knowing how to make art people want to buy or how to sell it. Second, even if you were born with that knowledge, it would quickly become obsolete, because exactly what people want to buy and how to sell it to them are constantly changing.

That means that running an art business, even if you've been in the game for years, is really a continual process of *learning how to run an art business*. We—myself very much included—are constantly trying to learn what is marketable and how to market it.

At this point you might be thinking, "Okay, but how do I learn those things?" Fortunately, again the answer is pretty simple. I call it the **Growth Ratchet**. Every time you share a design or launch a product or run an ad campaign, you are running an experiment. By paying attention to the outcome of that experiment, you will learn a little more about what people want to buy and how to sell it to them. What kinds of designs get the most attention? What kinds of ads get the best return? What's the right price point for this product? I can tell you what works for *me*, but at the end of the day, to find out what works for *you*, you have to *launch and learn!*

When you launch and learn, with every new idea you get a little more effective. This is where the Growth Ratchet kicks in, because as you gain experience, you'll get better and better at making art that sells. With each new launch, you bring along the lessons learned from all the launches that came before.

This is why staying in the Goldilocks Zone is so important for artists: Both overthinking and underthinking will jam up your Growth Ratchet. Overthinking will stop you from launching, and underthinking will stop you from learning. The Goldilocks Zone is where we keep the Growth Ratchet working at its highest potential.

STEP 1: MAKE ART—STOP OVERTHINKING IT AND BREAK THE THREE NEGATIVE PATTERNS HOLDING YOU BACK

When I'm coaching artists who are having trouble getting work over the finish line, there are three patterns I see time and time again: **lack of confidence**, **artist's block**, and **perfectionism**. All three of these will hinder your growth by slowing the pace at which you get to interact with your customers. The good news is that once we recognize that these patterns are happening, there are things we can do to break out of them.

Break Negative Pattern 1: Gain Skills and Confidence

I'm not going to sugarcoat it; sharing your art can be scary. You pour a bit of yourself into a piece and publishing it can feel like opening yourself up to the world for scrutiny. This does get better with experience, but when you're first starting out and have a shorter track record of successes to draw confidence from, the Chaos Goblin can camp out in your mind and try to convince you your art isn't good enough. This is totally normal. The important thing is to not allow fear to stop you from moving forward.

Vincent van Gogh once wrote a letter to his brother Theo trying to convince him that they should go into business together as painters. Theo was concerned that he didn't have the talent to make it, but Vincent was adamant that the level of skill needed to make a living as an artist is well within reach of anyone willing to put in the work.

To be clear, skill is important. But it's also true that skill can be learned through practice, and that getting paid as an artist does not require superhuman talent. I think the fastest way to build confidence is to level up your skill. Although a full course on the mechanics of making art is outside the scope of this book, I will give some practices you can use to build both skill and confidence.

- **Make one for yourself.** Not every piece needs to be made for publication. Sometimes I will sit down and make something just for me, not to share. Just knowing that I don't need to worry about making the results marketable (or even complete) frees me up to try new techniques. And sometimes the results end up being marketable anyway.
- **Draft with thumbnails.** I see a lot of beginners make the mistake of trying to create a perfect, finished piece in one go. It's tempting for side hustlers with limited time to skip drafts and dive straight into a final design. After all, drafts take time, and every stroke of the pen has to *really count.* But here is an artist's secret: Thumbnail sketches are *essential.* Even when you have an idea in mind about how to compose a piece, the odds are very good that that idea will require editing and refinement to ensure it says what you want it to say.

Thumbnail sketches are quick, small, and *cheap* drawings that allow you to try out different compositions without investing too much time in ideas that end up not working. They allow you to explore different realizations of your idea before committing. And thumbnails are not just a tool for beginners—working artists' sketchbooks are littered with studies for bigger pieces.

- **Face your dragons (or flowers)**. Every artist has at least a few dragons in their ocean of creativity; these are subjects that feel unnatural or daunting to work with. A big one for me was florals. I lack a green thumb and didn't feel connected to the subject, but I knew florals had significant demand in the art market. So, I challenged myself to approach them in my own style, and over time I developed what I now call my "Gingiber flowers." They're distinctly mine and show up as motifs in a lot of my work, and I'm proud of how I turned a weakness into a strength.

  What subject do you avoid drawing because it doesn't flow naturally? Put some concentrated practice time into it to build your muscle memory. Think about the subjects you've been avoiding—maybe it's drawing people, hands, animals, or even architecture. These are the areas where intentional practice will make the biggest difference in your work.

  Leveling up your craft and building confidence will require active effort, because growth happens at the frontier between ease and challenge. While it's important to lean in to what feels natural and enjoyable, avoiding what makes you uncomfortable can limit your potential.

Break Negative Pattern 2: Overcome Artist's Block

Artist's block happens to all of us from time to time. You sit down at your workspace with your art supplies, all ready to go, and—your mind draws a blank. One day you know exactly what ideas to pursue during your creative time, but the next it feels like the idea faucet has dried up; the inspiration has gone or at least gone into hiding. This is demoralizing when you know what it feels like to be in a flow state where the ideas just pour out. If you're like me, you might even panic a little—*What if I never have an idea again?!*

Don't panic! I'm here to tell you that artists' block is one of the easiest barriers to overcome, because having ideas was never all about getting inspired in the first place. It is true that some ideas seem to come from nowhere. But you don't have to sit and wait for them to arrive; there are specific practices we can incorporate to encourage them.

- **Pull out that sketchbook!** If you're following the S.T.A.R. Cycle, I hope you're carrying a sketchbook where you've jotted down notes, doodles, and thumbnail sketches. Now is the time to put them to work. Flip through the pages and see if there are any half-baked ideas that could be expanded into a full piece. It's easy for the contents of your sketchbook to feel impermanent and inconsequential—"small" ideas hastily scribbled in the in-between parts of life. Instead, I want you to think of your sketchbook as a steady supply of acorns waiting to grow into oak trees.
- **Impose a constraint on yourself.** Many artists like to draw on a tablet because it packs a lot of power in one small package. However, this power can also overwhelm—if I hypothetically could do *anything*, sometimes it's difficult to actually start on *one specific thing*. This problem is common for digital artists, but the cure is useful in any medium: Impose a constraint on yourself. For instance, you can use a limited or unusual or "ugly" color palette, or only use one type of brush (bonus points if it's an unfamiliar one).

  Pick an object and draw it upside down. Get two random words and draw something that represents both of them. Constraints enhance creativity because—and I don't have science to back this up, just experience—they seem to activate the part of your brain that looks for novel ways to subvert them.

- **Revisit an old piece.** Over time, you will build up a portfolio of both finished and unfinished pieces. Make sure you don't throw it out, because it's an absolute gold mine of ideas you can revisit, remix, and reimagine. There's no one correct way to do this; you might try remaking an old piece using the skills you've refined since it was first made or try building a collection around an old one-off piece or take an old motif and build a new piece around it.

Break Negative Pattern 3: Get Comfortable with Imperfections

A common attitude I see among early career artists is that making art requires being in the right mood for inspiration to strike. But to paraphrase Thomas Edison, creating art is 1 percent inspiration and 99 percent perspiration. When it's time to make art, *make art.*

One reason why I love *The Great British Baking Show* so much is that it doesn't shy away from those times when the soufflé falls, and the cake is dry, and the Swiss roll cracks. With editing, it would have been possible to present a baking process where the counters are always clean and everything goes just right. But baking is messy! Things go wrong all the time, and compromises have to be made!

The same is true for your art. When you see other artists' completed work, you're not necessarily also going to see all the mistakes and dead ends it took to get there, or the parts they really would like to have edited some more but didn't for the sake of finishing. If you get stuck thinking that a piece has to be perfect before it is done, *it will never be done.*

I think most if not all artists struggle with perfectionism at least sometimes; part of what makes an artist is an opinionated aesthetic sense and a compulsion to see it realized. I have a few tools I use to fight that urge and get work to "done."

- **Give yourself permission to make crappy art.** When I'm working on a piece that's just not working, sometimes I find myself falling into the sunk-cost mindset: I've already put so much time into this idea, I have to make it work so that time isn't wasted. But this is backward—the real waste of time is to keep spinning my wheels while getting nowhere. It's one thing if I'm actually making progress that happens to be slow. But "slow" is not the same as "stuck."

Sometimes I have to force myself to call the piece done, even if I don't really like it, and put it in my folder of unpublished work. I am totally okay with this because I have one golden rule when it comes to making art: *No work is ever wasted.* Even pieces that feel like failures can be revisited and repurposed later.

I can't even count the number of times I've been able to take a "bad" old piece and turn it into a new design that goes to market. If a piece isn't coming together, it's fine to put it in the duds pile and start fresh. You're not throwing away that effort; you're setting it aside for later so you can focus on something more productive now.

- **Set a hard time limit.** Only allow yourself a fixed time budget for editing. If time runs out and it's still not working, into the unpublished drafts it goes. But if it is good enough, call it done. I can't tell you exactly what "good enough" means because it depends so much on exactly what you're making. But if the remaining problems with a piece are difficult to resolve because there are multiple acceptable options, just pick one. Flip a coin if you need to!
- **Beware of diminishing returns.** Imagine your art as a big pile of dirt. (Stay with me here.) Your goal is to move the dirt from one pile to another, and you'd like to do it quickly. Now given the choice, is it better to dig with a shovel or a teaspoon? Tweaking a piece to death is like moving dirt with a teaspoon. Yes, it will probably work (eventually), but it's not the best use of your time. Part of being a professional artist is recognizing when you've picked up the teaspoon, and when it's time to step back and reassess.

  Remember that it's not actually possible for a piece of art to be perfect, because *perfection doesn't exist.* It was liberating when I really internalized this. To keep the Growth Ratchet cranking, we have to get comfortable knowing when a piece is good enough.

Lisa Bardot: Building Success One Digital Brush Stroke at a Time

"This path has shown me that big dreams can grow from even the smallest moments of dedication."

YouTube star and Procreate trailblazer Lisa Bardot didn't set out to build Bardot Brush into a full-fledged business. When I sat down to interview her for this book, she revealed to me that it all really started in the stolen moments of her life—late at night, squeezed between responsibilities, and layered on top of an already full schedule. She and her husband were wedding photographers, running a thriving but demanding business while also adjusting to parenthood.

Her entry into digital illustration was a side project, something she explored when time allowed. She created custom brushes for herself on the Procreate app, refining them as she experimented with the medium. When she put them up for sale, she had no expectations. But then people started buying them.

That initial success wasn't an endpoint; it was an opening. Lisa didn't wait for her brushes to be perfect before launching them. She put them out there, saw the response, and iterated. Over time, she built Bardot Brush into a second full-time business, gradually phasing out her photography work. Her ability to balance taking action while learning from each launch became the foundation for her success.

Today, Bardot Brush is more than a product-based business; it's the heart of Lisa's work as an educator. She's expanded into online courses, a membership (Art Makers Club), the daily drawing challenge Making Art Everyday, and a YouTube channel full of tutorials and creative inspiration. But it all started with that first small launch—a reminder that taking action, even in small ways, is what leads to real growth.

STEP 2: SELL THE ART—LESS UNDERTHINKING, MORE LEARNING

So, you've finished something. Great! Time to move to the next project, right? Well, yes, but also no. The second phase of the Growth Ratchet—and what turns it into an engine for continual improvement—is to observe and reflect on what happens after a launch. If you're action oriented like me, this might feel a little strange at first. After finishing a project, my mind is typically buzzing with ideas to try next. But with experience, I've learned to love this phase, because I've seen how valuable the launch-and-learn cycle is for long-term growth.

The concept of launching is not reserved for big product announcements. Launching just means publishing something to the world. That includes new products but also social media posts, newsletters, podcast episodes—any time you pick up the microphone to communicate with your audience, you're launching, and by being thoughtful about it, you can learn to make your launches as effective as they can be.

My most important piece of business advice is probably this: *Paint like a scientist.* I don't literally mean put on a lab coat and rubber gloves—although I suppose you could, and there are many scientists who also paint! What I mean is to plan your launches and then observe (and where possible, also *measure*) the outcome.

- **Have a launch plan and stick to it.** Exactly what your launch plans look like will vary, but the most important thing is to *have* a plan. Decide when and where to announce the launch, and write any posts in advance. Test your checkout and product pages to make sure customers won't run into problems—remember to check the mobile view! Use an incognito window to see what your site looks like for brand-new visitors.

  Bigger launches may also include ad spend and working with affiliates, and at that point having a plan is a must—big launches don't succeed by accident. I like to use a checklist to make sure I remember everything for the launch, and if anything goes wrong, I make a note to try to avoid it next time. Checklists also help me avoid anxiety during a launch because I'm not just throwing something against the wall to see if it sticks. I've got a *plan* and backup plans and a plan to adjust the plan.

- **Know where your analytics are, and keep an eye on them.** Every launch generates a trove of information. Like and share counts and changes in followers are coarse metrics for social media, and these are also affected by the time of day and day of the week. Your e-commerce platform or website probably has more data like your checkout conversion rate, where traffic comes from, and how visitors got there.

  When I have a timed launch window, I'll track daily stats to see the trajectory of the launch. In my experience, launch windows follow a pattern; by measuring the results in the beginning, I can make rough projections for the remaining days and adjust the launch plan as needed.

- **Adjust future launches to incorporate what you learn.** Over time, you'll see patterns in what your audience responds to. Now we need to close the loop by using what we learn to make the *next* launch more effective. Sometimes a particular subject does especially well. Maybe you get a large amount of traffic from a country; that is a good place to look for local retail partners. It can also be the case that some or all of the launch disappoints—I get my fair share of this too.

  Even if a launch doesn't convert as high as we'd like, we can still learn from it. Maybe an Instagram post gets less traction than I expected, or an ad campaign ends up targeting the wrong audience. Not everything in a launch is a hard and fast rule; running a business online involves so many variables, we can't possibly account for them all, and flukes do happen sometimes. Even so, the results we measure can help us refine our launch plans.

Developing the practice of setting up your launches to learn about your audience is an important step on the path from artist to art business. This might not sound like much fun if you haven't tried it before, but it's a tremendously useful tool for making your launches more successful.

Engaging Your Audience

The Internet provides us with an invaluable resource: direct engagement with an audience. This can happen on social media or in a dedicated community on your own website. However you interact with them, your audience is a wellspring of knowledge to help you better understand your niche.

- **Interact with them.** When you share your work on social media, respond to comments. Not all of them, necessarily, because that could get overwhelming, but some. Think of the comments under each of your posts as a little discussion board where the people have been brought together by a common interest in *your art*. The audience there has received what you are trying to say and is interested enough to respond. Cultivate a community there.
- **Listen to them.** Your audience can also be a tremendous source of both feedback and ideas. If you get the same questions over and over, that's a good sign that your message needs to be clarified or made more prominent. If you get subject requests, that's a sign of a potentially untapped niche for your style.
- **Bring them in.** Your community is a great place to share what goes on behind the scenes. Tease new product launches, show work in progress, even show two different drafts of a piece and poll to see which one the audience wants to see completed. When the audience feels a connection to your journey, they become invested in your progress.

STOP NITPICKING AND START FINISHING

A lot of artists stall out at the same moment: staring at a "maybe done" piece, unsure whether to tweak one more thing or finally release it into the world. When you're stuck in the weeds—second-guessing everything or endlessly reworking small details—pause and ask yourself: *Am I making a thoughtful improvement, or am I just avoiding the discomfort of declaring it done?*

Knowing when a piece is ready to launch comes down to a clear, intentional framework. That's where the Wait Versus Change Framework comes in. This is a gut-check tool to help you decide whether your work needs more refinement or whether it's time to hit Publish.

This framework doesn't aim for perfection. Instead, it helps you recognize when something is "good enough" when you're at a stage where progress matters more than polishing. It's about learning to trust your instincts *and* your process. *Good enough* doesn't mean lowering standards—it means recognizing when additional tweaks won't meaningfully improve the outcome and having the confidence to put it out into the world.

The Wait Versus Change Framework

Before you apply this framework, check in with yourself first. If your decision feels emotionally loaded—like you're anxious, second-guessing, or obsessing over small details—it's probably time to wait. Step back. Give yourself space. When your head is calm and clear, go through the questions in the framework with a critical eye.

- Does it communicate what you intended?
- Is it free of any obvious technical flaws that might distract from the message?
- Would you be proud to include this in your portfolio?
- Could you reasonably improve it within your time constraints?

If the first three answers are *yes* and the last is *no*, then it's good enough—ready to be released into the world.

If you see a specific, meaningful change that would improve the piece, then go ahead and make it. Just don't nitpick your way to perfection. You could "fix" something forever. If you've stepped away, come back fresh, and no obvious change jumps out at you, it's probably done. Let it go. Growth comes not from endless editing, but from *finishing*, sharing, learning, and moving forward.

REFINING YOUR PIECES BEFORE LAUNCH: HOW TO DEVELOP A CRITICAL EYE

It's important to get feedback on your work if you want to grow as an artist. Of course, when you publish on the Internet, feedback (from trolls) is not exactly in short supply—but that's not what I'm talking about. *Constructive* feedback is aimed at understanding what parts of a piece work well, and what parts need editing, with the goal of improving both the art and the artist.

The gold standard for feedback is to have a supportive community of peers who care about each other and about the craft and can critique each other's work. If you have a community like this, cherish it! Nowadays it is also possible to get a professional portfolio review, where an experienced artist will make a detailed critique of your portfolio for a fee. A third option, which doesn't cost anything and is available to everyone, is self-critique.

When I first started out, professional portfolio reviews weren't readily available. I had to learn to critique my own work, and frankly, it was a tough process. But I've come to believe that self-critique is one of the most essential and challenging skills an artist can develop. The purpose is not to nitpick every detail—it's to learn how to identify what makes a piece work. Being able to assess your own work allows you to move faster and eventually starts to impact your work as you're making it.

To critique a piece of art, we need to develop a critical eye. The word *criticism* might conjure images of blunt feedback tearing apart all the flaws in a piece, but this is *not at all* the purpose of criticism. Critique is not judgmental; it doesn't think in terms of good and bad but engages with the work as it is.

Having a critical eye means being able to understand how a piece is constructed, what makes it work (or not work), and how different choices would change the final product. Where a lay person might look at a chair and see a chair, a carpenter's critical eye sees how the grain flows, how the spindles were carved, the joinery holding it together, the proportions of the legs and arms, the species of the wood.

Visual art is also physically composed of smaller parts in a way that rewards craftsmanship. A critical eye can take the lessons learned from one piece and apply them to another. This cycle of self-assessment and improvement is what makes practice so effective.

The following list of questions is a simple rubric to help beginning artists productively critique their work. Each one focuses on a different element of composition. Take a finished piece and think about each question, then think about how changes to the piece might change the answer to the question as well as the overall effect of the work.

The Self-Critique Composition Rubric

- **Line:** Is the linework clear, purposeful, haphazard, timid?
- **Color:** How dynamic is the color palette? Is it vibrant or muted, playful, or austere?
- **Balance:** How is visual weight distributed across the composition? Does it feel homogeneous or lopsided?
- **Emphasis:** What is the focal point of the composition? What grabs the viewers' attention, and where is that attention directed?
- **Movement:** How do lines, shapes, and gradients guide the eye through the composition? Does the implied motion feel natural, stilted, graceful?
- **Contrast:** How are opposing elements juxtaposed in the composition? Big and small, light and dark, smooth and rough?

- **Pattern:** What repeating elements bring structure to the composition? Do these elicit an expectation in the viewer?

After having applied the rubric on a few pieces, the next time you are making thumbnail sketches to draft a piece, intentionally play with one or more elements of the composition to see which you prefer.

Beyond evaluating composition, I rely on a few other practical tools to determine if a piece is working:

- **The thumbnail test:** I shrink the finished piece to about one inch tall (either digitally or by printing it small). This helps me see if the main elements remain clear and legible when scaled down.
- **The flip test:** I turn the canvas upside down or mirror it. This often reveals hidden composition issues because I'm able to see the piece in a more abstract way, without my brain filling in what it *thinks* should be there.
- **The squint test:** I literally squint my eyes to blur the details. This allows me to check whether the values and focal points still stand out when everything is reduced to basic shapes and tones.
- **The walk-away test:** Stepping away for 24 hours before revisiting the piece gives me fresh eyes to immediately spot any glaring issues.

These simple yet effective techniques help refine a piece before launch.

Kristen Olivares: Building Dreams Before Dawn Breaks

"Every single day is 365 chances closer to where I want to be."

One of my Make Your Art Course students, Kristen Olivares, built her creative business in the early-morning hours before the rest of the world woke up. As a homeschooling mom to two boys, she didn't have long, uninterrupted stretches of time to dedicate to her art. But what she did have was persistence—and a commitment to taking consistent action.

She carved out her work hours at 4:45 A.M., picking away at her to-do list in small, steady increments. She learned through trial and error, adapting her approach as she went. Her first craft shows were a lesson in learning on the fly—she and her husband built display walls from 2x4s and pegboard, only to realize they were heavy, bulky, and a pain to assemble. Her first prints were framed with glass that was too shiny. She Scotch-taped prints to mat boards and, as she now admits with a laugh, used construction paper on the back to cover up the mess.

Despite the rough beginnings, she didn't stop. Kristen refined her materials, upgraded her display setup, and gradually shifted to higher-quality products. As she improved her process, her business grew alongside it.

Looking back, Kristen acknowledges that research might have saved her some time, but she also recognizes that experience was her best teacher. She didn't let perfectionism stall her progress, nor did she blindly repeat the same mistakes without learning from them. Instead, she stayed in the Goldilocks Zone—taking action, gathering feedback, and refining her approach.

Her advice to other artists mirrors her own journey: "The secret is to be persistent, hold a strong vision, and never give up."

TURNING THE GROWTH RATCHET

Not every problem you'll face as you grow your art business comes down to overthinking or underthinking. But by addressing these two points and making sure your Growth Ratchet is operating well, you can have a clear path to making progress. The launch-and-learn cycle is a simple and repeatable strategy for helping you find your place and your audience in the art market. By staying in your Goldilocks Zone and keeping your Growth Ratchet turning, you've set the foundation for a side hustle that is not only creative, but it's also strategic, sustainable, and built for real growth.

You've done the deep work—now it's time to build. In the next chapter, we're going to start assembling your Art Side Hustle Toolkit—the set of practical tools and systems that will support your creative business behind the scenes. These are the things that most artists *don't* talk about (like taxes, websites, and portfolios), but they're the quiet backbone of every thriving art business.

Don't worry, you won't have to tackle it all at once. We're going to take it step by step, tool by tool. Let's open the box and take a look inside.

7

YOUR ART SIDE HUSTLE TOOLKIT

As you transition from making art to making *money* from your art, you have to start viewing your creative passion through the lens of operating a business. If that sounds daunting, you're not alone! This part can get overwhelming for even the most talented artists.

Sales. Marketing. Networking. Taxes. Budgets. Profit Margins. Shipping. Portfolios. These are just *some* of the not-so-fun things that you have to wrap your head around to have a real, functional business—and that list doesn't even include making art!

When I teach these concepts to artists, I like to use the metaphor of a toolbox. Your typical toolbox will have a bunch of things in it, from general-purpose tools like mallets and saws to more specialized gadgets like right-angle clamps. The toolbox is versatile: Two carpenters can take the same set of tools and build two beautiful, functional, and *completely different* pieces with them. In the same way, as you build your creative business, there are some known problems you will encounter, and the Art Side Hustle Toolkit is designed to help you tackle them.

WHAT MAKES AN ARTIST'S TOOLKIT DIFFERENT?

Running an art-based business presents a unique set of challenges for an entrepreneur. Most obviously, the raw material we work with is our creative output, which is unpredictable and precious. Every product we sell first requires hours (sometimes weeks!) of creative development that you can't rush or automate, and which is hard to scale up. Then our market has a lot of natural cycles, which can lead to a feast-or-famine routine that is stressful to weather. We're creating a delicate ecosystem where creativity and commerce have to play nice together, learning to tell our story in a way that connects with our audience's hearts, and somehow being both the dreamer and the practical business owner that our company requires. It's like being the star of your own show while also handling the lighting, ticket sales, and concession stand.

I've divided the tools into two groups that I call *Strategic tools* and *Tactical tools*. Strategic tools are all about your plan and your long-term goals; these are big picture tools. Tactical tools are more technical; these get into the nitty-gritty details of the art business.

STRATEGIC TOOLS

Before you jump into the logistics of selling your art, you need a strong inner foundation. Strategic tools help you stay grounded, focused, and creatively fueled—especially when you're juggling your art alongside everything else in your life. These are the mindset anchors and long-term habits that will keep your business from burning out before it even begins.

Your Creative Battery

Running a creative business comes with one majorly unique challenge: You can't just restock your shelves with more art when you run low. When I managed inventory at the coffee shop, if we were about to run out of coffee beans, we'd just order more. However, I'm not aware of a service that will deliver creativity on demand. (Yet.)

Maintaining a fresh body of work that feels authentically "you" takes time, practice, and probably more cups of coffee than you'd care to admit—and we forget this at our peril. I learned this lesson the hard way in my early Gingiber days. One season I was so busy shipping orders that I completely forgot to refill my "creative cup." When I needed new products to release, I rushed the creative process, and it showed. My next release wasn't as successful because I hadn't given myself time to make the art I needed. These days I block out sacred creative hours each week—even if creativity that week is more akin to rearranging my living room or going to an art museum rather than sketching. Yes, even when my inbox is screaming for attention. Especially then! This is the engine of your business, and it's vital to keep it well oiled.

Not sure how to spend your creative time when you're not actively making new work? Think of it like cross-training for your imagination. You could flip through an old sketchbook, take yourself on a solo field trip to the library or antique store, listen to an artist interview podcast while on a walk, or even do something tactile like bake a new recipe or organize your studio. Creativity sneaks in through the side door.

Action Step:
Make Your Creative Battery Plan

Write down three to five activities that help you feel creatively refueled. Pick one and block off a time for it this week, just like you'd block off a dentist appointment or school pickup. Set a timer if needed. Protect this time like it's the most important meeting of your week—because for your art business, it just might be.

Lanette Yates: Balancing Healthcare and Creative Dreams

When you're balancing a day job, life responsibilities, and a creative side hustle, it's easy to burn out before you even get started. Lanette Yates, one of the members of my Creative Powerhouse Society Community, learned this the hard way. An art major turned healthcare professional, Lanette kept her creativity alive through small projects over the years. But when she decided to pursue art more seriously during the pandemic, she knew she had to be strategic about her time.

Instead of jumping in at full speed and risking exhaustion, Lanette made a key adjustment: She transitioned to a four-day workweek in healthcare, giving herself one dedicated "art day" per week. This shift allowed her to protect her creative energy, ensuring she didn't lose the joy of making art by cramming it into every spare moment.

She also set clear boundaries, reserving workdays for admin tasks like answering e-mails and listening to business podcasts, while saving creative work for her dedicated art time. This intentional structure kept her from feeling overwhelmed and allowed her business to grow at a sustainable pace.

"Don't overcommit too soon; strive for balance between hustling and rest. You don't want to lose the joy that creating brings you by stressing the business stuff too much."

Lanette's approach is a powerful reminder that hustling doesn't mean working yourself in the ground. By pacing herself and making deliberate choices, she built a sustainable creative business that still brings her joy.

Authentic Storytelling

Remember when you were little, and you eagerly showed your crayon drawings to a loved one, and they would ask you to tell them about your illustration? That excitement you felt explaining every tiny detail? That storytelling magic doesn't go away just because we've grown up! In fact, it becomes something like a superpower, creating value and meaning out of thin air. Your art isn't just about pretty pictures, the best composition, or perfect patterns—it's also about the story behind them.

When someone falls in love with a piece of art, they also fall in love with the spark that inspired it, the journey it took to create it, and the value they derive from it in their own lives. By embracing your role as an authentic storyteller, you build a business that doesn't just make money but makes meaning.

One of the best ways to start practicing this is by writing an *artist statement.* An artist statement is a short description of the *why* behind a particular piece or body of work. It can include what inspired you, what materials you used, and what the piece means to you. This isn't about sounding fancy or academic—it's about giving people a window into your creative heart.

Action Step:
Write a Mini Artist Statement

Pick one piece of your art–any piece that makes you feel proud or joyful–and write two to three sentences about why you made it, what it means to you, or what you hope others see in it. Don't overthink it. Just tell the story behind the art in your own words.

The Striving Artist Mindset

Putting your art out into the world feels about as vulnerable as that bad dream of showing up to class in your pajamas. The Chaos Goblin loves to show up (usually right before a big launch or important pitch), and creative blocks can feel like five alarm business emergencies. That's why the Striving Artist mindset we talked about way back in Chapter 2 isn't just nice; it's as essential as your favorite kneaded eraser.

I keep a folder labeled "love notes" filled with sweet messages from customers, and I browse through it on days when I need to remember why I started this journey. Sometimes you need a reminder that your art matters! And sometimes, you need a whole *toolkit* of reminders. Here are a few more ways to keep that striving artist energy alive—even on the hard days:

- **Keep a Wins Journal:** Write down every small victory, from finishing a sketch to getting a kind DM. Over time, you'll have pages of proof that you're making progress.
- **Create a Visual Reminder:** Post your favorite piece of art near your workspace and use your vision board to remind you what this journey is leading you toward.
- **Set "Feel-Good" Goals:** Not every goal has to be tied to money or followers. Consider goals like "enjoy my sketchbook for 30 minutes" or "try a new color palette just for fun."
- **Take Artist Dates** (credit to Julia Cameron's *The Artist's Way*): Visit a local gallery, spend an hour in a bookstore, or take yourself out for a coffee and quiet reflection—just you and your creativity.
- **Talk to Yourself Like a Friend:** When your inner critic shows up, try this: Would you talk to your best creative friend the way you're talking to yourself? If not, it's time to change the script.

Action Step: Build Your Own Creative Confidence Toolkit

Pick one of the ideas above (or create your own!) and put it into action this week. Whether it's starting a "wins" journal or hanging a favorite quote above your desk, take one small step that reminds you: You're doing brave, beautiful work–and that matters.

Multiple Income Streams

One month you're turning down pet portrait commissions, the next you're wondering if everyone on your commission waitlist simultaneously forgot that you exist. Artistic income is famously subject to feast-or-famine cycles, and after one too many panic attacks during those moments of famine, I learned that sustainable art businesses need multiple income streams.

Different parts of the industry ebb and flow at different times, so diversifying your business will help even out the ups and downs in revenue. These days, Gingiber has income flowing from physical products, licensing deals, teaching, and custom design projects. When one stream slows down, another one picks up the slack. It's like having a business safety net made of creativity! (We'll dive into how to set up your income streams with the three frameworks beginning in Chapter 8.)

Heart-Driven Business Models

Here's the beautiful mess of running an art business: We're essentially trying to build a bridge between creativity and commerce, all while keeping our artistic soul intact. Some days you'll feel like a walking contradiction—an artist who needs to think about profit margins, a dreamer who needs to send strategic marketing newsletters on the regular. It is not just possible to strike that balance, it is necessary. Keeping your heart at the helm of your career is how you stay focused on your Personal Why.

So how do you actually let your heart lead in business? It starts with asking what truly lights you up. What parts of your creative practice make you lose track of time? What messages do you feel called to share through your work? What problem do your creations solve for others—or what joy do they spark?

Your heart-driven business might start with a single sketch, a phrase that feels important, or a quiet pull toward a purpose you can't yet fully name. Sometimes, following that spark leads you to something bigger than you imagined.

Debby, one of my Leverage Your Art course alumni and now a Creative Hive Mastermind member, shares a wonderful example:

Debby Lightman: Building a Heart-Driven Business

For many artists, the business side of things can feel overwhelming—but what if you let your passion lead the way? Debby Lightman, founder of the brand Mindfulnice, didn't start with a grand business plan. She started with Post-it notes.

With a background in psychology and education, Debby was teaching mindfulness and meditation in local schools when she noticed something: Students and teachers wanted tools to help them practice mindfulness outside the classroom. She began scribbling down activities, turning her ideas into small, shareable resources.

At first, she didn't think of this as a business; it was simply a way to help others. But as demand grew, she turned those scribbled notes into Mindful Minute Activity Cards, a product that would later define her creative business.

Her first sale? A handmade gemstone necklace at a small local art show. But the moment that changed everything came at her second show, when a couple approached her in tears. They shared how her Mindful Minute Activity Cards had transformed their relationship, helping them connect in ways they hadn't before.

"What started as a way to share mindfulness and help others turned into a creative side hustle."

That moment gave Debby the confidence to keep going. But running a business while raising children meant working in small pockets of time—early mornings, late nights, and school hours. Instead of focusing on what she didn't have (like a full workday), she broke her tasks into manageable steps, proving that meaningful businesses can grow even in the margins of life.

Debby's story is a testament to the fact that you don't have to force a business idea—sometimes, your purpose naturally becomes your business.

Action Step:
Follow the Spark

Take 10 minutes today to reflect on what lights you up most about your creative practice. What themes or causes do you care about deeply? What conversations does your art seem to naturally start? Write a few notes or journal entries about how your art could make someone's life better. You might just uncover the heart of your business.

TACTICAL TOOLS—THE ARTIST'S POWER TRIO

Strategic tools are important for your art business, but they are also pretty abstract. Now we're going to get into the weeds. *Tactical tools* are concrete things that will take time to develop, but this time is well-spent. These tools will be aimed at defining three key characteristics of your business I like to call the Power Trio: your Style, your Brand, and your Portfolio. Together these form the foundation of your side hustle, and once that foundation is solid, you can build a stable business framework on top. These are the tools that turn amateurs into professionals.

Tactical Tool 1: Your Unique Style

When your art tells a story, your personal style is the accent it speaks with. It's what makes someone look at a piece and say, "That's a Gingiber illustration." It's what less scrupulous brands will try to copy, and what you'll one day teach to your apprentices. I cannot overemphasize the value of identifying and developing your personal art style.

By nature, style isn't something that will ever be "done." It evolves as you evolve. But it does stabilize—and in a world overflowing with visual noise, having a distinct and recognizable point of view is one of your greatest assets. It's time to embrace your inner unicorn and get wildly weird with it.

I like to call artists in this stage *Discoverers*. This is your time to create boldly as your unique voice begins to emerge. You'll share with friends and family, post online, and most importantly, enjoy the journey of developing your creative fingerprint.

How I Found My Personal Style

My own artistic journey proves how style develops naturally when you give it time and space to grow.

I've loved drawing dogs for as long as I can remember. My first attempts—around age four—were joyful crayon chaos: wobbly circles for heads, stick legs, triangle ears the size of their heads, and tails wherever I felt like putting them. My dogs had 17 legs and came in all colors of the rainbow—especially purple. They weren't technically correct, but they were full of joy.

By age 10, I had entered what I call my "cartoon phase." Inspired by Spottie Dottie (a major influence!), I drew dalmatians using a formula: circle head, bigger circle body, floppy ears, and tons of spots. Still far from realistic—but deliberate.

In college, I found myself stuck. My portfolio was a mix of artist studies, drawings of friends, and work that clung tightly to realism. It was technically fine, but it lacked soul. I was so afraid of creating without a reference that I never gave myself the freedom to explore what made my work uniquely mine. And the result? My work, while polished, felt flat and forgettable.

Everything shifted when I started designing my daughter's nursery. Late nights, a sleeping baby, and piles of sketches gave way to a new style—pen-and-ink lines, muted colors, animals with attitude, and those now-signature Gingiber cheek dots. That was the moment things clicked.

Why don't my animals smile? Why the distinctive cheeks? Because that's what made them mine.

How to Find Your Personal Style

Here's the truth: The most successful artists in the market usually develop their style before they try to monetize it. Every hour you spend now exploring your style is an investment in your future business.

Give yourself *three to six months of pure creative exploration* before trying to sell anything. Your only job is to create consistently, notice patterns, and document your journey:

- What subjects make you lose track of time?
- What techniques feel natural?
- Which pieces make you think, *This feels like me*?

When you develop your unique artistic voice before the pressure of sales goals and customer demands, you're building an unshakable creative foundation. Your art and business can grow in tandem, but the creative foundation comes first.

Your art business journey can have two parallel tracks running simultaneously. While you spend these months developing your style through consistent creation, experimentation, and documenting what feels authentic, you can also lay the groundwork for your business. Your art and business can grow together.

The Personal Style Discovery S.T.A.R. Cycle

To kickstart your exploration, try using the S.T.A.R. Cycle as a one-month intensive. (And remember—you can always stretch this timeline if needed!)

Even if you've been making art for a long time, you might not know what your personal style is. That's okay! We're going to adapt the S.T.A.R. Cycle into a style discovery machine. It's time for a scavenger hunt, and we're gathering clues about what makes your art uniquely yours.

Here's how we will adjust the S.T.A.R. Cycle.

- **Week 1: Explore and Make**

  Create a variety of pieces using different mediums. Document what brings you joy in each one. What tools feel natural in your hands?

- **Week 2: Deep Dive**

  Draw what you love most. Try new subjects. Revisit favorite pieces and create variations. Push beyond your comfort zone.

- **Week 3: Play with the Details**

  Test new color palettes. Take your "safest" piece and remake it—then get weird with it. Draw the same subject in three totally different styles.

- **Week 4: Refine and Reflect**

  Note which techniques energize or drain you. Identify which pieces feel most like "you." List your favorite go-to materials and recurring themes.

Reminder: If a weekly cadence doesn't work for you, adapt the cycle to fit your life. The goal is consistent exploration, not perfection.

Action Step:
Explore Your Personal Style

At the end of the month, lay out all your work–yes, even the cringey ones! Print your digital pieces. Spread them out on the floor or a table and look at them away from a screen. Look for patterns, preferences, and artistic DNA. What's emerging? That's your unique voice–trust it, nurture it, and let it guide your creative journey.

Tactical Tool 2: Your Brand

When you commit to your side hustle, it's no longer enough to simply make art and share it. You have to craft *how* you share your art with the world in a narrative that makes sense to both you and your audience. You have to build your personal art brand—and you are the *only* person who can do it. (Don't worry. I've got your back.)

The day I learned the true meaning of a brand story was life changing. It also involved crying in public in front of one of my heroes. It was a big day.

I was only three-ish years into running Gingiber, but I already knew that if I wanted to grow, I needed to learn from an expert. Enter Grace Kang, a former buyer for Bloomingdale's and the founder of Pink Olive, a boutique known for supporting independent artists and makers. She was one of the first store owners to reach out to me on Etsy, asking to carry my products in her shop, so it felt like fate when she accepted me into her brand coaching program.

Part of the coaching process included me coming to New York City for an in-person workshop on brand building. It was a rainy day in NYC, and I had no umbrella or boots. I showed up at her headquarters soaking wet, but I refused to let that stop me from making the most of this meeting.

Grace sat me down, and we began working through worksheet after worksheet about my business. But these weren't factoids about how much I had sold or questions I could answer about my big Gingiber dreams—those I could have handled. Instead, she looked me straight in the eye and asked a simple question that would unravel my entire self-conception as an entrepreneur: "What is your true, authentic Brand Story? If someone were to ask you to describe Gingiber in a single sentence, what would you say?"

I froze. The silence stretched out, growing from awkward to agonizing. My nose began to sting, and I felt tears welling up behind my glasses. I couldn't cry in front of a mentor. I was trying to be a real professional business lady. *There's no crying in business.* I just needed to focus, push through, and dazzle Grace with my vision.

But the floodgates gave way, and I burst into tears. To her credit, Grace was kind and patient as I had a minor mental breakdown in her office. Here I was, already selling successfully on Etsy, but I couldn't articulate what my business even *was*, or who it served. In my rush to start selling, I had somehow skipped this incredibly basic step.

When Grace gently pressed me to describe my brand, I realized I had never stopped to think about what Gingiber truly meant—not just as a business, but as a creative force in the world. I had been telling myself a false narrative, unwilling to accept the full weight of the business I had created. Somewhere deep down, I didn't truly view Gingiber as a *real* business—it was a glorified hobby, and my success was just sheer luck. It wasn't worth articulating, and if I did, wouldn't that be oversharing? Professionals don't talk about their feelings.

I had built a perfect Catch-22 out of a lifetime's worth of toxic thoughts around the value of art and even my own value as an artist and a person. No wonder I started crying!

I'm so glad she challenged me that day. I sat down, reflected on pretty much everything I've shared with you so far about my journey, and then looked even deeper. I wrote down every milestone that had happened from the moment I found the word *Gingiber* in an old Latin dictionary, to the very first time I heard the *cha-ching* sound coming from the Etsy app telling me I made a sale, to the first blog that featured my art, to this very moment in NYC.

(About that blog post: *Hi, Holly from Decor8! Did you know you changed my life?*)

You don't usually recognize a life-changing moment until it's already passed. But those memories helped me recognize the power of a brand story that was entirely my own. A brand story isn't just a description; it's your creative DNA. It's the narrative that transforms a business from a collection of products into a recognizable entity that people can root for and connect with. In a very real sense, your Brand Story *is* your brand.

Two Ways to Tell Your Brand Story

What Grace was asking me for on that day was my Brand Story. We're going to walk through how to create this *right now*, so that if anyone ever asks you to describe what your company is all about (and they will! often!) you will know exactly what to say. There are going to be two versions of this story: the elevator pitch for when time is short, and the extended brand story for when it's not.

Your Elevator Pitch is your creative introduction. It should be short enough to pitch to a stranger while riding the elevator—concise, engaging, and memorable. Here's mine:

Hi, I'm Stacie Bloomfield, an illustrator and entrepreneur with over a decade of industry experience. I run Gingiber, a creative business that produces items sold in over 1,000 brick-and-mortar stores. I've licensed artwork to companies like Williams Sonoma and Crate & Kids. My goal? To create artwork that encourages people to live their most creative lives.

Let me pull back the curtain on how I built my elevator pitch—because trust me, it didn't just magically appear! I remember feeling lost writing it, so here's a little guide to the elements it should include.

- **Who You Are:** "Hi, I'm Stacie Bloomfield, an illustrator and entrepreneur . . ." (This establishes both my name and my professional identity.)
- **What You Do:** "with over a decade of industry experience. I run Gingiber." (This shows that I've been doing this awhile and have built something real and successful.)
- **Your Achievements:** "I've licensed artwork to companies like Williams Sonoma . . ." (Mention something that builds trust and shows your experience—this could be a brand collaboration, completing a portfolio, selling your first print, hosting a pop-up, or even teaching a mini class online.)
- **Your Purpose:** "My goal? To create artwork . . ." (This is the heart—why you do what you do.)

When I first started, my pitch was just "I'm an artist who draws animals." Accurate, but pretty basic. But as my business grew, my pitch evolved. Your pitch will too, and that's exactly how it should be! Start where you are, and let it grow with you.

Even if you're just starting out, you need an elevator pitch now! Having a quick way to tell people what you do is super valuable no matter where you're at, from the coffee shop to the craft fair.

Action Step:
Elevator Pitch Practice

Write down your elevator pitch and practice saying it to three people this week–friends, fellow artists, or even your pet if you're nervous. The goal is to get used to owning your identity out loud.

Your Extended Brand Story: Once you've got your elevator pitch, it's time to expand it into a longer version—perfect for your website, portfolio, or press kit. This version gives more context, personality, and backstory to your creative brand. Here's mine:

> Gingiber is the work of artist Stacie Bloomfield. Her goal is to encourage and inspire you to live your most creative life. Our original designs feature bold colors and unexpected patterns. We have a teensy sentimental streak and a healthy obsession with vintage children's books and stories you never outgrow.
>
> Our goods are made to be timeless and enjoyed by the young and the young at heart. Once upon a time, Stacie couldn't find artwork for her daughter's nursery, so she decided to take matters into her own hands. She kept being drawn to the irresistible essence of animals—their furry faces, perky ears, and plethora of colors and textures.
>
> Animals simply have a way of being adventurous and fun, both figuratively and literally. At Gingiber, we believe life should be that way too.

They may be short, but writing both your elevator pitch and your extended brand story will take thought and introspection; they deserve time to marinate. This extended version helps people connect with not just *what* you do, but *why* you do it. It makes your brand feel human and memorable.

Action Step: Write Your Brand Story

Write a two- to three-paragraph version of your brand story. Include the following aspects:

- What your business stands for
- Where the idea came from
- What kind of artwork you create
- What you want people to feel when they see your work

Building Your Brand Story S.T.A.R. Cycle

We can adapt the S.T.A.R. Cycle to give space for this work.

- **Week 1: Find Your Voice.** Write down three words that describe your art. Practice introducing yourself as an artist, and document what makes your work unique.
- **Week 2: Craft Your Story.** Draft your first elevator pitch. Test it on two people you trust, then refine it based on their reactions.
- **Week 3: Expand Your Narrative.** List your artistic milestones. Write your creative origin story and collect meaningful feedback from trusted sources.
- **Week 4: Polish and Share.** Refine your elevator pitch and draft your extended brand story. Practice telling both versions.

Don't feel like you're ready for a full brand story? No worries! For now, just document your journey. Jot down one cool thing that happened in your art each month. Save nice comments people make about your work and take photos of your creative process. These little details will become the building blocks of your brand story when you're ready to tell it.

Remember: Your story will grow and evolve with you. Start collecting the pieces now, and you'll be amazed at how naturally they come together when you need them.

Tactical Tool 3: Your Portfolio

The third part of the Artist's Power Trio is your portfolio. This is a curated catalog of finished projects showing off what you can do—but it's also more than that. Your portfolio is your creative handshake. It's your introduction to the world as an artist. Think of it as the ultimate first impression, one that can open doors to opportunities you've only dreamed of.

I know building a portfolio can feel overwhelming. My first professional portfolio wasn't perfect; it was just a quick collage of Etsy prints, Spoonflower designs, and a couple of handmade fox pillows. When I e-mailed it to The Land of Nod (now Crate & Kids), my pitch was simple: "Hi, I'm Stacie Bloomfield. Here's my art. Want to work together?" To my surprise, they said yes.

Looking back on it now, that messy little collage wasn't polished or cohesive—but it worked because my art spoke for itself. The lesson I took from that experience is to just start. Pick your best 10 to 12 pieces, arrange them in a way that makes sense to you, and get them out there. You can use a simple PDF, a basic website, or even a curated social media grid.

Start wherever you are with the tools you have—but know that eventually, you'll want to build a professional online portfolio that gives you more control over how your work is presented and discovered. A website becomes essential when you're ready to pitch to clients, apply for licensing, or get serious about building your brand presence.

Depending on your niche, you might also consider a printed portfolio, especially if you're attending trade shows, art fairs, or in-person licensing meetings. A well-designed PDF can also bridge the gap while you're building your website.

Remember that your portfolio is a living document. Update it regularly with new work, and don't be afraid to remove older pieces as your style develops.

Your Professional Website Portfolio

The most important part of your portfolio is just that it exists, whatever form it takes. But eventually, as you continue to grow your business, you'll need a portfolio that works hard for you and is shared easily during pitches.

In the 21st century, that means a website. You'll need an online headquarters where your art can shine from a laptop or phone screen.

Your website is your base of business operations. It's the one space you truly own, free from social media algorithms. Social platforms change their feeds constantly, shuffle which posts they show, or update their search rankings without warning. But your website is *your* territory. You decide how to present your work, who sees it, and how they find it. In a world where platforms come and go, your website is your creative home base; it stays steady while the world shifts around it.

Your online home should do more than display artwork. It should showcase your unique creative voice, build trust with potential clients, create multiple pathways for connection, and reflect the personality behind your brand. It's your creative living room, a place where people can get to know you and your work.

When I first created Gingiber.com, I was terrified of getting it "wrong." I thought every detail needed to be perfect, every pixel precisely placed. But websites are living, breathing spaces. They're conversations. They're invitations. Naturally, I launched my site with a huge typo on my homepage. But I fixed it and kept going. The world didn't end, and history forgot my blunder. (Until now.)

Start simple. I wish someone had told me this in the beginning. Don't get caught up in the technical details. Either hire a web designer who gets your vision or use a user-friendly platform like a website builder that offers templates for creatives. The important thing is getting your work online in a way that feels true to you. Your site will grow and evolve just like your art does. This first version will change at some point when you gain traction, so there's no need to invest a ton into it right now; basic is fine. The goal is progress, not perfection.

The S.T.A.R. Cycle for Building Your Portfolio

We'll adapt the S.T.A.R. System to help build a portfolio step by step, allowing ourselves to be perfectly imperfect.

- **Week 1: Gather and Review.** Pull *all* your finished work together in one place and sort it into categories that make sense to you. Notice which pieces make you excited to share, and mark your top 20 favorites.
- **Week 2: Select and Refine.** Narrow your selection down to the strongest 10 to 12 pieces. Take quality photos or make clean scans, or for digital work, export a high-resolution image. Write simple descriptions for each piece and create titles that reflect your brand voice.
- **Week 3: Structure and Story.** Organize your pieces into a logical or narrative flow. Write a short artist statement and add context about the techniques you use. Get feedback from two trusted sources.
- **Week 4: Polish and Present.** Choose your portfolio format—PDF, printed binder, website, or social media grid. Create a clean and consistent layout. Make sure to include your contact information! Do a final review and edit pass.

If you're just starting out, pick the format that feels most doable. A simple PDF or social grid is a great beginning. But when you're ready to pitch clients or grow professionally, building a dedicated website will give you the most control over how your work is seen and shared.

Like everything else in your creative journey, your portfolio is a work in progress. Start with what you have now, knowing you can (and will!) update it later.

PREPARE TO WORK!

You now have a solid set of tools to start building your art business. You've got the striving artist's mindset, a compelling and authentic story to tell, and strategies to keep your creative energy flowing. You're thinking long term with multiple income streams in mind. And now, you've developed your Power Trio: Style, Brand, and Portfolio.

These tools might still feel a little unfamiliar—and that's okay. Your style will evolve with every piece you make. Your brand story will gain richness as you connect with more people. Your portfolio will shift and grow as your body of work expands. Just by working through this chapter, you've laid the creative and strategic foundation your business needs to thrive.

Now let's talk about how to turn all of this into real income.

8

UNDERSTANDING THE 3 FRAMEWORKS

If you've been following along with the book and implementing what you've learned, congratulations—you're well on your way to building a solid art business foundation. Up to this point, we've done important mindset work: valuing your art, allowing yourself to dream big and take action, and taming the Chaos Goblin. We've also assembled an art business toolkit designed to support a side hustle that fits your life. At this point, I hope you're excitedly wondering—*what comes next?* In the next few chapters, we're going to take a detailed look at three models for turning your creativity into a sustainable income. You'll learn how to get started, avoid common pitfalls, and grow a thriving art business that aligns with your dreams—with only five hours a week.

Your path to success will be as unique as your art. Trust me, that's a good thing! There's no one-size-fits-all strategy here because let's be real, when has that ever worked for creatives? That's why I've outlined three distinct frameworks to guide you. Think of them as different routes to the same destination: making money from your art without losing your mind or your creative spark.

THE FRAMEWORKS

Each framework offers a different approach to turning your creativity into sustainable income. Which one is right for you? That depends on your *why*. This chapter will help you start thinking about it. In the next, we'll go deeper.

Because your why is more than a business goal—it's the story that shapes the way you show up, serve, and succeed. And yes, it will evolve. Because growth isn't just about the work; it's about who you're becoming in the process.

- **The Passive Income Framework:**

  Create once, earn repeatedly. This includes licensing your art, selling digital products, and setting up royalty-based income streams that continue to generate revenue long after the work is done. This might be your path if you dream of creating from anywhere and letting your art travel farther than you do.

- **The Product Sales Framework:**

  Turn your art into physical products or custom commissions you can sell directly to customers or retailers. This path is ideal if you love seeing your designs come to life in tangible ways, including physical goods in stores.

- **The Teaching Framework:**

  Share your expertise through workshops, courses, coaching, or creative consulting. Perfect for artists who love connecting with people, helping them learn, and guiding others through a transformation.

Each framework can work independently or in combination with the others; I've used all three at different points in my journey. While my focus has been primarily on using my own art and designs for physical products that I sell myself and for licensing with brand partners, I've met artists who've built thriving businesses using these frameworks in completely different ways: writers selling both books and coaching services, photographers combining print sales with passive income through art licensing, fiber artists mixing custom commissions with teaching workshops, and many, *many* more.

My colleague Shannon McNab conducts an annual survey of artists, and publishes statistics on what it reveals about the industry. Her 2025 survey includes data from 475 hobbyists and part-time hustlers. It gives a peek into what income streams folks are seeing the most activity in. In the 2025 data, the top sources of income are print on demand, with 50.1 percent of respondents using it, followed by physical products (40 percent), licensing (21.9 percent), digital products (16.2 percent), and freelance surface design (14.9 percent). Two things jump out immediately: First, the percentages don't add up to 100 percent because many artists are using multiple income streams. Second, both passive and product sales models are well represented.

As your business matures, I expect you will eventually explore all three frameworks to different degrees at one time or another. However, when you're first starting out, I recommend focusing on just one, and finding your footing before branching out. But how do you decide which one? To help you make this decision, and before we get into the details of each framework in the next three chapters, we'll see a brief overview of how each one works and some case studies of students who've found success using them. The short quiz at the end of this chapter will help you reflect on your goals, strengths, and lifestyle so you can make the right choice for you.

IN A NUTSHELL: THE PASSIVE INCOME FRAMEWORK

Imagine creating gorgeous artwork once and getting paid for it again and again—while you sleep, binge-watch *Anne of Green Gables* for the 100th time, or chase your potty-training puppy around the house. That's the magic of the Passive Income Framework.

The most well-known version of this is art *licensing*: Basically, you rent your art to companies who use it on their products (think greeting cards, fabric lines, puzzles, calendars . . . the works!). But that's just the tip of the creative iceberg. Your work could also show up as digital downloads for phones, wall art on Etsy, stock illustrations for books and magazines, or designs on print-on-demand sites.

Best part? You keep the copyright—your art is still your baby—and you can license it in multiple ways, letting the same design do a whole lot of heavy lifting across different streams of income.

Who this is for: This framework is ideal for artists who want creative freedom, location independence, and a business model that skips the logistics of inventory and shipping. It's especially great if:

- You want to work from anywhere (even your favorite café).
- You'd rather spend time making art than packing boxes.
- You love the idea of your work showing up on products all over the world—without having to manufacture them yourself.

It's also a strong choice if you're just starting out and want a low-cost, low-risk way to dip your toes into creative income.

How it works: Your portfolio becomes your hardest-working employee—the one who never calls in sick and doesn't need coffee breaks. You might license your work to manufacturers for royalties (fancy!), upload your designs to print-on-demand platforms like Society6 or Spoonflower, or sell digital downloads on Etsy. Those same designs could also find new life as stock illustrations, digital planner stickers, or surface patterns in an online library. Once you've built up a strong body of work, you can remix and repurpose it across multiple channels. The beauty of this approach? You get to mix and match strategies like you're crafting the perfect playlist, choosing what works best for your style, goals, and season of life.

Startup needs: You don't need to take out a business loan or turn your guest room into a shipping zone. The upfront costs are relatively low compared to other paths, especially if you already have:

- A way to create and digitize your artwork (like using the Procreate iPad app, a scanner, or a drawing tablet with design software)
- Access to the Internet
- A willingness to test, pitch, and grow

You won't need inventory, packaging, or a studio filled with products. Most of your investment will be time: building your portfolio, polishing your pitch materials, and experimenting with platforms that can get your work out into the world.

While you're sharing your artwork online and building a following (trust me, they are out there waiting to champion you!), you can test different passive income streams until you find your sweet spot.

And once you're set up? You can run everything from your kitchen table, a corner of your favorite coffee shop, or even overlooking the twinkling lights of a holiday market from Edinburgh Castle (yes, really).

Where this can lead: This framework rewards persistence. Art licensing often takes time to build up consistent income—especially since royalties typically aren't paid until after the product hits the market. But once those partnerships are in place, they can last for years.

I pitched one of my dream clients for three years before they said yes. That relationship? It turned into a long-term licensing deal that helped fund my business growth. Another client sent me consistent royalty checks for eight straight years. That's the kind of compounding effect passive income can offer—your older work keeps working for you, even while you're making something new.

Want a real-world reference point? According to the 2024 Surface Design Industry Survey Report by Shannon McNab, part-time and hobbyist artists earn on average $5,200–$6,800 a year from licensing. That might not replace your day job just yet, but it's a powerful step toward steady, scalable creative income. And yes—it is possible to grow from there (I did!).

Lissie Teehee: From University Teacher to Worldwide Art Educator

"I can do this. I don't know how, but I'll figure it out."

Lissie is a dear friend and one of the most consistent side hustlers I know. She built a thriving design business using art licensing, all while raising three daughters as a single mother and while working part time as a university instructor in Edmond, Oklahoma. I'll let her tell her story in her own words:

"I set out three goals for the first six months. I needed to begin making illustrations and designs, get a website up, and find out how to market myself. I had freelanced and worked with clients while I stayed home with my kids, but looking to build a full creative business was different this time. With quiet tears, I thought, *Start my design career over? From scratch? Am I crazy? I don't even know where to begin anymore.* I had about six months' worth of savings and about two to three hours a day to make it happen.

"I spent my days designing and researching business and my nights creating the artwork. What I didn't expect was to quickly find other artists and designers like me, to join communities, to take free courses, to invest in business classes, to find treasured friends who were doing the same as me. I jumped all the way in.

"Within a year, I was licensed with one of my favorite companies, and it gave me all the fuel I needed. Even better, I was able to continue teaching online as another stream of revenue. Now, I am a licensed artist and graphic designer, and a worldwide art educator with large online programs. I'm so thankful I can say that I believed in myself enough to jump all the way in. I get to stay home with my kids, do art, and take film classes. I couldn't have asked for anything better."

IN A NUTSHELL: THE PRODUCT SALES FRAMEWORK

Product sales is the first thing most people think of when they hear "art business"; if Richard Scarry ever needed to depict an entrepreneurial artist as a Busytown resident with a beret and old-fashioned cash register, this is what they would be doing. If customers buying something tangible that you made excites you, the Product Sales Framework might be a perfect fit. This path is the most direct way to turn art into income and encompasses everything from homemade goods and craft shows to online sales to manufacturers and wholesale contracts.

Who this is for: This framework is for artists who are excited to see their work come to life in physical form—whether that's as nursery art, stickers, tea towels, or journals. You don't need a giant following or massive budget to begin. You just need a few pieces you're proud of, a way to produce them (like printing at home or working with a vendor), and a willingness to try.

If you enjoy the hands-on part—packaging up orders, sharing your work online, and imagining your art out in the world—this may feel like home. I started with a few tea towels and a dream at my dining room table. You can start right where you are too.

How it works: This framework includes a range of opportunities. You might begin by selling original works or prints of your art, then expand into handmade goods or small-batch manufactured products that you design from start to finish—and sell yourself. As your confidence and capacity grow, you can explore wholesale opportunities to place your work in shops and boutiques, moving beyond one-on-one sales. Even a small but engaged audience is enough to get started—especially if you've developed a signature style and are ready to invest in that first round of production.

Startup needs: Product sales often require more upfront investment than passive income streams—but what you'll need depends on your specific products and process. At a minimum, you'll need a way to make your products, materials, or inventory to sell; basic packaging supplies; and a method for shipping. That might look like a home printer and cardstock for art prints, or a sewing machine and fabric for handmade goods. It could also mean working with a trusted local vendor or ordering a small batch from a manufacturer.

And yes—storage matters! Plan for a place to keep your supplies and finished products, even if it's just a shelf in the garage or a closet-turned-shipping station. As your business grows, so will your need for space (a good problem to have!).

The good news? You don't have to go all in right away. Many successful product-based artists start with just a couple of items listed on Etsy and reinvest their early profits as they grow.

Where this can lead: This is where things get exciting. At first glance, this framework might seem similar to passive income—they both result in customers getting products with your art on them. But here's the key difference: With product sales, you steer the ship. You're responsible for everything from product development to packaging and marketing—which also means you get more control, more flexibility, and a bigger slice of the profits.

When I couldn't find artwork I loved for my daughter's nursery, I made my own. That one decision sparked an idea—and soon I started sharing my nursery art on Etsy. Just a few listings. A few sales. But over time, this framework took me from sewing tea towels at my dining room table to building Gingiber into a thriving full-time business.

Sixteen years later, we've sold over $2 million a year in products. I've seen my art in national magazines, featured in holiday gift guides, and stocked in stores around the country. We've had giant wholesale orders. And my favorite part? Customers who come back year after year—for ornaments, for calendars, for tea towels that feel like tradition.

And you don't have to go full-time to experience those wins.

This book is all about the side hustle. You can work a few hours a week from your kitchen table and still build a brand that brings in real income, loyal fans, and joyful impact.

This path isn't about perfection—it's about possibility. If you love the idea of seeing your art in the hands of customers around the world, this framework is ready when you are.

Jennifer Knight: Math Teacher Finds Product Success

Jennifer Knight, a Leverage Your Art alumni and longtime student of mine, didn't start out in the art or product world—she came from a background in math and education, running two successful tutoring businesses. But creativity had always been part of her life, and in December 2015, a five-day beach trip with her husband gave her the space she needed to reconnect with drawing. That was the moment her art business quietly began.

Like many artists stepping into product sales for the first time, Jennifer started with what felt attainable. She invested a few hundred dollars from family savings to place her first greeting card order with a local printer. "When I started, I didn't know much about the art industry, so I didn't really have the capacity to dream as big as I do now," she recalled. "I focused on something I thought I could create." The logic was sound; cards were affordable to produce, easy to store, and had a built-in market. She took the leap.

It didn't take long to realize that getting greeting cards into stores was much harder than she had imagined. But each challenge taught her something new about the art industry and product-based businesses. Over time, Jennifer began to recognize that while greeting cards were a great entry point, they weren't her long-term passion.

"Fast forward to last year, when I introduced my apron line. That moment marked a significant shift for me," Jennifer explained. "I didn't just make something because I thought I could. I made something that at first felt totally out of reach because I really wanted to." This time, she went all in, working closely with boutique cooking stores and restaurant owners to design the perfect apron. She refined prototype after prototype, listening to feedback and fine-tuning every feature. She learned how to source high-end materials, how to get her designs onto fabric, and how to manufacture at scale without cutting corners.

Jennifer's approach to business growth has always been rooted in sustainability. "Start small, make a little money, reinvest it into your business, and repeat on a little bit larger scale," she advised. "Don't overlook the resources you already have—your community, your creativity, and your willingness to work hard and learn. These are worth way more to you than start-up funding."

Her business has since grown beyond a side hustle—so much that her husband was able to leave his full-time job to join her. As her operation expanded, she had to find ways to maintain creative momentum while managing the day-to-day logistics of a larger business. One of her solutions? Regular "drawing retreats" where she rents a home or room and steps away from operations to focus solely on creating.

For Jennifer, success isn't just measured in sales; it's about the impact her work has on people. "There's nothing like watching someone burst out laughing, then run to grab a friend or spouse just to share in the moment. Even if they don't buy a thing, the fact that I created something that made someone smile—that brought a tiny moment of delight into their day—is such a rewarding part of what I do."

Through years of trial, error, and evolution, Jennifer has learned that product success isn't about luck—it's about systems, habits, and mindsets that encourage balance. "It all comes down to balance—between the creative and the practical, between discipline and experimentation, and between planning and creating space for inspiration."

Her story is proof that product-based businesses can grow from small, strategic beginnings into something far bigger than imagined—with persistence, adaptability, and a willingness to take the next step, even when it feels out of reach.

IN A NUTSHELL: THE TEACHING FRAMEWORK

Sometimes, your art isn't just about what you create—it's about how you help others create or grow. The Teaching Framework is all about turning your creative skills into opportunities for connection, transformation, and income.

This might look like teaching workshops, leading online classes, offering creative coaching, or consulting with fellow artists. It's a flexible path with room to grow—from intimate one-on-one support to scalable online courses you can sell again and again.

This framework is perfect for artists who want to start generating income quickly from their creative skills. It works especially well if others already ask you for help or admire how you do something—and you genuinely enjoy connecting and teaching. The project-based nature of this work offers freedom and variety, making it ideal for busy side hustlers.

Who this is for: The Teaching Framework is a strong fit if:

- You love connecting with others and sharing what you've learned.
- You enjoy guiding people through a transformation—whether that's helping someone paint for the first time, coaching a fellow artist, or building a curriculum that turns your know-how into results.
- You're looking for flexible, project-based income you can generate with just a few hours a week.
- You want to work from anywhere without managing inventory or dealing with shipping logistics.
- This is also a great entry point for artists who want to earn income quickly using the skills they already have.

How it works: The Teaching Framework is all about turning your unique skills into valuable services that help others grow. You might teach locally or online, lead workshops, coach fellow creatives, or offer critiques and consulting. Many artists also support their peers through services like brand audits, design help, or launching strategies.

Startup needs: You likely already have what you need to begin:

- A laptop or tablet
- Internet access
- Your creative expertise (which may feel invisible to you—but others are already looking for it)

If you're teaching online, you'll eventually want a simple camera setup and a way to record or host content (Zoom, Skillshare, or Kajabi, for example). But don't let the tech scare you off—start with what you have and improve over time.

Where this can lead: Offering services creates unique opportunities for your creative business. You can generate substantial, project-based income more quickly than with other frameworks, while simultaneously building your reputation as an expert in your field. This path also offers flexibility to work on your own schedule and be selective about the clients you take on, making it ideal for balancing with other commitments.

Teaching and services also scale beautifully. You can remain intentionally small and part-time—or grow into group coaching programs, full courses, and even your own online education platform. Thanks to the Internet, your classroom can be global.

When I first offered a simple vision board course, I made a few thousand dollars—and that felt like a huge win. My Skillshare classes have brought in around $12,000 (and that's without much promotion). But when I launched my signature course and fully stepped into teaching what I knew? That course earned over $500,000 in its first year alone.

Some artists begin with one-on-one offerings like portfolio reviews, art critiques, or creative mentoring—meeting over Zoom and sharing honest, practical insights. That kind of support is deeply valuable, especially for newer artists looking for direction. I've seen it turn into consistent monthly income *and* lasting client relationships.

And yes, this path can support big dreams. My friend and fellow educator Cat Coquillette went from teaching Skillshare classes on the side to licensing with major retailers and educating over half a million students online.

The Teaching Framework begins with generosity—showing up to serve others using the skills you've worked hard to build. Whether your goal is to bring in an extra $500 a month or build a thriving education brand, this framework invites you to start small, show up with heart, and let your expertise open the next door.

Cat Coquillette: From Design Agency to World Travel

My friend (and industry colleague) Cat was able to turn her constraints into a thriving education platform. Here's part of her story in her own words.

"Back when I was working full-time at a design agency, I spent my nights and weekends building up my side hustle. It was tough—in addition to my limited time, I also had a bank account that was slowly depleting and bills to pay. Rather than seeing these constraints as obstacles, I turned them into catalysts for creative problem-solving. I found innovative ways to grow through strategic partnerships. For example, I didn't have the finances to invest in much of my own inventory (besides what I could reasonably sell through weekend craft fairs), so I focused on selling my designs through print-on-demand websites. I didn't have a platform to teach online classes or even much of an audience, but Skillshare had that covered for me. As my business evolved, I expanded into art licensing with major retailers like Target, Anthropologie, Urban Outfitters, HomeGoods, Nordstrom, and more. My students grew to over a half a million, and I expanded my classes to my *own* website.

"Looking back now, I realize that what seemed like obstacles at the beginning of my self-employment journey actually shaped my business into something more sustainable and scalable than if I'd had unlimited resources from the start. By leveraging existing platforms and partnerships rather than trying to build everything from scratch, I created a solid foundation that served as a launching pad for my brand. Over time, this approach allowed me to gradually expand my business on my own terms, growing from print on demand to licensing deals, and eventually creating my own independent teaching platform. The journey taught me that success doesn't always mean having everything figured out from the beginning—sometimes it means being clever about working with what you have."

HOW I'VE LEVERAGED THE FRAMEWORKS

When I first started Gingiber, my goals weren't as lofty as quitting my day job and immediately turning my art into a full-time career. It was much simpler: My family needed groceries. The path from this simple starting point actually taught me the power of each framework in different ways.

My first breakthrough with the Product Sales Framework came when I sold my tenth nursery print on Etsy. That sale wasn't just about the money; it showed me I could create something once and sell it multiple times, turning my nursery art into a sustainable product line. Even better, each customer's feedback helped me understand exactly what parents were looking for in nursery decor.

The Passive Income Framework clicked for me during my first licensing meeting with a prominent kids' home decor company. I remember sitting there, realizing that instead of printing and shipping everything myself, I could "rent" my designs and reach thousands more customers while focusing on creating new art. That one licensing deal taught me the power of making money while I sleep—literally! My art would be earning money even during those late-night nursing sessions with my daughter.

The Teaching Framework revealed itself when other artists started messaging me on Instagram, asking how I'd built Gingiber. After my fifth "coffee chat" explaining licensing and product development, I realized I could help other artists skip the years of trial and error I'd gone through. Teaching and consulting didn't just create another revenue stream; it gave me the chance to help other people find the same creative freedom I'd discovered.

Today, my life looks completely different. By understanding and implementing all three frameworks, I've built a business that supports my family and creates opportunities for others. I even get to create jobs for other mothers who want to fit part-time creative work around their family life, something I never imagined when I was just trying to decorate my daughter's nursery.

QUIZ: YOUR PERSONAL ALIGNMENT WITH THE THREE FRAMEWORKS

Looking at the three frameworks, you can see there are a lot of opportunities out there for creatives like us. Maybe one of them immediately speaks to you. Or maybe you're still not sure what to pursue. That's okay! This short quiz will help you reflect on your goals, strengths, and lifestyle so you can find the best starting point.

For each question, choose the answer that most resonates with you right now:

What excites you most about building an art business?

a. Creating art that can earn money while I sleep

b. Seeing my work become physical products people can hold

c. Helping others grow and sharing what I know

Which best describes your current situation?

a. I want to create art without managing inventory

b. I love the idea of making and selling my own products

c. I enjoy teaching and connecting with other creatives

What's your ideal workday?

a. Focusing purely on creating new art

b. A mix of making art and handling business tasks

c. Splitting time between creating and helping others

What's your biggest constraint right now?

a. Limited startup funds

b. Limited storage space

c. Limited time to create

What Your Results Say

Mostly A's?

The **Passive Income Framework** might be your sweet spot! You're ready to create art that can work for you through licensing, digital downloads, or print-on-demand platforms. This framework is ideal if you want low overhead and love the idea of making money while you sleep.

Head to Chapter 9 to learn how to set up income streams that keep paying long after the work is done.

Mostly B's?

The **Product Sales Framework** could be your perfect match! You've got the energy and enthusiasm for turning your art into tangible goods that people can hold, love, and gift.

Flip to Chapter 10 to discover how to build a product-based business that fits your life.

Mostly C's?

The **Teaching Framework** is calling your name! Your combination of artistic skill and teaching spirit could help other creatives thrive—while earning income from your expertise.

Start with Chapter 11 to explore how to teach, coach, or guide others through transformation with your unique skills.

There's no wrong answer here—just the path that fits your life right now. Many successful artists eventually blend all three frameworks together as their businesses evolve. But the best way to begin is to start with the one that excites you most today.

Take that first step. Your future artist self will thank you.

9

THE PASSIVE INCOME FRAMEWORK

Imagine: Your designs are out in the world brightening up someone's day. A cozy throw pillow, a coffee mug, maybe a plush toddler-sized chair because why not. Somewhere in the world, someone is walking out of a shop having just purchased a real, physical product with your art on it—and you got paid. *But wait!* How can this be? You don't have a warehouse full of goods or relationships with any retailers. You certainly don't have contacts at any factories. Where did all this *real stuff* come from?!

That, my friend, is the power of art licensing.

Of all the ways to grow your art business, licensing is one of my favorites. It allows you to get your art on products and see what sells while someone else manages the logistics. It helps you build a solid portfolio of work you can show to other clients. It lets you gain experience with the world of manufacturing at no risk. And best of all—it *pays*.

Next time you're in a retail store, pay attention to the number and variety of products that have designs printed on them. Those designs largely got there in one of two ways. The first way is that they were made by a salaried in-house artist for the supplier. The second way is that they were licensed or outright purchased from a third-party artist—that could be *you*!

An art license is basically a copyright rental agreement. For a negotiated price, a company gets the right to use your design on their products, typically for a fixed period of time. You still retain the copyright and—depending on the terms of the contract—can also license it to other companies making other kinds of products. One design could simultaneously appear on bedding, a calendar, maybe a wine label—all generating income for you.

It gets even better. The upfront cost required to get started with licensing is tiny compared to other ways of getting art on product, but because there is an enormous diversity of companies looking to license art, as a business model it can also scale. With licensing, you can learn firsthand how to create marketable art, build lasting partnerships, and even pivot into manufacturing, if that's where you want to go. Have I mentioned that I *love* art licensing?

In this chapter I'm going to show you what you need to know to start licensing your art and present a framework for getting your own contracts. We'll start by covering some industry lingo and then dive into the process that I use to find, pitch, and land licensing deals. It's not magic—in fact it's mostly tenacity and spreadsheets. Finally, we'll see how to adjust the S.T.A.R. Cycle to make it a contract generating machine. By the end, it's my goal that you will feel confident pitching your own licensing deals.

THE IMPORTANT TERMS OF LICENSING

The world of art licensing is very big and very old, and so it has developed some jargon with meanings specific to the industry. Knowing these terms will help you communicate with art directors and negotiate contracts like a pro. Rather than alphabetically, these terms are introduced in a way that builds upon each concept you need to know.

- **Artwork:** The design itself, along with the actual digital files or physical copies. Contracts may specify that the artwork be delivered in a particular format, such as layered PSD files or high-resolution TIFFs.
- **Collection:** A group of related artwork pieces that form a cohesive set. Licensing contracts often cover a full collection rather than a single design.

- **Copyright:** The legal protection that gives you ownership and exclusive rights over your artwork. In the U.S., your work is automatically protected the moment it's created and fixed in a tangible form. You can also register it with the U.S. Copyright Office to make it easier to enforce those rights in court. If your artwork were a house, copyright would be the deed to the land and building.
- **License:** A legal agreement that grants another party permission to use your artwork under specific conditions (how, where, and for how long). You retain ownership (copyright), while the client receives limited usage rights. In our house analogy, licensing is like renting out a room—you're not giving away the whole house.
- **Buyout:** A contract in which the buyer purchases the full copyright of the artwork. This means you no longer own the rights to the work, and you can't reuse or resell it. In the house analogy, it's like selling the deed, the house, and the furniture—unless otherwise agreed upon.
- **Flat Fee:** A one-time, upfront payment for the use of your artwork. This payment structure is common for short-term or limited-use licenses.
- **Royalties:** Ongoing payments based on the number of products sold that use your artwork. You may also encounter deals that combine royalties with a flat fee.
- **Territory:** The geographical area where the license is valid, such as North America, Europe, or Global. Broader territories typically command higher fees.
- **Exclusivity:** Defines whether you're allowed to license the same artwork to others. An exclusive license means you cannot sign another license in the same category or territory, while a nonexclusive license allows more flexibility. Exclusivity usually increases the value of a deal.
- **Sell Sheet:** A one-page promotional document that showcases your artwork, includes your contact information, and often features a short artist bio or pitch. It's essentially your art's résumé and is what you'll attach when sending licensing pitches.

Licensing as a solo artist means signing contracts, and I *strongly* encourage you to read them carefully. Learning the lingo empowers you to understand what's happening in a negotiation and to protect your work while maximizing its potential.

THE PITCHING PIPELINE

Most of the work involved in art licensing will be in securing deals; you'll largely be pitching art that already exists, and the manufacturing, marketing, and product sales are out of your hands. The process I'll be presenting here is what I call the Pitching Pipeline, a five-phase framework for landing contracts:

1. the Quest
2. the Pitch
3. the Follow-Up
4. the Boomerang
5. the Negotiation

Getting steady income from licensing is a numbers game. For every company that says *yes*, there will be a lot that say *no*, or *some other time*, or *it's not a good fit*. And that's fine! A company turning down your licensing pitch doesn't mean there's something wrong with you or your art; it doesn't even mean they'll never say *yes* in the future (more on this later). Companies get a lot of pitches and can't say yes to all of them. All this really means is that in order to turn licensing into consistent income, you'll need to keep lots of potential client relationships at different stages of the Pitching Pipeline, since many of them won't work out.

There's going to be a lot of information to keep track of: companies, names, contact information, important dates, proposed terms, and more. I use spreadsheets to organize this and recommend you do the same. We're going to interact with a lot of people, and being able to communicate accurately helps you to present as a serious professional.

It's also important to remember that we'll mostly be interacting with art directors who are, above all else, *people*. The contracts are just the formal reflection of the relationships you've nurtured. Your reputation is worth a lot in this industry. Art directors talk to each other and move between companies all the time, so treating each interaction with care and professionalism will serve you well.

If you cultivate a reputation for being prompt, reasonable, fair, and pleasant to work with, you'll find it much easier to land new clients and get repeat business from existing ones. On the other hand, if you are unresponsive, difficult, rude, or pushy . . . Well, there are other artists out there who won't make the art director's life harder. All that is to say, be a good human!

PHASE 1—THE QUEST: FINDING LEADS

Before we can even think about pitching our work, we need to have someone to pitch to! Finding them is what the Quest is all about. For this phase we're going to be part detective, part treasure hunter.

I always imagine that when a company chooses an artist to license with, there's a room of people looking at several different possible collaborators. If they're going to pick me, it's because someone in that room likes me and my art enough to advocate for it. You want to find that person and give them a reason to root for you.

To keep yourself organized, I recommend creating a pitch tracker spreadsheet to contain all the information you'll be collecting in the next three steps.

Create Your Dream Target List

First make a list of companies that align with your art and goals, and with whom you'd like to collaborate. Start with what you already love: brands you shop with or admire. Look for clues from other licensed artists online; when they announce collaborations, note the companies they're working with. Search social media for hashtags like #licensedart or #artlicensing and save posts of brands that catch your eye. When you're in a retail shop, take note of the brands making things you like. Add these lists to your spreadsheet.

Hunt for Submission Guidelines

Most companies that license art have a preferred way to receive pitches from new artists, and many will include submission guidelines on their websites. Look for links with names like "Contact Us," "Work with Us," or even just "Submissions." If you can't find instructions there, you probably can find a customer service e-mail address, send an e-mail, and ask! Here's a script you can use.

> **Subject:** *Licensing Inquiry*
>
> *Hi! My name is [your name], and I'm an artist exploring licensing opportunities. Could you direct me to the appropriate person or department at your company to receive artist submissions? Thank you for your time!*

If you still haven't found submission instructions, pick up the phone. Yes, actual phone calls still exist, and they're underrated! Call and politely ask for the contact information for their art or licensing team; reach out and ask directly. You might be surprised by how helpful they are. Put any instructions, websites, contact information, etc., in your spreadsheet.

Find the Decision-Makers

Next, we're going to head over to LinkedIn for some sleuthing. Pick one of the companies on your list; our goal now is to find the people in charge of licensing decisions at that company. What makes LinkedIn so useful is we can see the names and titles of all the employees that have a profile, which is usually a lot of them. Look for titles like "Art Director," "Product Developer," or "Licensing Manager"; these are the people you need to reach.

Once you've found a potential contact, craft a brief, polite LinkedIn message stating who you are and that you're interested in licensing opportunities and ask if they are or can direct you to the person who handles artist submissions. Here is a template you can use:

Hi [Their First Name],

My name is [Your Name], and I'm an artist specializing in [brief description, e.g., nature-inspired patterns, whimsical illustrations]. I'm very interested in licensing my artwork and would love to explore potential opportunities with [Company Name].

Could you let me know if you're the right person to speak with or direct me to whoever handles artist submissions?

Thanks so much for your time!

Best,

[Your Name]

Finding the right contacts takes time and patience. Some companies won't respond, and some will tell you they do not accept submissions. Keep looking, celebrate the small wins, and don't forget to record the results of this research in your spreadsheet!

Sachiko Yoshikawa: Finding the Right Market and Investing in Visibility

Sachiko is an alumna of my course Leverage Your Art. Sachiko Yoshikawa's career as an illustrator took an unexpected turn when a newspaper review of her group exhibition at the Uganda National Museum described her work as "humorous, vibrant, and full of life, in contrast to the darker themes of war and suffering often seen in local art." That one sentence changed everything. After many detours, she discovered that storytelling was her true strength. She realized that instead of trying to fit her art into existing industry trends, she needed to lean into what made her work unique.

With this new perspective, Sachiko made a bold move: She invested $6,000 to showcase her work in the *American Showcase*, a marketing directory for illustrators. It was a major financial risk, but it paid off almost immediately. Within a month, five major licensing representatives reached out to her, including one from New York specializing in children's books, who flew across the country just to meet her. Her first deal with *National Geographic* recovered her entire investment in a matter of weeks.

Sachiko's experience highlights an essential truth about art licensing—success isn't about changing your work to fit the market; it's about finding the right market for your work, one that excites and moves your soul. Just as the pieces she exhibited in Uganda reflected the vibrant life she experienced there, art directors are constantly looking for fresh, distinctive voices, and sometimes, the key to breaking in is making sure your work is seen by the right people.

PHASE 2—THE PITCH: SELLING YOUR PORTFOLIO

Now that we have a list of contacts and know how to submit inquiries to them, it's time to craft our pitch. For this phase we're entering salesperson mode. If you haven't made many sales in the past, get ready; this can be one of the most thrilling (and slightly terrifying) parts of art licensing. The Pitch is a proposal, typically sent via e-mail, where you say, "Hey, look at my art! Isn't it *fabulous*? Wouldn't it be great on your products?" (Maybe not phrased exactly like that!)

Our main goal in this phase is to sell licenses to parts of our portfolio, but from the art director's point of view the pitch is also about you as the artist behind the work. You're selling your ability to be a professional creative colleague. They have production deadlines to meet and need to have confidence you'll be a good partner.

This might sound a little daunting. Pitching feels very vulnerable. *What if they say no?* But don't worry; pitching is a skill just like drawing or painting, and you will get better at it with practice. It's less about doing everything perfectly and more about showing up, taking action, and embracing the learning curve. And yes, sometimes they will say no. Maybe most of the time! That's okay; not every pitch leads to a contract, but we're going to cultivate the attitude that every pitch makes us more comfortable showcasing our work—whether it leads to a sale or not.

Way back in Chapter 7 we crafted our brand story and elevator pitch. Pull those out now; we're going to adapt them into a well-written love letter to a potential client—except with less romance and more business proposals.

Adopt the Mindset of a Successful Pitcher

Let's talk about confidence, because it really is a vital ingredient in every great pitch. To succeed you need to recognize your value as an artist. Your work is unique, and nobody else is going to promote it for you like you can. Confidence doesn't mean being cocky, or pretentious, or having all the answers. It means showing up even when you're nervous and believing that your art has something to share with the world. Low confidence will manifest itself in your pitch in a few ways; here are some common pitfalls to avoid.

- **Belittling yourself or your work.** Saying things like "I'm just starting out" or "I'm not sure if this is good enough" doesn't build confidence—it undermines it. Instead, own your talent. Try this instead: "My work is unique, and I'm excited to share it with you."
- **Speaking poorly about others.** Criticizing other artists or companies in your pitch is a major no-no. Focus on your strengths instead.
- **Minimizing your accomplishments.** You don't need to apologize for being proud of your work. Say it with confidence: "I've seen great growth in my work and business, and I'm excited to collaborate."

I won't lie to you; sometimes it will be difficult to maintain your confidence when rejections come in. That's why we're not going to focus on the rejections. We accept rejections as part of the process and choose to focus on successes and learn from each pitch. This phase is about opening a door and starting a conversation.

Assemble a Mini Collection

The foundation of every art-based business is the portfolio. It's the artist's résumé, showcasing samples of what you can do for clients. For the pitch though, we're not going to just send the entire portfolio. Instead we're going to curate a *mini collection*—a small group of pieces that form a cohesive and thematic whole.

This format has a lot going for it. It demonstrates both your technical ability to compose and execute art and your aesthetic ability to build a collection, and it does so succinctly—art directors are busy and probably won't have time to flip through an entire portfolio. We're going to make an executive summary that lets them see what they need to see quickly. Mini collections are also more manageable for you; you don't need a ton of work, just a few thoughtfully chosen pieces.

I've had the most success with mini collections of three pieces that each play a specific role.

- The *hero illustration* is the centerpiece, the star of the show that grabs attention and says, "I'm fabulous."
- The *secondary pattern* is a sidekick that complements the hero without stealing the spotlight.
- The *blender pattern* is a solid team player, adding depth and versatility.

You can tweak the format a bit, adding a blender or secondary pattern or swapping the secondary for two blenders. But as a template this structure is pure gold. Even industries that will eventually ask for larger collections, like fabric manufacturing, love to see mini collections. For instance, I licensed a small collection to Moda Fabrics with just a few blender patterns and one large hero illustration. Mini collections are like appetizers—they give a taste of what you're capable of while leaving clients wanting more. The mini collection should also be curated for the client; pay attention to their aesthetic and craft your pitch to blend with it.

Build a Sell Sheet

Once the mini collection has been assembled, we're going to design a sell sheet. This will be a one-page document saved as a PDF, and we're going to compose it like a piece of art on its own.

> You can download your own sell sheet template by visiting **staciebloomfield.com/bookbonus**.

The sell sheet needs to include:

- A clear, high-quality image of your mini collection
- Your name
- Contact info (make it easy for them to reach you!)
- Logo, if you have one
- A short brand-aligned description of your art and why it's a perfect fit for this client

This is where your brand story comes in! Adapt the elevator pitch version of your brand story and tailor it to the company you're pitching. Look at their product line, values, and aesthetic—and show how your art naturally fits into their world. If they lean whimsical, highlight that in your tone. If their line is sophisticated or minimalist, match that energy.

Your description doesn't need to be long—two to four sentences is perfect. Focus on what makes your art memorable, what kinds of products it's well-suited for, and how your work resonates with their customer base. Here's an example:

> I'm an illustrator whose work is known for bold colors and playful storytelling. This collection is inspired by childhood nostalgia and designed to shine on stationery, textiles, and giftables. My work connects deeply with customers who want warmth, wonder, and whimsy in their everyday items.

You should also include a link to your full portfolio or website. This gives the art director a chance to explore further if they're intrigued. A simple line at the bottom of the sell sheet like "To view my full portfolio, visit **www.YourWebsiteHere.com**" works beautifully.

If you want to go the extra mile, you can include a second colorway of the mini collection to show off its versatility; this just means using the same art with a different color palette. If you've ever done any publication design, think of the sell sheet like a tight single page spread—it should feel polished, professional, and easy to digest at a glance.

Send It—and Then Wait

When your sell sheet is ready, it's time to share it! Be sure to follow the submission guidelines you found during the Quest phase—each company may have different preferences for how they want to be contacted.

In the e-mail or message accompanying your pitch:

- **Briefly introduce yourself with a personal greeting.** Mention your name and a line or two about who you are as an artist.
- **Include your brand elevator pitch**, ideally tailored to the company. This can echo or build on the short description in your sell sheet, reinforcing why your work is a great fit.
- **Address the message to the specific decision-maker** you identified during the Quest phase.
- **Attach your sell sheet** as a PDF—make it easy for them to view your work at a glance!
- If you've met the person you're pitching to—whether in person, online, or at a conference—**wait about one week from the interaction to send your pitch**. Reference your meeting and remind them where and how you connected.
- And now, we wait. I don't mean sitting still. I mean: **Move on to your next task**, because this pitch is now out of your hands.

This is a great moment to keep your portfolio evolving. If your sell sheet features a general-purpose mini collection, one that isn't overly customized for just one company, consider adding it to your online portfolio or website. You can also include a standalone PDF link if you want to showcase your licensing readiness.

And—this part is important—update your pitch tracker spreadsheet. Record the date, the contact's name, the company, and any notes about the pitch.

You'll typically receive one of three responses:

- **"Tell me more"** (hooray! Head straight to Phase 5—The Negotiation),
- **A clear no** (time for Phase 4—The Boomerang), or
- **No response at all** (very common—which is why we move to Phase 3—The Follow-Up).

PHASE 3—THE FOLLOW-UP: START CONVERSATIONS AND STAY ORGANIZED

If you're like me, when you send a pitch e-mail and don't hear back, your natural assumption might be something like, *"Oh no, they hated my pitch so much they won't even write back to reject me! It's like a super rejection!"* But hang on for a minute. There's another explanation that's much more likely: The art director is busy and either hasn't responded yet—or just forgot. The only way to tell the difference is with a Follow-Up.

Following up can feel vulnerable—trust me, I get it. You don't want to come across as pushy. But think of the follow-up as a gentle nudge; **persistence is powerful**, and art directors respect professionals who send polite reminders.

Use the following guidelines to help you confidently and clearly follow up.

Use a Pitch Calendar

You've probably noticed by now that the Pitching Pipeline involves sending a lot of e-mails to specific people and following up on them at specific times. Do not rely on your memory to keep all of this organized! Use your pitch tracker spreadsheet to track when and to whom you send follow-ups, and mark your calendar with the best times to reach out.

To make it even more efficient, I like to batch my artwork and e-mail prep and schedule a specific day in the quarter to send pitches and follow-ups. Treat it like a creative ritual—grab a coffee, cue up your favorite playlist, and get pitching.

Space Out the Timing of Your Follow-Ups

Remember that date we logged when we sent the pitch? That's your starting point. If you don't hear back, wait *two weeks* to send your first follow-up, and *another two weeks* for a second. After that, scale back to sending *quarterly updates.*

Use the Follow-Up Message Formula

You don't need to resend your elevator pitch or attach your sell sheet again—keep your message short, kind, and professional. Here's a simple structure I recommend:

1. Greet them by name.
2. Reference your original message.
   "I'm following up on the e-mail I sent two weeks ago about my *Woodland Creatures* mini collection."
3. Express continued interest.
   "I'd love to hear your thoughts or send along additional pieces if that would be helpful!"
4. Offer a next step.
   "Would you like a printed sample or a short catalog of my work?"
5. Include a link to your social media or portfolio.
6. Thank them for their time.
   "I really appreciate you taking the time to review it!"

Adjust the tone as needed based on how well you know them, but stick to the core message: You're professional, excited about the potential, and respectful of their time.

Quarterly updates can include new or updated sell sheets, but otherwise, the goal here is simply to **start (or restart) a conversation.**

Why the Follow-Up Is Shockingly Effective

Sometimes your initial pitch doesn't get a response because the timing just isn't right. Art directors are often looking for something specific, and one of your follow-ups might land at *just* the right time. By staying on their radar, you increase your chances of getting that yes when the stars align.

Longevity and persistence will help you stand out. The artist who stays top of mind—politely and professionally—is often the one who gets the gig.

PHASE 4—THE BOOMERANG: NATURALLY NAVIGATING NO

Rejection is an inevitable part of pitching your work. And I'll be real with you: It can feel like a gut punch. It's normal to feel sad after a rejection. But I have a secret weapon for handling it that I like to call the Boomerang Technique.

I imagine making a pitch like throwing a boomerang into a wide-open field; I'd like for it to come back to me. But if you've ever tried throwing a boomerang, you know that sometimes it smacks into a tree or catches the wind and falls or just hits the ground. Rejection is like the boomerang not coming back. It *feels* like failure, but it's not—not yet. You can redirect your sadness in a new direction: Pick up the boomerang, adjust your form, check the wind, and try again. The purpose of the Boomerang Technique is to turn the sting of *no* into momentum for your next pitch.

One of my toughest rejections came early in my art-licensing journey. I'd spent weeks crafting what I thought would be the perfect mini collection to pitch to a company I admired, but the response was a polite but firm *no.* I was crushed. For a little bit I allowed myself to feel all the feels: doubt, disappointment, frustration. But I also realized at that moment that I had a choice: I could let that rejection define me, or I could use it as fuel to move forward.

This was the birth of the Boomerang Technique. I promised myself that for every rejection I got, I would send out a new pitch to another potential client. Feel sadness but no spiraling—just action. This simple habit turned every rejection into a stepping stone. And because I was also continually refining my pitches, eventually some of those boomerangs started coming back.

Here's how you apply the Boomerang Technique to turn rejection into action.

- **Acknowledge the rejection.** Allow yourself to feel disappointment, whether that means journaling, venting to a friend, or taking a walk. You wouldn't have sent that pitch if you didn't want it to work, and it's okay to feel sad.
- **Redirect negative energy.** Don't dwell on the rejection. Open your spreadsheet of leads, pick the next one, and get to work.
- **Craft a new pitch.** Write a fresh pitch e-mail to the new lead. Use what you've learned to make it polished, professional, and personalized.
- **Send and record.** Once the new pitch is done, send it—immediately. Record it in the spreadsheet for follow-up in two weeks.
- **Celebrate your action.** Yes, celebrate! Every pitch is a step forward regardless of the outcome. Get a fancy coffee, take a dance break, or just take a moment to think, "Look at me, I'm doing it!" This is positive reinforcement to trick your brain into wanting to do this again next time.

Why the Boomerang Works

Rejection can be quicksand for your confidence. The purpose of the Boomerang Technique is to keep yourself moving by meeting the rejection with positive forward motion toward your goals. By taking action, you stay in charge of your creative career and aren't just passively waiting for opportunities. To this day I still use the Boomerang Technique when I get a rejection; it's a ritual of hope for me.

Not all rejections are created equally. Sometimes you'll get a *hard no*: responses like "We do not accept submissions," or "We prefer to use in-house creative," or "We don't think your style is a good fit for our brand." (Ideally, that last one won't happen because you've designed your pitch to be a good fit.) When this happens, make a note in your spreadsheet and move on.

But sometimes the rejection is a *soft no*. It comes with an asterisk—the answer is *no* right now, but if you come back in 3, 6, 12 months, it might not be. *Soft nos are solid gold.* A soft no means the art director looked at your proposal and decided it wouldn't fit with any current projects but could imagine your art working on something and respected your pitch enough to send you a response. Make a note of this and treat these contacts like your long-term nonresponders. Send an updated pitch every quarter or so. You might be surprised how often a *soft no* can turn into a *yes*, and then into a long-term collaboration.

PHASE 5—THE NEGOTIATION: SO YOU'VE CAUGHT THE CAR

So far, all the steps in the Pitching Pipeline have been at least a little scary, but this last one might be the scariest of all. *What if you make your pitch and they say . . . yes? What now?!*

You've entered the Negotiation.

Like the dog that finally caught a car, after making so many pitches and getting so many rejections, when you do get a *yes*, you need to be prepared to do something with it! The conversation has now started, and your goal is to get a signed licensing contract that matches your worth.

Sometimes the company will have a standard licensing contract they start with, and sometimes they will ask you to propose one. In either case, the initial proposal is just an opening offer. The other party will look at the terms and may request reasonable changes.

Pricing Your Work

The one question I hear most often about licensing negotiation is what price to set. To be frank, this depends on so many factors, I can only give general advice; any specific numbers would probably be out of date by the time you're reading this anyway. Here are things to consider during the negotiation that may affect the price.

- **Payment structure:** Flat fee, royalty, or both? Flat fee means getting the money faster, but royalties can end up being more valuable in the long run. If you're unsure, ask what the company usually uses.
- **Scope of use:** Where will the artwork be used—a single product, multiple products?
- **Territory:** Where in the world does the license apply? Globally, or scoped to one region?
- **Length of use:** How long is the license effective? Is there an option to renew?
- **Complexity:** Complex, layered pieces command higher prices than simple ones.
- **Nonmonetary perks:** This is an underrated part of the contract. You can ask for samples of the finished product and the right to purchase it at a wholesale discount, which allows you to sell the product in your own store. You can also ask that your name and brand be included in marketing, which helps build your brand.

Document the negotiation process for future reference. You can use the negotiated price as a starting point when you need to set prices for the next negotiation.

Keep the Copyright (and When to Not Keep the Copyright)

Remember the difference between a licensing agreement and a buyout—when selling a license, you keep the copyright, but a buyout transfers all ownership of a piece to the buyer. There are situations where a buyout is fine; for example, book cover illustrations are usually bought out. But when licensing for products, a buyout might mean leaving money on the table.

I learned this the hard way early in my career. I had landed a deal with a dream client—a company loved my pitch and offered me a $1,000 flat fee for a buyout of a design that was in my portfolio. At the time I really needed some money for my business, and I didn't know yet that the design had the potential to earn 10 times what they offered to pay me. I sold my copyright instead of licensing for a specific royalty in a single category.

The flat fee structure meant that later, when that design was put on hundreds of products and sold in big box stores, instead of earning, say, $1 per product sold across dozens of product categories like I would have gotten with a royalty, I got paid once—then never again. And, because the buyout gave them my copyright, I could never license that design to another different client ever again. Buyouts are always good for the buyer and nearly always cut the artist out of revenue share.

If you're just starting out and the full licensing pipeline feels a bit overwhelming, here's how to begin with a simpler version of the S.T.A.R. Cycle—no fancy portfolio or extensive experience required.

A SIMPLER S.T.A.R. CYCLE: PITCH YOUR FIRST LICENSING DEAL

Here's how to use the S.T.A.R. Cycle to begin licensing your artwork—even if you don't have a big portfolio, a mailing list, or tons of industry experience:

This is proof that you don't need to wait until you're "ready." You just need to start. By taking consistent small steps, you're building confidence, momentum, and visibility. You can always scale up your strategy later—but for now, get your art out into the world.

Week 1: Strategize

Pick three to five companies you'd love to work with. These can be brands you already shop from or admire. Do a little digging: What kinds of products do they sell? What art styles do they use? Add their names, websites, and any contact info to a simple spreadsheet.

Week 2: Think and Create

Assemble a mini collection. Start by choosing one of your best finished pieces of art for your hero illustration (an eye-catching, standout piece of artwork that serves as the anchor or focal point of your mini collection, showcasing your unique style and strongest visual elements, and setting the tone and theme for the entire collection). Then create two supporting pieces (a secondary pattern and a blender). Name the collection, and save the images in high resolution.

Week 3: Adapt

Create a simple sell sheet in Canva or Illustrator. Include the following and export it as a PDF:

- Your mini collection images
- A short two- to three-sentence bio or brand story
- Your name, e-mail, and website or portfolio link (if you have one)

Week 4: Reach Out

Send your sell sheet to two or three of the companies you researched. Keep it short and polite—introduce yourself, mention why you love their brand, and share your attached collection. Log when and who you pitched in your pitch tracker spreadsheet so you know when to follow up.

LEVERAGING THE S.T.A.R. CYCLE FOR LICENSING

With a few tweaks, we can adapt the S.T.A.R. Cycle as a workflow for licensing.

Week 1: Strategize

For Strategy week, your focus should be on researching leads for new collaborations. You'll be questing after companies, submission guidelines, and art director contact info. For each of your target companies, research their aesthetic and what they sell. What kind of artwork does well on their products? What is their vibe? If you feel inspired, you can sketch out a collection of ideas that you think would be a good fit. Track all this information in a pitch tracker spreadsheet and build a pitch calendar to keep yourself organized.

Week 2: Think and Create

For Think and Create week, your focus should be on filling any gaps in your portfolio. Pick a standout piece to serve as the hero illustration and build a mini collection around it—this will serve double duty. You can feature the mini collection in your online portfolio and later adapt it into a sell sheet for pitching. Or make a new holiday-themed mini collection to align with seasonal trends. Round out your portfolio to show clients you've got range, and name your designs. To increase licensing potential, aim for high-resolution, scalable files that are flexible for different formats and product types.

Week 3: Adapt

For Adapt week, your focus should be on creating new sell sheets and keeping your portfolio up to date. Make sure your portfolio represents your best work.

Week 4: Reach Out

For Reach Out week, your focus should be on pitching and following up! Craft those e-mails, send those sell sheets. Check your calendar to see who is overdue for a follow-up. Send your quarterly updates. Double-check that your materials meet each company's submission requirements; think of this as a preflight checklist. Don't forget to update your pitch tracker spreadsheet and pitch calendar.

Kirsten Katz: Persistence in Licensing

When Kirsten Katz, a prolific Australian artist, first started sharing her work on Instagram, she had no idea what art licensing was. But when people began reaching out to ask if they could license her designs, she knew she needed to learn everything she could. What began as an exploration quickly turned into a business, and by 2018, she was exhibiting at the Blue Print Show in New York, a major milestone for an artist who had only recently discovered the industry. Kirsten later joined my Leverage Your Art course and eventually became part of my Mastermind group, where I helped her develop her licensing strategy and grow her art business.

Her journey, however, was anything but smooth. Kirsten secured licensing partnerships for fabric and greeting card designs, but when the pandemic hit in 2020, many of those deals stalled or disappeared entirely. It was a devastating blow.

Instead of giving up, she adapted. She pivoted to selling prints and tea towels on Etsy, determined to keep moving forward. The first few sales felt like a miracle. "Those first ten sales were the hardest," she recalled. "Then the next milestone was twenty-five, then fifty, then one hundred." Each win built momentum, reinforcing the lesson that persistence is everything in licensing.

For Kirsten, the key to success wasn't avoiding rejection; it was learning how to push forward despite it. Every *no* was an opportunity to refine her work, pitch again, and find the right partnerships. Through years of steady effort, she built a thriving licensing career, proving that setbacks aren't the end of the road; they're just part of the journey.

OVERCOMING SETBACKS

Sometimes, disappointment comes in the beginning of your career, when you realize you've made a mistake with one of the above tips. And then, sometimes disappointment hits—not when you're starting out, but when you're already "successful."

In 2023, just days before I was set to embark on my vision-board-come-to-life dream trip (two months in Europe with my family), an art licensing agent decided to no longer represent me. On paper, this shouldn't have devastated me. After all, I'd already licensed my artwork with major brands, written a book, built a seven-figure product-based business, and taught countless artists how to launch their own licensing careers.

But there I was, after that Zoom call, walking through my neighborhood listening to the moodiest Nickel Creek album I could find, trying to make sense of it. I had a killer portfolio. A solid reputation. Fifteen years of experience. How could this still be happening? I found a quiet spot and just sat there, trying to slow my racing mind, remembering all the advice I'd given other artists in similar situations.

It took me a full month to come to grips with this rejection. One of my mentors reminded me that my path has always been different. I've always found a sideways path into this industry. Those twists and turns are what enabled me to create Leverage Your Art, a comprehensive art business course I teach every year with up-to-date advice to help other artists launch their careers.

Looking back a year later at the video I took that day, I can see the blessing in the setback. While I was off on that summer trip feeling like I'd failed, a member of the Creative Powerhouse Society, an art business membership that I have run since 2020, e-mailed me her résumé. Jessica Hobbs has since joined our team, helping with collaborations and product development—a hire that wouldn't have been possible if that licensing deal had gone through. Sometimes the *no* makes space for an unexpected yes.

The lesson? Your path might look wildly different from what you're anticipating. And maybe that's not so bad. The world needs our art and our voices, even (or especially) when the route to sharing them takes unexpected turns.

Art licensing isn't about avoiding rejection; it's about what you do next. So grab your portfolio, rehearse your pitch, and remember: For every no that knocks you down, there's a yes waiting to change everything.

As you continue your journey, be sure to read Chapters 10 and 11. They'll walk you through two more powerful ways to generate income from your art—so you can build a business that's not just creative, but sustainable too.

10

THE PRODUCT SALES FRAMEWORK

For many artists, the details of what happens in between a licensing pitch getting accepted and customers taking your art home is a little mysterious. From the artist's perspective it looks something like:

1. Pitch Portfolio

2. ???

3. Profit

The Product Sales Framework is all about unpacking that second step. And there's plenty to unpack—becoming a product-based business means having to learn a bunch of new skills, from marketing to shipping to working with manufacturers. I'll be real with you: It's a lot of effort, and the risk is higher. But the upside of that trade-off is that you gain a lot more flexibility and control over your products, and you get to take home a much larger cut of the profits.

Translating your ideas into products isn't always straightforward. It's not enough just to pick the right design or product; we'll need to tackle a much larger strategic process called *product development*. You need to think about your audience, pricing, production, testing, and shipping; how to market in a way that feels both authentic and rewarding; and how to do all of this in a sustainable way that builds stable income.

Whether you're just starting out or you're ready to scale up, this chapter is your guide to turning your art into products that work for you.

I'll never forget the moment I held my first tea towel design in my hands. It was soft and sturdy, printed with a playful illustration of a fox that I'd spent weeks perfecting—and it went on to clean up countless spills and cover many batches of cookies and loaves of banana bread in my kitchen for years to come.

Seeing my art transformed from a sketch on paper to a tangible and useful product felt like magic, as if all the pieces of my creative journey had finally clicked into place. But that moment didn't happen overnight. It was the culmination of years of trial and error, starting small, and learning to balance my passion for creating with the practical realities of running a business.

In this chapter, I'll guide you step-by-step through my process for turning art into products that resonate with an audience and generate consistent income. You don't need a fancy studio, expensive equipment, or even a huge audience to start. What you need is a plan, a bit of courage, and the belief that your art deserves to exist in the world.

THE ART TO PRODUCT PIPELINE

Going from an idea to a profitable product might feel a little overwhelming if you've never been through the process before, but it doesn't have to be! It helps me to break up the problem into five phases:

1. Understanding the audience
2. Finding a product idea
3. Production and pricing
4. Testing the market
5. Launching and marketing

We will go into detail about each step. Together, they are a repeatable blueprint for turning creativity into products and products into stable income.

PHASE 1: UNDERSTANDING YOUR AUDIENCE

If you want to create products that people love, you first need to know *who* you're creating them for. I've learned this the hard way: It's not enough to make something beautiful and hope it sells. Real magic happens when you understand your audience so well that your products feel like they were made just for them.

Take a moment to think about your ideal customer. What are they like? What makes them tick? When I first started creating art, I had no idea who my audience was. I thought I could make art that appealed to *everyone*. Spoiler alert: That's not how it works. Trying to please everyone meant I wasn't really connecting with anyone.

Everything changed when I narrowed my focus. I began to picture one person—someone who loved whimsical, uplifting designs with a vintage flair. Someone who valued handmade, meaningful products. With that image in mind, I created my first cohesive collection, and suddenly my work started resonating with people on a deeper level.

Create Your Customer Persona

To identify your audience, start by creating a customer persona—a fictional representation of your ideal customer. Sometimes this is also called an "ideal customer avatar," or ICA for short. Think of this persona as your muse. To help paint a picture of your customer persona, think about the following questions.

- **Who is your ideal customer?** What is the age range of your target audience? Where do they live? What is their gender? What are their interests and hobbies? What is their occupation? What is their income range? What is their lifestyle like? What inspires them?
- **Where does your ideal customer spend their time?** What social platforms do they use? What websites do they frequent? What events or activities do they attend? What restaurants do they patronize? What are their favorite television shows? Who do they follow on Instagram or TikTok? What kind of media do they consume?

- **What are your ideal customer's pain points and needs?** What problems does your product solve for them? What desires does your product fulfill? What kind of information are they searching for online? What kind of products or services are they currently buying? What feedback have you gotten from existing customers?

  For example, let's say you're an artist who creates delicate floral illustrations. Your ideal customer might be a 30-something homeowner who loves decorating her space with calming, nature-inspired decor. She shops at local boutiques, enjoys gardening, and appreciates high-quality, eco-friendly products. Having a specific persona in mind will help when making product and marketing decisions later.

Research Your Audience

Once you've sketched out your persona, it's time to do some research. Social media is a goldmine for understanding your audience. Follow accounts and hashtags that align with your style and notice what kinds of products people are sharing, commenting on, and buying. If you already have a small following, don't be afraid to ask your audience directly—send out a survey or ask questions in your Instagram Stories to gather insights.

One of the best tools I've ever used is a simple Google Form. Early in my career, I created a quick survey and sent it to my e-mail list, asking some basic questions. What kind of products do you wish existed? What price range feels reasonable for handmade goods? What's most important to you when choosing decor for your home?

The responses didn't just give me ideas; they gave me *confidence.* I learned that my audience loved practical products with a touch of whimsy, like tea towels and art prints. I also discovered that they were willing to pay a bit more for items that felt unique and meaningful.

Action Step:
Download Your Free Bonus Audience Building Chapter

If you want even more guidance on growing your audience and building your e-mail list, I've created a special bonus chapter you can download for free at stauciebloomfield .com/bookbonus.

Harness the Power of Niche

The more specific you get about your audience, the easier it becomes to create products that they can't resist. It's tempting to think that narrowing your focus will limit your sales, but the opposite is true. By speaking directly to a specific group, you can create a stronger connection, and that connection is what turns casual browsers into loyal customers.

Let's go back to my tea towels as an example. Setting aside some variables like material and manufacturing quality, tea towels are basically a commodity—all else being equal, if someone wants to buy a tea towel, they likely won't be very concerned about who made it.

However, printing a design onto that same towel turns it into something very different; it becomes something closer to a book or a song than to the plain fabric it was cut from. For example, imagine three different printed tea towels: one with flowers, one with cats, and one with an image of Mr. Darcy and a Jane Austen quote; each appeals much more strongly to very different audiences.

Art transforms the tea towel by making it represent something. This is why we talk about the *audience*—not just customers, they are people receptive to what our art has to say, and they communicate back to us.

PHASE 2: FINDING A PRODUCT IDEA

Where do you even begin designing a product? Should you create something functional, or go for something purely decorative? The good news is that you don't have to figure it all out at once. The process of finding your first product idea is a mix of creativity, research, and a little trial and error.

The best product ideas are often rooted in what you already do well. Think about the kind of art you love to create. Are you a painter, an illustrator, or a graphic designer? Do you have a particular style or theme that runs through your work, like bold colors, intricate patterns, or whimsical characters? If you love painting botanicals, consider turning your work into stationery, like notebooks or greeting cards. If you're great at lettering, think about creating inspirational prints or even calendars featuring your designs. If your art has a playful or humorous tone, stickers or enamel pins could be a perfect fit.

When the time comes to market your products, you'll have a much easier time if you choose a product type that feels authentic to you and showcases your art in a way that's both appealing and practical for your audience.

Start by dreaming big; we'll narrow down our options later. Think about all the ways your art could translate into products. Here are a few ideas to spark your creativity.

- **Home goods:** tea towels, mugs, throw pillows, coasters, rugs, pillowcases, blankets, dishes (including decorative plates), lampshades, wallpaper, wall decals, magnets, art prints, nursery decor.
- **Stationery:** journals, greeting cards, calendars, washi tape, planners, reusable book covers, postcards, notepads.
- **Apparel:** T-shirts, hoodies, tote bags, scarves, bandanas (pets can wear these too!), onesies, bibs, aprons.
- **Accessories:** enamel pins, stickers, phone cases, patches.
- **Gifts:** puzzles, gift books, subscription boxes.
- **DIY kits:** fabric, art kits (embroidery, paint-by-number, crochet, knitting).

Think About Your Audience's Needs

Now it's time to consider how your art can solve a problem or meet a need for your audience. This doesn't mean your product has to be utilitarian, like a tool or gadget. The "problem" your product solves might be as simple as brightening someone's day, being a gift for a friend, or adding a personal touch to their home. Ask yourself:

- What would make my audience's life more joyful, meaningful, or beautiful?
- Are there specific moments or occasions (like birthdays, holidays, moving to a new home, or new baby arrivals) where my art could play a role?
- How can my art help my audience express themselves or connect with others?
- What products do they already buy?
- What problems can my art solve for them? (e.g., beautiful cards for heartfelt messages, tote bags for eco-friendly shopping)
- What products would complement my brand style?

Research What's Popular (But Stay True to Yourself)

It's tempting to jump on trends when you're deciding what to create. While it's important to know what's popular, your product idea should still reflect your unique style and vision. Trends can be a helpful starting point, but don't let them overshadow what makes your art special. There are several ways to research product ideas.

- **Look at your own purchases.** Think about the types of products you're drawn to as a consumer. Are there categories that overlap with your artistic style?
- **Browse platforms like Etsy, Pinterest, Amazon, and even TikTok or Instagram.** These are goldmines for seeing what's trending in the handmade and creative product space. Pay attention to what's popular in your niche and read both written and video reviews

to understand what people love (or don't love) about similar products. What are customers raving about? What complaints come up again and again? Let that insight inform how you approach your own product line.

- **Check out local markets and boutiques.** Visit craft fairs, farmers' markets, or small shops to see what's selling well in your area. This can also give you ideas for packaging and presentation.

A word of caution: While researching, resist the urge to compare yourself to other artists. Use their success as inspiration, but remember that your unique voice is what will set your products apart.

Start Small and Test Your Idea

Don't just imagine your products—bring them to life with mock-ups and prototypes. Create digital mock-ups using tools like Canva or Photoshop, or order physical samples from print-on-demand (POD) platforms. Seeing your design on an actual product helps you evaluate its appeal and functionality.

The best way to figure out if your product idea is viable is to test it on a small scale. This doesn't mean you have to commit to a huge production run or spend a fortune up front. Start with a limited batch or a single product and gather feedback from your audience.

- **Create a mock-up.** Mock-ups are images edited to feature a design, sort of like thumbnails for physical items. For example, I have several photos of blank tea towels being held up or laid on a table, and I use Photoshop to put new designs on them. This is a cheap way to visualize how a design will look in context.
- **Create a prototype.** If you're making something like an art print or a sticker, you can easily create a few samples at home or through a local print shop. For more complex products like textiles or ceramics, consider partnering with a small-batch manufacturer.

- **Ask for feedback.** Share your prototype with friends, family, or your social media audience. Be open to their thoughts, and use their input to refine your idea.
- **Sell a small batch.** If the feedback is positive, produce a small batch of your product and list it for sale on platforms like Etsy or your own website. This will give you valuable insights into pricing, demand, and customer preferences.

When I tested my first screen-printed tote bags, I started with just 25 units. I hand-printed them myself with a screen-printing kit, took photos in my dining room, and listed them on Etsy. They sold out within a week, and I used that momentum to produce my next batch. Testing your idea on a small scale not only reduces risk but also builds confidence as you move forward.

One of the biggest barriers to getting started is the fear of spending too much money up front. But you don't need a huge budget to create your first product. Start with what you have and keep your costs low. Use local or online printers for small runs of prints, cards, or stickers. Look for manufacturers that offer low minimum order quantities (MOQs) for items like mugs or textiles.

When creating prototypes, repurpose tools and materials you already own. If you want to go full DIY, screen printing is very accessible, especially when validating an idea with low-quantity runs and can be done in your home. This technique can be used to prototype and produce all kinds of paper and fabric goods. Your community might already have a makerspace with access to prototyping equipment like sewing machines, laser cutters, and printers (both 2D and 3D), as well as other artists experienced in using them. The makerspace may be in a business in which you pay for access, a cooperative where you volunteer your labor, or even a local library that offers access to this equipment for free.

The goal isn't to create a perfect product right away; it's to take that first step and learn as you go. It is much easier to edit than to create from scratch; the sooner you get a prototype made, the sooner you can refine it. Your first product is a starting point—a way to dip your toes into the world of art products without overcommitting.

PHASE 3: PRODUCTION AND PRICING

Once you have your product idea and a proven prototype, it's time to bring your product to life. Our first step is to choose the right production method. There are two basic options.

- **Handmaking:** This means managing it all yourself. This approach is ideal for prototyping, for small batches, or for unique high-value items. Handmade products also more easily allow for customization and personal touch but can be time-consuming.
- **Manufacturing:** This means finding a supplier that specializes in making a product more efficiently than you can. This approach is perfect for larger runs or scaling your business. Print-on-demand platforms and local print shops don't require much initial investment but also offer you limited control over the final product.

At a certain scale, most businesses start looking into working directly with a factory for manufacturing; however, this topic is complicated, advanced, and outside our scope. For many kinds of products, you can get pretty far going all handmade. Also remember handmade does not necessarily mean making everything on your own; when scaling up, consider hiring local artisans to help with production. For years I contracted with local seamstresses on a per-piece basis to make pillows before scaling that product line up to manufacturer-level volume. Making products by hand is also a great way to understand your product.

Once you've found an appropriate production method for your product, you'll need to price it. Pricing can be one of the most challenging parts of selling your art on products. Set your prices too high, and you'll scare off customers. Too low, and you'll barely cover costs—or worse, undervalue your work. I wish I could give you a 100 percent foolproof way to set prices, but unfortunately, it's not quite that simple.

Wholesale/Retail Pricing Formula

Many artists use this simple formula to set prices.

- First, calculate the unit cost of production for your product; this number should include materials, manufacturing, labor, and shipping.

- Then calculate your wholesale price by doubling the unit cost; this covers your production cost with a modest profit to help cover marketing and the cost of keeping your website running.
- Finally, calculate the retail price by doubling the wholesale price. This is the price you would charge in your own shop.

For instance, say you have an item with a unit production cost of $5. Then wholesale customers would pay $10 for this item, and retail customers would pay $20. If you produce small batches, your production costs might be higher. Adjust your pricing to account for the added expense, but communicate the value of limited-edition or handmade products to your audience.

Pricing is as much about perception as it is about math. A higher price can signal quality, while a lower price might suggest your product isn't worth much. Don't be afraid to charge what your art is worth.

Think of this wholesale/retail calculation as your price floor; this is the margin you need to make the business profitable. I also recommend gathering around 10 comparable products that compete directly with yours to get a price range that the market can support. If this number is lower than your price floor, you'll need to adjust your marketing plan to get your product in front of people who can afford to pay a price you can afford to accept.

PHASE 4: TESTING THE MARKET

Before diving headfirst into a full product launch, it's essential to validate your ideas. Testing ensures your products resonate with your audience and gives you a chance to refine your offerings based on real feedback. Product development is exciting, but it's also a financial investment.

Testing helps you gauge interest before committing to large production runs, gather feedback to improve your products, and build anticipation among your audience. This is also a good time to test the checkout flow wherever your product is being sold; there's nothing worse than hyping up a big launch only to have a website bug that prevents customers from actually buying!

Every product idea comes with assumptions. For example, you might be assuming that your audience wants a calendar featuring your artwork, that they will pay $25 for it, and that they prefer neutral, minimalist designs over bold, colorful ones. By identifying these assumptions up front, you can design your test to determine whether they're accurate. If they're not, you'll know what to adjust before launching. I've used a few different methods to market test a new product. But pick *one*, and move forward. Don't try them all at once.

- **Preselling.** Create a landing page or use social media to showcase your product idea. Offer an exclusive preorder discount to gauge interest; this also lets your followers feel like they're in an exclusive club. Be transparent with your audience—let them know this is presale and when they can expect to receive their items. Set a minimum sales goal (e.g., 10 orders) to confirm that it's worth moving forward with a bigger launch.
- **Surveys and Polls.** Ask your audience about their preferences, ideal price points, color preferences, and what they'd like to see next. Post two or three product mock-ups and ask your audience to vote for their favorite.
- **Feedback Groups.** Share prototypes with a small group of trusted customers or peers and encourage honest feedback on the design, functionality, and pricing.

Once you've gathered feedback, take time to review it carefully. Look for patterns or recurring themes such as concerns about the price point or stylistic suggestions. Use this information to refine your product. If your audience prefers bold designs over neutral ones, adjust your artwork accordingly. If they're hesitant about the price, consider reducing production costs or adding value by, for instance, bundling your product with a bonus item.

At Gingiber, we've tested products by running Instagram polls and sending e-mail surveys to our subscribers. For our embroidery kits, we started with a small in-house batch to gauge demand before moving into larger-scale manufacturing. Testing not only helped us refine the product but also created buzz and buy-in from our audience.

PHASE 5: LAUNCHING AND MARKETING

No matter how big or how small, you can launch your product successfully—right where you are.

Simpler Launch Plan

Don't have a mailing list or a big social media following yet? That's okay. Here's a basic launch plan to help you get started:

- **Start with your personal network.** Let friends, family, and creative peers know what you're working on. A few personal messages can go a long way.
- **Post in local or online communities.** Share your product in groups you're already part of, whether they're Facebook groups, Slack channels, or neighborhood forums.
- **List your product on a platform like Etsy or Gumroad.** These tools are beginner-friendly and help you handle payments, listings, and fulfillment.
- **Tell a story.** Share what inspired the product or how you made it. Use your own voice. It's okay if only a few people see it—you're building trust and planting seeds.
- **Offer a small incentive.** A freebie like a digital print or free shipping for early buyers gives people a reason to support you now.
- **Ask for a share or review.** Word of mouth from even one or two people can kick-start your momentum.

More Advanced Launch Plan

Once you're ready to level up, you can start layering in more advanced strategies like the ones below. These steps will help you create more excitement, boost engagement, and build long-term momentum.

- **The planning and marketing for a launch starts weeks before your product goes live.** The goal of marketing is to create anticipation for the new product, engage the audience, and drive urgency.

- **Tease your product.** Share behind-the-scenes content that hints at what's coming. Sneak peeks of your creative process bring your audience along for the journey. Post close-up shots of the product without revealing the whole design and stories about the inspiration behind the product; use captions that invite curiosity, like "Can't wait to show you what I've been working on! Any guesses?" Add a countdown to your website or social media to build urgency.
- **Build buy-in.** Involve your audience by sharing how their feedback shaped the product and ask for their input on final details if appropriate (for instance, color palettes). When people feel invested in your process, they're more likely to buy your product.
- **Use your newsletter.** Your e-mail list is one of your most powerful tools. Send a series of e-mails a few days apart leading up to the launch. A sequence I've had luck with is the announcement ("Something exciting is coming!"), the sneak peek (Share behind-the-scenes photos or a teaser), the countdown ("Just 3 days until the big reveal!"), and the launch (announce that your product is officially live with a clear call to action like "Shop now!").
- **Create urgency.** We want to encourage quick action. Some ways to do this include releasing limited quantities or with an exclusive bonus—a small freebie for early buyers like a sticker or digital download. Time-sensitive discounts are also effective, for instance a 20 percent off coupon valid for the first 48 hours.
- **Go live!** For your launch day social media plan, post the announcement across all platforms and encourage followers to share. Respond to messages in this period to drive engagement. Thank your followers for their support and share customer testimonials or action shots. Giveaways can be effective for encouraging shares. Not everyone will buy right away; continue promoting periodically for at least a week.

- **Evaluate and refine.** After the launch, reflect on the results. How many units did you sell? Did you meet your goals? Which posts or e-mails generated the most interest? What did buyers love? Were there any issues? Use these insights to improve future launches.

A good product launch creates an experience for your audience. Launching is a skill that improves with practice. Each launch teaches you something new, and every step brings you closer to mastering the art of selling your creations.

A SIMPLER S.T.A.R. CYCLE: LAUNCH YOUR FIRST ETSY LISTING

We can adapt the S.T.A.R. Cycle to support a product-based business—and in fact, we already did! Follow the S.T.A.R.s as you bring your products to life. This chapter ends with two further S.T.A.R. Cycles to guide you no matter where you're starting from. It ends with an artist's story containing another adapted version of the S.T.A.R. Cycle—Start, Test, Assess, and Refine—for inspiration.

Here's how to use the S.T.A.R. Cycle to launch a single art print—no e-mail list or fancy marketing needed: This is proof you can build momentum without needing to be "ready." Just start small and stay consistent.

Week 1: Strategize

Choose *one* finished piece of art. Who is it for? Think of one person who'd love it (like a plant mom or cozy homebody). Set a small goal: "List this print on Etsy by [insert date]."

Week 2: Think and Create

Use Canva or Placeit to create a mock-up—your print in a frame, styled in a room. Write a short, clear description that includes size, colors, and how it ships.

Week 3: Adapt

Upload the listing to Etsy. Price it using the Wholesale/Retail Pricing Formula in this chapter. Add one to three clear product photos. Double-check spelling and shipping times.

Week 4: Reach Out

Share the link on Instagram or with a few friends. You don't need a huge following—just let people know it's out there. Celebrate this milestone!

Now that you've seen how this works on a simple scale, let's explore how the S.T.A.R. Cycle supports artists ready to launch or scale up their product-based business.

LEVERAGING THE S.T.A.R. CYCLE FOR PRODUCT SALES

One important note: Developing and producing a product takes time, and so we might need to be flexible about how long "a week" is in the S.T.A.R. Cycle when making batches of a new product. That's okay. The real power of this cycle is less about rigid schedules and more about maintaining intentional focus—especially if you're building your side hustle in the margins of life.

That said, if you're reading this and thinking, "Whoa, I don't even have an e-mail list yet!" or "I haven't sold *anything* before," don't worry. You don't need a full-blown launch machine to start. This next section walks you through the full STAR approach—but if you're newer, the previous section shows how to use this same framework in a super simple way.

Week 1: Strategize—Ideation and Planning

For Strategy week, your focus should be on laying the groundwork for your launch by refining ideas, setting goals, and planning the timeline. Brainstorm product ideas and consider current trends or gaps in the market. Look at potential competitors and identify what is working for them (like price points and product bundling). Reviews on competitors' listings are valuable resources for understanding what customers love or want more of. Define your success metrics like units sold or a revenue target. Set your launch date and reverse-engineer deadlines for design, production, and marketing.

Week 2: Think and Create—Design and Prototyping

For Think and Create week, your focus should be on preparing prototypes for review and feedback. Use a print-on-demand service to make samples in multiple colorways as appropriate. Take flat-lay photos of your prototypes and prepare a social media poll or e-mail survey to gather input on favorites. This is a good time to engage the audience with some behind-the-scenes content. Incorporate feedback, adjusting scale, colors, or patterns as needed. Draft your prelaunch content calendar.

Week 3: Adapt—Production and Prelaunch Prep

For Adapt week, your focus should be on preparing for launch by producing your final product and finalizing marketing. Place your bulk order, or if you're making by hand, schedule time to complete production (e.g., printing, sewing, or packaging). Write SEO-friendly product descriptions, prepare online product listings, and take professional photos. Schedule your prelaunch e-mails: I've had success with a first e-mail announcing the launch date with a sneak peek of the design, and a second "last chance" preorder e-mail with a discount or bonus incentive.

Week 4: Reach Out—Launch Week

For Reach Out week, your goal should be to successfully launch your product and gather momentum for scaling. Schedule launch day social media posts and send your launch e-mail with a clear call to action, like "Shop the collection now!" Respond to messages on social media and share live updates, like packing the first orders. Announce a limited-time offer, like free shipping for the first 24 hours. Analyze sales data and prepare for restocking based on demand.

Julie Byrne: Nurse Transforming Artistic Experimentation into a Thriving Business

Julie Byrne's journey into creative entrepreneurship didn't begin with a grand plan. It started with small, intentional steps and a willingness to test what worked. Though she had long dreamed of a life filled with art, practicality led her to a career in nursing. For years, art remained a personal passion, woven into the fabric of her life through murals, DIY projects, and seasonal crafts.

As her children grew, so did her creative ambitions. She explored embroidery, digital art, and printmaking, yet still saw these pursuits as hobbies rather than a potential business. That changed when she took the Leverage Your Art course, realizing that what she had once called an "expensive hobby" could actually be something more.

Her approach followed an adapted interpretation of the S.T.A.R. Cycle—Start, Test, Assess, and Refine.

Start: Julie didn't begin by trying to launch a full-scale business. She started by experimenting—monogramming towels for neighbors, creating prints, and sharing her work.

Test: She gauged interest by casually selling pieces and taking note of customer reactions. The real turning point came when a neighbor saw her work and insisted, *"You should sell this!"* That feedback gave her the confidence to push forward.

Assess: Encouraged by early sales, Julie took a strategic look at what was working. She built a Shopify store and focused on print on demand to scale her efforts without overwhelming herself with inventory.

Refine: With experience, she refined her approach, setting three nonnegotiable daily tasks to keep momentum. She adopted batch working—setting aside time for creation, marketing, and administration separately—so that her creativity didn't get lost in the logistics of running a business.

This process didn't eliminate challenges. Julie wrestled with imposter syndrome, worried she wasn't *really* an artist, and faced skepticism from those around her. But persistence and a willingness to iterate helped her push through.

She now teaches workshops, mentors other creatives, and has built a thriving business that brings her joy. As she puts it: *"The real beauty is in the trying—the bonus is in the good results."*

Her advice to aspiring artists? Start small, test your ideas, and surround yourself with people who challenge and encourage you. Or as she puts it: *"Find your mentor . . . a snowplow in advance makes a smoother path."*

Product sales are one of the most rewarding ways to bring your art into the world—and into your customers' homes. Whether you're hand-printing your first tea towel or preparing for your next wholesale order, remember that every product is more than just an object. It's a little piece of your creative story.

And while this chapter focused on selling physical goods, don't stop here! If you haven't yet read Chapter 9 on licensing, or Chapter 11 on offering teaching, I encourage you to take a look. Each income stream offers different benefits and challenges, and when layered together, they can create a truly resilient art business. You don't have to choose just one path—you get to build the mix that fits your life and your goals.

11

THE TEACHING FRAMEWORK

In our third and final framework, we'll explore a different way to turn your creative experience into meaningful income: teaching others. This can take many forms—from offering live workshops and online courses to consulting, critiques, coaching, or custom commissions. The teaching framework is broad, but for the purposes of this book, we'll focus on teaching in the most accessible sense: guiding others through what you know via workshops, classes, or memberships. Think of it as monetizing your expertise through what you *know* and how you can *share* it, not just what you *make*.

Compared to product sales and art licensing, teaching can start generating income relatively quickly. The skills you develop teaching will give you more perspective when approaching your own art. Some of the most successful artists I know have built their careers by sharing their knowledge alongside creating their art.

I'll be real—I never thought teaching would be a good fit for me. You might be in the same boat, but before you write it off, I want you to try something. Think back to the people who've helped you grow, whether they were teachers, mentors, or other artists. What made them special? Was it their technical perfection? Their fancy equipment? Or was it something else—perhaps their ability to break down complex ideas, their enthusiasm, or the way they made you feel capable of achieving your goals? There is a niche where you can provide that for others.

Teaching was never on my radar when I first started side hustling. I had this rigid idea that creating art for myself or for sale was the "real" path. Teaching was for others—those mythical beings with perfect mastery of their craft or natural-born educators with unshakable confidence.

If you'd asked me years ago, I would have told you that I was a terrible teacher. I'm naturally impatient, always wanting to get things done quickly and efficiently. I had this image in my head of myself as an overly rushed, ineffective teacher. Plus, when people heard I wanted to be an artist, they'd immediately assume I meant teaching art in schools. That wasn't my dream at all.

My journey into teaching began unexpectedly during a retreat I organized with friends in northwest Arkansas. I was finally out of the "having babies" phase—all my children were potty trained and could survive without mommy 24/7. I desperately wanted to reconnect with my art after being consumed by managing my life with a fixer-upper house, three kids, and a husband changing careers. That creative hunger led me to impulsively invite some local artist friends to join me in a cozy cabin for a weekend of artmaking.

Picture a group of accomplished artists—fine artists, fiber artists, watercolorists, curators—all gathered around a kitchen table with their supplies. And there I was with my tablet, wondering if my digital illustrations even "counted" as real art. That weekend was transformative, filled with good wine, cheese, and deep conversations about our creative dreams.

Someone jokingly suggested we do it again as a teaching retreat with each of us leading different workshops. When the subject of teaching came up, I suddenly felt like a kid sitting at the grown-ups table—the others all had teaching experience, and while I was full of ideas, I had never even attempted teaching before. What could I possibly offer someone who is looking to learn? But the idea stuck in my mind.

When it came time to advertise the retreat, I scrambled to figure out what I could possibly offer. My friends kept saying, "Just pick anything! Teach what you know." So, I dug back into my college years and dusted off block printing, something I used to do for fun.

In the weeks leading up to the retreat, I bought pink block printing kits from the local craft store and started practicing in the evenings. I carved simple designs—hands with flowers, deer, owls—narrating each step aloud to myself. I even recorded myself on my phone making a block print from start to finish, studying the recording to break down my process into clear steps. Slowly, I started to feel like I could do this.

When 12 women arrived at our retreat, my friends insisted I teach first so I could stop being nervous and start enjoying myself. Despite having run Gingiber for 7 years at this point, I was filled with doubt. Making art while people watched had never been my strong suit. In college, I'd freeze up whenever professors walked by during studio sessions. One professor even accused me of cheating because I couldn't create anything under observation. But alone at night, my creativity would flow freely. My fear of being watched had convinced me I couldn't teach.

Standing in front of our makeshift classroom, my heart raced. But as I picked up my carving tools, something shifted. I took a deep breath, set aside my fear and ego, and began talking. My muscle memory took over.

I'll never forget what happened next. These women didn't need me to be a master of block printing or a polished teacher with a detailed five-step plan—they just needed a guide. Someone who'd walked the path before, and could say: *This way—I'll show you.* As they carved their designs and pressed them onto paper, I watched joy and excitement light up their faces.

The session exceeded my wildest expectations. When my co-retreat leaders announced, "Can you believe this is the first thing Stacie has ever taught?" The group was stunned. "Really? This is your first time teaching? You were great!"

The revelation hit me: *Teaching wasn't so challenging when I leaned in to something I already knew how to do.* With hindsight this made perfect sense, but the Chaos Goblin had convinced me I couldn't do it. But effective teaching didn't require perfection—it just needed to be real. That retreat became the foundation for a path I never expected to love: becoming an online art educator.

THE ART TO TEACHING PIPELINE

Even after hearing my unlikely path to education, you might be having a hard time imagining yourself in the role of teacher. But I'd like to challenge you to consider that you have already held that role in *some* capacity. There is some topic or niche where you've developed expertise that is recognized by others—this is your teaching sweet spot. To help figure out what your niche is, ask yourself these questions:

- **What things do people already ask you to help them with?** Think about the DMs, e-mails, or coffee conversations where other artists seek your advice. These questions are gold—they reveal what others see as your expertise, even if you take it for granted.
- **Which processes come naturally to you?** Consider the techniques or approaches that feel like second nature. Maybe it's your color selection process, your way of creating patterns, or how you plan your collections. These natural skills are your starter teaching topics.

MAKING YOUR TEACHING PLAN (WITHOUT THE OVERWHELM)

Probably the biggest misconception about teaching is that you need to have everything perfectly mapped out like a college professor. This isn't a calculus class with complex formulas written across multiple whiteboards. Think of yourself more like a nature guide leading others down a trail you've walked many times before. You know where the path gets steep, where to pause for breath, and (most importantly) where the most beautiful views are. You're simply showing others how to reach that amazing destination you've already discovered.

That's your *curriculum*. It's really just a fancy word for "What should I teach first, second, and third?" Start by writing down what you wish someone had told you when you were beginning. What are the tricky spots where people might need extra guidance? What shortcuts or viewpoints have you discovered that others might miss on their own? These insights become the trail markers of your teaching plan.

Think of building a piece of IKEA furniture. The instructions show you step one, then step two, with clear pictures along the way. Your teaching can follow the same pattern: Break down your process into clear, manageable steps, each building on the last. When students see early success, they're motivated to tackle bigger challenges.

Action Step:
Pick Your First Workshop Idea

Grab your notebook and jot down three potential workshop topics you'd feel excited to teach. Don't overthink it—just brainstorm! Then, circle the one that makes you say, "Yes, I could teach that." That's your first step toward sharing your knowledge and building income through teaching.

Judy Havrilla: Turning Local Need into Art Camp Magic

Judy is one of my students. Judy's creative business began with a gap she noticed in her hometown. After moving back, she found there wasn't anything like the children's art program her son had loved when he was six or seven years old, so she decided to create one herself. This program would become the most enduring part of her art business.

Her first children's art class took place in a small studio she'd rented for her graphic design business, with everyone sitting and working on the floor. From there, she helped found an art business incubator, which provided free space. When the incubator didn't take off, she moved her graphic design business into her bedroom and rented space at a symphony school, where her rent was calculated as a portion of tuition.

As a single parent at the time, Judy ensured the program remained profitable from the start. After remarrying and moving, she rebooted her art program as Bull Run Mountain Art

Camp, initially renting the local community center for summer sessions. When repairs forced the center to close one summer, she moved the camp to her home on a wooded mountain, complete with a tiny house studio and treehouse. The space she had thought needed to be somewhere more professional turned out to be perfect—she saved on overhead. Parents have described the setting as "magical."

Throughout the years, Judy has balanced the art camp with multiple commitments: serving as an Army reservist, raising her son (who later worked as her camp assistant), and now accompanying her husband on business trips, living half the year in Guam. She describes the camp as "confiscating her life" for about a month each summer, but she loves the intensity and looks forward to it each year. Looking ahead, she and her husband plan to expand into adult art camps after his retirement, with him putting his culinary school training to use as camp cook.

And her practical business advice: "Get going with as little overhead as possible. Commit to the least expenditure as you can. It's so much more manageable and inspiring to keep going when you aren't 'spending your own money,' meaning the family money, on your business."

UNDERSTANDING TEACHING FORMATS

Teaching is not a one-size-fits-all process. Let's talk about three different models that I (and other artists) have found success with: *live workshops, comprehensive courses,* and *membership programs.*

- **Live Workshops:** One of the easiest ways to start teaching is through live workshops, whether in person or virtual. These are especially great for beginners because they allow for immediate feedback and real-time interaction with students. Teaching live helps to build your confidence, sharpen your skills, and gauge student interest. Workshops can also be recorded and repurposed for future content. If you're unsure whether a topic is course-worthy, a live workshop is a great way to test the waters before committing to a full course.

- **Comprehensive Courses:** For a more structured learning experience, comprehensive courses provide students with a complete journey through a subject. These courses combine multiple lessons, offering a deeper dive into a topic. They can be self-paced, giving students flexibility, and can include live elements for added support. Because of their in-depth and self-directed nature, comprehensive courses typically have a higher price point and the potential to generate passive income over time.
- **Membership Programs:** The membership model offers an ongoing way to teach at a higher level while building a tight-knit learning community. With a recurring revenue model, memberships provide financial stability while fostering deep connections with students. However, they require consistent content creation to keep members engaged. If you enjoy teaching regularly and love the idea of nurturing a long-term learning environment, a membership program could be a great fit. As higher level and higher cost offerings, membership programs are typically most successful after you've built a reputation and credibility as both a teacher and a practitioner.

STARTING SMALL: YOUR FIRST WORKSHOP

I recommend starting with live workshops, even if your ultimate goal is creating comprehensive online courses, because live teaching gives you immediate feedback. You can see exactly where students get stuck, what questions they ask, and which explanations resonate most. This insight is invaluable when you're ready to create prerecorded content. The following steps will help you design, plan, and pull off your first class.

Choose a Specific Focus

Instead of "Watercolor Painting," try "Creating Loose Floral Wreaths in Watercolor." Rather than covering all of pattern design, focus on creating a repeating pattern from a single motif. The more specific the topic, the better. Aim to give your students one clear win they can achieve in a single session. Nothing builds confidence like seeing results. The outcome we'd love to see is our students leaving the session excited and empowered to continue learning after class is over.

Structure Your Teaching Time

Practice your workshop activity to ensure that you can achieve your teaching goals in an appropriate time frame; 90 minutes is a good length to aim for. Teaching often takes longer than expected; what seems like a quick demonstration in your head might need extra time for student questions and hands-on practice. When you're starting out, students will almost certainly come up with questions you wouldn't have predicted! You might structure your class time like so:

- 15 minutes: Welcome and demonstrate the technique
- 45 minutes: Guided practice time where students create
- 15 minutes: Troubleshooting and questions
- 15 minutes: Sharing and celebration of work

To keep your lesson structured and effective, have examples of work at different stages so students can visualize the progression of the technique.

Create Simple Support Materials

Even a basic workshop benefits from a simple handout. Think of this like your syllabus, and include the following information:

- Materials needed
- Basic steps covered
- Common mistakes to avoid

- Resources for learning more
- Your contact information

A simple checklist of things to bring or prepare will help ensure you don't forget essential materials, whether it's supplies, reference images, or tech equipment. Lastly, think about how you'll document student work—always with permission—so you can share success stories and showcase real-life transformations. Capturing these moments not only builds credibility but also inspires future students to take part in your workshops.

Gather Your Equipment

If you're teaching virtually, or if you're teaching in person but want to record the session, you don't want your technology setup to get in the way. Recording yourself teaching the main technique can also be incredibly useful—not only does it help you catch areas where you might need to slow down or clarify instructions, but it also gives you a chance to see how your explanations translate on camera. Keep the following in mind for the basic technical supplies you'll need:

- **Good lighting** makes a big difference in your video quality; natural light from a window, a well-lit room, or a ring light can all work. Next, **clear audio** is just as important as visuals. A simple lapel mic can greatly improve sound quality.
- You'll also need **a way to show your work** effectively. Use a smartphone camera or webcam to capture your process, and a tripod to hold it steady. Finally, gather **your regular art supplies** so you can teach comfortably with the tools you already use. Keeping things simple ensures you can focus on sharing your expertise rather than worrying about complicated equipment.

Test Your Setup

Practice your lesson with a friend or family member. Teaching in a low-pressure setting allows you to refine your approach, identify potential gaps in your content, and build confidence. Focus on clarity rather than perfection. Can they follow your instructions? Do they end up with a completed project? That's what matters.

TIPS TO MAKE YOUR FIRST WORKSHOP A SMASH HIT

Don't try to teach everything at once.

You're excited to share everything you know, and you want your first workshop to include *all the things*. (Actually, I'm still there! Even writing this book, I catch myself wanting to cram in every single thing an aspiring art side hustler could possibly need to know.) But information overload leads to inaction, and that doesn't serve anyone.

Imagine teaching someone to swim by explaining the history of swimming, competitive techniques, and advanced diving all at once—they'll likely sink before they even learn to float. Even after years of teaching, I have to remind myself to slow down and focus on what's most important right now. Remember: You can always add more advanced workshops later. Start by teaching one thing exceptionally well and let your teaching grow organically from there.

Know what you're really worth (and charge accordingly).

Can we have a heart-to-heart about pricing? When I first started teaching, I made a classic mistake. I looked at my two-hour workshop and thought, "Well, it's just two hours, so I should charge accordingly." Oh, friend, was I wrong!

I forgot to factor in the three hours I spent preparing materials, the years of experience that made those two hours valuable, the time answering student questions afterward, and most importantly—the transformation I was offering my students. They weren't just paying for my time; they were paying for the confidence and skills they'd take home with them.

Start now, perfect later.

I used to think I needed a proper studio setup before I could teach. This is a trap—there is literally no limit on how much time and money you can spend setting up the "correct" recording environment. When I finally made my first online course, I filmed with my iPad propped up on a stack of books and recorded with a $20 lapel mic. Was it perfect? Not even close! But you know what? My students learned, created beautiful art, and many of them are still in my community today.

The truth is, if I'd waited for the "perfect" setup, I'd probably still be waiting. Your phone camera and some good natural light by a window are enough to start. Trust me—your knowledge is way more valuable than fancy equipment. The launch-and-learn cycle applies here!

Build your creative cheer squad.

Here's my favorite part about teaching—those magical moments that happen between the "actual" teaching. You know, five minutes before class starts when everyone's chatting about their latest projects. Or the group chat where someone shares their first successful pattern design and everyone celebrates together.

I've watched lifetime friendships form in my workshops, and some of my most successful students credit their growth not just to my teaching, but to the community they found there. Whether you're teaching online or in person, make space for these connections. It could be as simple as a WhatsApp group or a few minutes of sharing time at the end of each session.

Build confidence through preparation.

While great teaching evolves through experience, your students deserve a well-prepared instructor from day one. Master your material thoroughly enough to demonstrate it flawlessly and explain it multiple ways. Create and test a detailed lesson plan, practicing your full demonstration at least three times. I write out my full scripts that I am going to teach and read them aloud so I can catch anything that sounds off or rushes over an important step.

Put yourself in your most beginner student's shoes and create a document with the frequently asked questions (FAQs) based on any questions or problems they might have; update it as new questions come in. This will allow you to have solutions ready for common student challenges. Test all equipment and materials thoroughly, and prepare clear handouts and reference materials. Set up a system for student questions and feedback; even a simple Google Form or an e-mail that says, "Reply here with any questions" will give your students an invitation to interact.

Remember: Your students are investing their time and money in your expertise. While you'll continue growing as a teacher, they shouldn't have to pay for your learning curve.

True confidence as a teacher comes through mindful experience built on this foundation of thorough preparation. Each session will reveal new insights about your teaching style and your students' needs, but these insights should refine an already solid approach. Your students' questions will help you identify areas to clarify or expand. Their successes will validate your methods, and their challenges will help you develop even better teaching strategies.

Your first workshop doesn't need to be perfect, but it does need to be professional. Think of it as a structured conversation where you're sharing proven expertise with people who have invested in learning from you. When you approach teaching with both thorough preparation and genuine enthusiasm, you create an environment where both you and your students can thrive. Each workshop brings opportunities to serve your students better, and these insights become invaluable as you expand your teaching offerings.

The most successful workshop I ever ran wasn't the one with the most polished presentation; it was the one where students felt so comfortable sharing their work that they kept posting progress photos weeks after the class ended. That's the kind of energy you want to create.

TEACHING AS A WAY OF BUILDING COMMUNITY

Here's something I've learned after years of teaching artists: The courses that create the most income aren't necessarily the ones with the fanciest production value or the most extensive curriculum. They're the ones where students feel connected and supported. Why? Because these students don't just complete one course and disappear—they become loyal supporters who take your future courses, recommend you to friends, and actively participate in your artistic ecosystem.

When students feel part of a community, they're more likely to stick with the challenging parts of learning, more likely to share their successes (and tag you in them), and more likely to come back for more advanced courses. I've watched students from my early courses become my most effective marketing channel, sharing their progress on social media and bringing their friends into our next session. That kind of organic growth is priceless.

If the phrase "building community" makes you want to hide under your desk, you're not alone. Here's the good news: Building this kind of community doesn't require complicated systems or constant attention. Start with tools you probably already use. A simple WhatsApp group can become a vibrant space for sharing works in progress. Google Classroom offers a free, straightforward way to share materials and foster discussion. Even a dedicated Instagram DM group can work wonders to keep students connected. I've seen thriving communities built on each of these platforms.

What happens in these spaces? It's surprisingly simple. Students share their latest projects, asking, "How did you get that effect?" or "Does anyone else struggle with this technique?" They celebrate each other's wins ("Look what I finally finished!") and troubleshoot challenges together. One of my students posted about struggling with a particular brush technique, and within hours, three others had shared videos of their process. That kind of peer support is pure gold.

The secret is this: Artists love talking to other artists about their work. Your job isn't to manufacture connection—it's just to create space for it to happen naturally. That might mean setting aside the last 15 minutes of class for sharing works in progress, or starting each session with a quick round of "what are you stuck on?" Some of the strongest creative communities I know started with just a handful of people who felt safe enough to share their struggles and celebrations.

Maja Faber: Stockholm Move Launches Creative Career

Maja Faber has become one of my trusted industry friends. Her journey into teaching began with an unwavering belief that she could carve her own path in the creative world. For two years, surface pattern design was her passion, but not yet her career. She juggled up to three part-time jobs, earning between $1,000 and $3,000 per month, which gave her the financial cushion to experiment, refine her skills, and build confidence in her craft. "My part-time jobs gave me the financial cushion to experiment, learn, and get truly skilled at my craft before making the leap," she said.

Despite doubts from friends and family, Maja's father—a lifelong entrepreneur—remained her biggest supporter. His advice was simple but profound: persistence wins. She couldn't imagine a life spent working for someone else's dreams, so when an opportunity arose to move to Stockholm to be with her husband, she saw it as her chance to go all in. With $12,000 in savings, she gave herself a one-year runway to make her creative business work.

The leap was perfectly timed. After two years of sharing her work online, she landed her first two licensing deals—worth a combined $4,500—the same week she officially launched her business. Soon after, she started teaching on Skillshare, earning just $300 in her first month. But by month six, that number had grown to $1,100, and her teaching career continued to expand from there.

Through licensing and online courses, Maja not only built a thriving creative business but also discovered her true passion: helping others turn their artistic skills into careers. She embodies the balance of persistence, preparation, and seizing the right moment to step into a teaching role that now fuels both her creativity and her business.

BUILDING YOUR FRAMEWORK

This is the mindset I want you to adopt: Ask yourself, "What do I need right now? How can I create income using what I know right this minute?"

Every successful teacher begins with a single class or workshop. Your initial offerings don't need to be perfect; what matters is starting with what you have and refining as you go. Teaching, like any skill, improves through experience, and the best way to gain that experience is by simply beginning.

Listening to your audience is key to creating impactful lessons. Pay attention to the questions people ask you, whether it's through social media, e-mails, or in casual conversations. Even if you don't have a large following, survey the people who are already engaged in your work. Their needs and interests should guide the content you develop, ensuring that your teaching remains relevant and valuable.

Building authentic connections is what sets great teachers apart. Sharing your own learning journey, including challenges and breakthroughs, makes your teaching more relatable. Transparency about your creative process invites trust and engagement, fostering a sense of community around your work. When students feel connected, they're more likely to return and recommend your lessons to others.

Teaching is an evolving process, and adaptation is essential. Start with simple offerings and add complexity over time. Pay close attention to student feedback, as it can provide valuable insights into what's working and what needs adjustment. Be willing to pivot when necessary—flexibility allows you to refine your approach and continue growing as an educator.

Above all, focus on delivering value. Prioritize student success and aim to provide more than you promise. By consistently offering high-quality instruction and meaningful experiences, you build trust with your audience. The more you invest in their growth, the more they will invest in you.

You've started to think about how your experience and creative voice can serve others—and now, it's time to put that into motion. Let's walk through a simple, beginner-friendly plan using the S.T.A.R. Cycle to help you outline, prepare, and launch your very first workshop. No overwhelm. Just four small steps to build momentum.

A SIMPLE S.T.A.R. CYCLE FOR PLANNING YOUR FIRST WORKSHOP

Here's how to use the S.T.A.R. Cycle to go from "maybe I could teach" to having a real workshop offering—whether it's in-person, on Zoom, or even prerecorded. No fancy tools needed—just start with what you have.

Week 1: Strategize

Pick a topic you feel confident about—something you already know how to do. Ask yourself: What could I teach in one hour that would help someone make real progress? Set a simple goal: "Teach a free live Zoom class on watercolor flowers by [insert date]." That's your milestone.

Week 2: Think and Create

Map out the basic structure of your class. What are the three to five steps you'll guide students through? Gather your materials, create a rough outline, and make one or two sample projects to show during class.

Week 3: Adapt

Set up the logistics: Where will you host it? (Zoom, in-person, Instagram Live?) What tools will you use? Create a basic signup form and simple promo image. Keep it low-tech. You can use Canva and a free Mailchimp form or even just a Google Form.

Week 4: Reach Out

Start spreading the word! Share about your class with your e-mail list, on social media, or in your local community. Let people know why this class matters and how it will help them. Show your sample project, and invite them to sign up!

LEVERAGING THE S.T.A.R. CYCLE TO LAUNCH A MINI COURSE

If you've already taught a simple live workshop—or if you've got a bit of teaching experience under your belt—you're ready to build something more structured that keeps working even when you're not.

What if that same material could become something you sell again and again—without having to teach it live every time?

That's where your first mini course comes in.

A mini course is a slightly more polished offer: three to five short lessons that walk your students toward a clear, tangible result. It doesn't need to be fancy. But it *does* give you the freedom to prerecord your content, expand your reach, and create repeatable income.

And the best part? You've already done the hard part: You taught it live. Now we're just packaging it up.

Let's walk through how to bring your mini course to life using the full S.T.A.R. Cycle—one week at a time.

Week 1: Strategize

Define the focus of your mini course. What specific outcome will your students achieve? Outline the key lessons you'll teach—aim for three to five lessons that build on each other. Think of it like a workshop turned into a step-by-step guide.

Decide how you'll deliver it. Will it be prerecorded video lessons hosted on a platform like Kajabi or Thinkific? Will you offer a student workbook? What's the timeline you need to create it?

Week 2: Think and Create

Record your lessons! Keep them short, clear, and focused on student results. You don't need fancy tech—a smartphone, a quiet space, and natural lighting will do.

Also start building your student experience: a welcome e-mail, a simple checklist, or downloadable resources that make the course feel supportive and complete.

Week 3: Adapt

Upload your course content and finalize your sales page. Keep the copy clear: What's the transformation? Who is this for? What will they walk away with?

Add testimonials from your workshop (even just one!) if you have them, or include some enthusiastic quotes from DMs or e-mails if students have shared appreciation in the past.

Test everything—make sure your payment system works, your content uploads correctly, and your e-mails send.

Week 4: Reach Out

It's launch time! Send an announcement to your e-mail list or post on social media. Keep the messaging personal: "If you loved my workshop, you're going to love this course."

Give your audience a reason to take action now—a limited-time discount, a bonus, or early bird pricing. And remember to follow up! Most people don't buy the first time they see something. Be proud of what you've created and keep inviting them in.

WHEN YOU'RE READY TO GROW: THE FOUR-PART LAUNCH FRAMEWORK

Once you've run a few successful workshops and built a small following, you might be ready to launch a bigger program. You won't need complicated funnels, fancy equipment, or a marketing MBA. Coming up, you'll see how Amber, a Leverage Your Art course alumna, began her most successful launch with a simple Christmas tree tutorial on Pinterest. Or Maja, who started on Skillshare making just $300 her first month but grew her income to $1,100 by month six by focusing on genuine connection with her students.

The truth is that successful courses and workshop launches often follow a surprisingly simple pattern that puts connection and authentic teaching first. Here's a framework I learned from my mentor Jeff Walker that I've adapted specifically for artists.

- **The Why (Video/Post/E-Mail #1)** Share what inspired you to create this course. Think about how Rebecca Woolbright found her calling after her honeymoon in Japan; that personal story of discovering washi tape became the foundation for her teaching. Your story helps others see themselves in your journey.
- **The What (Video/Post/E-Mail #2)** This is where you give real value and teach something meaningful that gives students a quick win. When Myra taught her first art workshop with just basic block printing supplies from the craft store, she wasn't trying to be perfect; she was focused on helping her students create something they'd be proud of.
- **The How (Video/Post/E-Mail #3)** Paint the bigger picture of transformation. Share concrete examples, like how Judy turned a gap in local children's art education into a thriving summer program. Your students need to see what's possible.
- **The Invitation (Video/Post/E-Mail #4)** Finally, invite them to join your course. Be clear about what you're offering and why now is the time to start. As Jennifer Knight discovered, you don't need a massive following—you just need to serve the right people well.

The secret sauce of this approach is that by the time you make your course offer, you've already proven your value through teaching. You're not just selling a course; you're inviting students to continue a journey they've already started with you. Let me share with you what Leverage Your Art course alumna Amber Fife discovered when she ventured into teaching:

Amber Fife: Building a Global Watercolor Movement

Amber Fife's story perfectly captures what's possible when you combine creativity with consistent action. She didn't start with a massive following or fancy equipment—just a love for watercolor and a desire to share it with others.

Her journey began simply: by teaching basic watercolor techniques through live sessions. But what made Amber's approach special was her focus on community and seasonal creativity. She created a watercolor membership program that offered both live instruction and self-paced learning, making it accessible to students with different schedules and learning styles. She wanted to help women establish a practice of creative living, calling her business *Women Create Weekly*.

The turning point in Amber's business came from an unexpected source: Pinterest. She had shared an image of a Christmas tree project she'd created—nothing fancy, just a simple watercolor tutorial. For almost two years, that pin circulated quietly until suddenly it went viral, garnering 22 million views.

But crucially, Amber was ready for that moment when it arrived. She had already built a solid foundation with her membership program, so when that wave of traffic came, she had something valuable to offer her new audience.

What I love most about Amber's story is how it rippled beyond her immediate community. Her own mother, who had stepped away from art due to life's pressures, was inspired to return to her calligraphy and art practice. She even began teaching in-person classes from her home. Several of her mother's students later joined Amber's online membership, creating a beautiful cycle of creativity and community.

Today, her watercolor club is more than just a teaching platform—it's a nurturing space where members connect, grow, and share their artistic journeys. By sharing what she knows with an eager audience, she's made high-quality art education accessible while building a sustainable business.

Remember: You don't need to be the world's greatest expert to offer valuable services. You just need to be able to solve problems for people who need help. Start with what you already know and can do well.

As we close this chapter, I want you to think about the impact your knowledge and creativity can have. Teaching isn't about having the perfect setup; it's about showing up and sharing what you know in a way that helps others grow.

The best teachers didn't start with flawless systems or unshakable confidence. They had doubts. They faced challenges. But what set them apart wasn't fancy equipment or natural talent; it was their decision to begin anyway. To experiment. To refine. To keep going. Because in the end, the most powerful thing you can offer isn't perfection; it's your willingness to show up and serve.

Your journey as a teacher doesn't need to mirror anyone else's. Maybe you'll start with simple live workshops and discover you love the energy of real-time teaching. Perhaps you'll create a series of focused mini courses that generate passive income. Or you might build a membership community that becomes your primary business. The path you choose should align with your strengths, circumstances, and goals.

What matters most is that you take that first step. Your experiences, your unique perspective, and your artistic journey are valuable. Someone out there needs to learn exactly what you know, in exactly the way you can teach it.

Remember, the most important step is to start—no matter how small. Begin now and focus on serving your students with authenticity and intention. Prioritize building genuine connections, as strong relationships foster trust and engagement. Allow your teaching style to evolve naturally over time, embracing the learning process as both a teacher and an artist. Most importantly, trust in the value of your experience; your unique journey and perspective have the power to inspire and guide others.

The world needs more artists sharing their knowledge, breaking down barriers, and helping others find their creative voice. Your teaching journey isn't just about generating income—though that *is* important—it's about contributing to a larger creative community and helping others achieve their artistic dreams.

If you haven't yet read Chapters 9 and 10, I encourage you to take a look. Each income stream offers different benefits and challenges, and when layered together, they can create a truly resilient art business. You don't have to choose just one path—you get to build the mix that fits your life and your goals.

Now go create something amazing. Your future students are waiting!

12

HOW TO KEEP GOING (AND GROWING)

Imagine this: You're looking at a blank page. Or maybe it's a canvas, a new product concept, or the draft of a pitch e-mail. Rather than focusing on all the possibilities, your mind fixates on what can go wrong. *What if it's not good enough? What if they say no? What if this is a huge waste of time?*

I've found myself trapped in this spiral of paralyzing negativity more times than I can count. The longer we allow our doubt, uncertainty, or fear of failure to ferment, the bigger it gets—until it feels insurmountable. But a similar magnifying effect applies to positive focus: When we shift our attention to what excites us, what inspires us, and what we can do right now, those things start to grow too.

My sister and I share so many core memories, but the one we come back to even now as adults is how our dad always cheered us on with the phrase: *You're a winner!* He said it so often that it became an automatic loop in our heads. Even now, when we're together laughing about something ridiculous, we'll echo his words: *We're winners!*

Looking back, I see now how intentional my dad was with those words. He saw me struggling. I've always been a little too good at putting myself down. As a kid, I stood out in ways I didn't want to. I was tall—too tall, I thought. My classmates nicknamed me "the Jolly Green Giant" and "the Eiffel Tower." (Kids, right?) I carried that sense of not-enough-ness into adulthood, where anonymous Internet trolls were all too willing to pick up the mantle of my childhood bullies.

By my mid-20s, with two daughters of my own, I realized I couldn't keep living in that negative loop. I wanted to be better—for me, yes—but especially for them. So, I started a simple but life-changing practice: **mirror work and daily affirmations**. Every time I looked in the mirror, instead of dissecting my flaws, I placed my hand over my heart and said: *"I love you. You're doing a good job. And you. Are. A winner."*

At first, it felt forced and downright awkward. (Talking to yourself in the mirror? Really, Stacie?) But I kept at it. Over time, those words became my truth. My dad's voice became my own. And what I focused on started to grow.

When I first began Gingiber, my focus was clouded with insecurities. "My work just isn't in style." "I have no idea how to sell myself." "Other artists are much better than me." It was a negative feedback loop running nonstop through my head. But one day, I decided to reverse the roles. I wondered: "What's already working, and how can I do more of that?"

In my case? Tea towels. I'd begun making them as a trial in 2012, and customers loved them. So, I leaned all the way in. Instead of stressing over all the other products I *could* or *should* be making, I focused. I perfected my designs, refined the packaging, and honored the story behind them. More than anything, I brainstormed new tea towel designs, letting them take center stage in my business.

And you know what? That focus paid off. Sales skyrocketed, and those tea towels became a signature part of my brand.

Focus and consistency, over time, yield the best results. In 2012, I sold maybe 100 tea towels. Flash forward to 2024—we sold over 100,000 tea towels to tens of thousands of customers around the world! But that wasn't the real win, the tea towels. It was the discovery that the more I leaned in to the things that brought me joy, the more aligned everything felt.

I love this quote from a 2017 blog post by author Ryan Holiday titled, "Tell Me Who You Spend Time With, And I Will Tell You Who You Are." It hits the nail on the head about where we should put our focus:

A lot of productivity advice is similarly flawed—it's about doing what you do better instead of getting you to do better things. How much you get done is far less important than the type of activities you participate in and what you're willing to spend your life on. Because that's what we're doing when we put toward something—spending our limited amount of life.

HOW I GET UNSTUCK: FOUR QUICK PRACTICES TO REGAIN MOMENTUM

These are the exact mindset shifts and small actions I return to when I'm feeling stuck, overwhelmed, or unsure of my next move. You don't need to do them all at once. Just choose one, try it today, and see what shifts. Over time, these tiny practices can create big movement. Keep this list somewhere visible—on your phone, taped to your mirror, or inside your sketchbook—for those days when doubt or burnout creeps in.

- **Gratitude practice.** On both good and bad days, reflect on at least one thing you're grateful for. Perhaps it's electricity or running water. Gratitude, like any other skill, is learned and improved over time.
- **Turn envy into inspiration.** Perceived competition stems from a scarcity mindset. Turn it on its head: They have what I want—and I can have it too.
- **Choose a goal.** Visualize the accomplishment of a significant goal. What does it look like? What does it feel like? Visualize the specifics and use them as motivation.
- **Focus on action.** Rather than getting hung up on all the things that could go wrong, ask: *What's one small thing I can do today that moves me closer to my goal?* Then do it.

Think of a goal that feels out of reach. Write it down. Now, break it into the tiniest possible step you can take today: sending an e-mail, sketching an idea, or writing down three affirmations. Do it. Then celebrate that small win.

Patricia Efunsade: Finding Joy Through Small, Consistent Steps

Patricia Efunsade's creative business wasn't born out of perfect circumstances; it emerged from grief, uncertainty, and the need to heal. In 2019, after the unexpected loss of her sister Ayotola, Patricia found herself searching for something that would bring light into the darkness. Her sister had always found joy in the little things, even in difficult times, and Patricia wanted to carry that spirit forward.

With just $300, she took a leap and bought her first materials: die cutting supplies, paper, and a small storage unit for her supplies. She had no grand plan, just a desire to create something that would bring joy. At first, her work was squeezed into late nights, weekends, and early mornings before her full-time job. She made space wherever she could, tucking supplies into corners and repurposing parts of her living area into a makeshift studio. Growth was slow—painfully slow—but she kept showing up.

"Consistency is more important than perfection." This became Patricia Efunsade's guiding mantra. Even when progress felt invisible, she kept going—attending local vendor shows, reaching out to small shops, and refining her craft. After three years, she finally recouped her initial investment. Soon after, a small retailer agreed to carry her products. By 2024, her work was stocked in three retail shops, and she was teaching sold-out classes at the local art center.

Patricia's story is a testament to the power of small, consistent steps. Success didn't come overnight, but each small action compounded over time. She didn't wait for the perfect moment. She simply began, adjusting as she went. She has been a member of my Creative Powerhouse Society for many years, and I've had a front-row seat to her bravery and tenacity.

Her journey echoes the message of this chapter: Keep going, even when the road feels slow. Each step forward is still progress.

BUILD A LIFELINE OF COMMUNITY AND ACCOUNTABILITY

If you've ever told a friend about a goal and suddenly felt more committed to it, you've experienced the power of accountability. A study conducted by Gail Matthews at the Dominican University of California found that writing down goals increases the likelihood of achieving them by 42 percent. Sharing your creative journey—whether through social media, newsletters, or an accountability group—keeps you motivated and makes your progress more tangible.

Confession time: If you had asked me 15 years ago to give you advice on community and friendship, I would not have been the best resource. Because I was a lone wolf. People wanted to be there for me, but I just didn't know how to let them in or maintain long-term friendships. And I know I'm not alone in this. Many entrepreneurs and side hustlers fall into the same trap, believing they have to go it alone. Sometimes it's about control—feeling like no one else can do things *just right.* Other times, it's a form of self-protection. We downplay our efforts, keep things small, and don't let people in because if we fail, at least no one watches. If no one knows how much we're trying, then no one can judge if it doesn't work out.

Let's be honest—it's not easy to find a community of creatives openly *bragging* about their side hustles. Most of the artists we admire? They're full-time. Their success stories feel miles away from where we are. So where do you go when you're building something in the margins of your life? When you're trying to make it work between a day job, family, and the fear that maybe this won't be enough? Because if you don't find that space, if you don't seek out people who *get it,* isolation isn't just a possibility—it's inevitable. And that comes at a cost.

When I first started Gingiber, I thought I had to do everything alone. I didn't trust people. I was so self-reliant that I didn't seek community. I believed that no one could do it better than me, so I had to do it all myself. Let me tell you—it was lonely.

Then, something shifted. I stumbled upon a community, and it changed everything.

At this point, I had moved on from the coffee shop and was working at the local university. My husband was finishing his PhD, and soon, I thought, Arkansas would be a quick detour in the grand scheme of our lives. (Spoiler alert: As of the time of this writing, I'm still living in Arkansas.) Because of this, I had intentionally made zero effort to make friends, figuring I'd rather not get attached, only to have to eventually say good-bye.

I decided to try my hand at a local craft show, which is where I found Vanessa, a mosaic artist and vintage seller who just so happened to be set up next to me. She was warm, open, and encouraging. Before the craft show ended, she insisted I join her Thursday coffee group. My introverted self screamed, "*No!* Weekly meetings? With strangers?" I had been focused on *not* making friends.

Going to these meetings was the best decision I could have made. Thursday coffee became a lifeline—a space to share struggles, swap tips, and celebrate wins. Over time, these women became my sounding board and accountability partners. They reminded me to "be nice to our friend, Stacie" when I spiraled into self-doubt. They gave me courage when I needed it most. They became my community. And, because I surrounded myself with inquisitive, creative, deeply motivated women, I matured. And I started to find myself.

Building Community: Start Small

As a side hustler, you don't need to dedicate large amounts of time to community-building. You just need to start small. Vanessa taught me that just being present can be an entry point. Here's how you can do it too:

- **Start with one connection.** Try getting in touch with one person that you admire or feel connected with, however tenuously—why not even just on Instagram? Comment on something they've done; ask them a question; DM them to tell them about something you love about what they've done.
- **Set up a mini "Thursday Coffee" crowd.** Encourage one or two people to meet weekly (virtually or in person) for an informal check-in. Discuss your goals, wins, and challenges. Make it low-pressure and regular.

- **Find or build a community.** Look for local meetups, workshops, and online forums in your niche. If it does not exist, make one. A monthly Zoom call with like-minded creatives can work wonders. Looking back at it all, I can see how my community has been there for me at every step of my journey. When I was featured on *Good Morning America*, the Thursday Coffee Gals spread the word and told everyone and their mama to purchase tea towels.

They folded towels and assembled products for me while I was on bedrest, pregnant with my son, Dexter. They picked up my other kids from nursery school and watched them when Nathan and I traveled to a product trade show in New York City. They continue to cheer me on (and comment on every Instagram post), reminding me of my "why" when I've lost sight of it.

The right people will catch you when you can't catch yourself. They'll remind you of your victories when you remember only the defeats. And sometimes, they'll just come to your house, coffee in hand, and sit next to you while you cut out pillow fronts and simply listen to your processes, hopes, and frustrations of side hustling.

But community isn't just about receiving—it thrives when you give too. And giving doesn't have to be complicated. Share someone's new product launch on social media. Leave a thoughtful comment hyping up their work. Buy from a fellow artist when you can or refer them to an opportunity that might be a better fit for them than for you. Invite a creative friend to co-work over Zoom or meet up in person to sketch and brainstorm.

If you've learned something helpful, pass that knowledge along. Encouraging words, a quick tip, a shared resource—these small acts of generosity strengthen your network in ways that come back tenfold. Because when you invest in your community, you're not just helping others—you're creating a space where support flows freely, and that's the kind of community that will always have your back too. We are all stronger together.

EXERCISES FOR BUILDING YOUR CREATIVE COMMUNITY

Here are a handful of exercises you can use to cultivate and support your creative community:

- **Exercise 1—Who's in Your Corner?** List three people you admire or to whom you feel a connection. Connect with at least one this week—comment on their post, DM them, or e-mail them. Keep it simple and genuine.
- **Exercise 2—The Coffee Chat Experiment:** Arrange for a 15-minute virtual coffee chat with one person. Share about one victory, one challenge, and something you're looking forward to. Invite them to share too.
- **Exercise 3—Celebrate the Small Wins:** The next time you meet up with a creative friend or group, bring three small wins from the week to share. If it's sending a pitch e-mail or completing a doodle, celebrate them together. Watch how the energy shifts.
- **Exercise 4—Dream Together:** Find a creative colleague and take 10 minutes to discuss each other's wildest dreams. No restrictions, no judgments, simply encouragement.

Community is the lifeline of creativity, especially for side hustlers. It's not just about art or business; it's about connection, accountability, and having people who remind you to keep going when the road feels tough. Find your people. Be their cheerleader and let them be yours. (Tallness and gangly arms welcome.) Together, you'll go further than you ever could alone.

FIND YOUR HYPE RITUAL

Self-doubt is inevitable, despite all your preparation and good intentions. But here is what I have learned: You don't need to drown in it. And sometimes the best thing to shake it off isn't a lengthy journaling session or a heart-to-heart with your BFF. Sometimes, it's a song. A very specific song.

I have a ritual before I launch anything—a new product, a new course, or even just a licensing pitch e-mail. I dance and sing to my hype song: "I Believe in a Thing Called Love" by The Darkness. I turn it up as loud as my speakers will go. I bounce around like a wild woman. I belt out every word as loud as I can. It's not for the sake of looking cool (spoiler: I don't). It's shaking off the nerves, releasing that physical tension, and reentering my empowered body. It's a reset button with a killer falsetto. If one hit doesn't do it, I repeat. And if there's something I'm really unsure about, I play it on loop until the doubt gets smaller and my courage gets stronger.

Maybe The Darkness isn't your bag after all (although, if it isn't, I have questions). But I encourage you to develop your own hype ritual. Maybe it's dancing alone to Beyoncé in your kitchen, reading a power mantra aloud, or even hitting a power pose in front of a mirror. Anything that gets your blood pumping and reminds you of your inherent worth is valuable and something to be treasured.

Because the truth is this: Confidence is made by action. And when you are going to take action, sometimes you need a little ritual encouragement to get your mind right. This ritual is not about perfectionism. Some days, you'll hit them all out of the park. On other days, life will intervene. It's not perfection; it's consistency.

By showing up for yourself, you affirm your value and worth, no matter the outside results, and you create a container for your commitment to yourself—body, mind, and spirit—in any way you can to get you through the ups and downs of creating your art business. So, pick one ritual to try, get out your notebook, and begin where you are.

DO THE RIGHT WORK

We spoke earlier about focus, but without execution, focus isn't going to get you far. This is the work of doing the right work—that which distinguishes dreaming from doing. It's the difference between the artists who sell their artwork and the artists who have hundreds of paintings in their home that no one has ever laid eyes on.

I've witnessed far too many artists trying to skip over the unglamorous, ground-level work of building their business. They want to get into the fun, creative stuff—designing new products, coming up with fun ideas, rearranging the layout of their Instagram page. But as fun as those things are, they don't always affect the bottom line of your business.

The truth is that *the right work* is very boring. It's sending that pitch e-mail, updating your portfolio, or researching manufacturers. Sometimes it's talking to your accountant. It's the unglamorous things that prepare you for opportunities later on. If you want to license your art, then the right work is refining your pitch, working on your potential licensees, and sending sell sheets consistently.

When your goal is to write an art book, the right work may involve writing a book proposal, getting information about publishers, and networking with agents.

If you're working to increase your side hustle income, the right work might look like managing an online shop, marketing your products, or reaching out to potential wholesale clients.

Whenever artists tell me, "I haven't been able to license my art," my first question is, "When's the last time you sent a pitch e-mail?" Nine times out of ten, the answer is a sheepish *never* or *a long time ago*. They're not actively pursuing opportunities and instead are waiting for opportunities to come to them.

It's totally fair to admit that crafting pitch e-mails isn't half as fun as drafting new designs or browsing Pinterest for inspiration. But if you're serious about building a profitable, successful art business, it's work that has to get done.

Follow the "One Small Thing" Rule

When I'm feeling stuck or overwhelmed, I ask myself: What's one small thing I can do right now to help me move forward? It's sometimes as simple as e-mailing a client or reorganizing my workspace. Little steps lead to momentum, and momentum drives confidence.

When I started thinking seriously about licensing, I didn't have a presentable portfolio. I didn't know what I didn't know and had no idea where to even begin. So, I took one step: I sent a photo collage of my work to a company I was inspired by. That small action led to my first licensing deal, which led to more opportunities.

Stay Aligned with Your Goals

One of my favorite quotes is from Sir Isaac Newton: "My powers are ordinary. Application is my only key to success." Success does not require extraordinary talent or resources—all you need is a little effort, sustained over the long term.

Here's a helpful exercise to turn fear into action: Write down your top three goals, then for each goal, list three concrete actions you can take to move closer to achieving it. Finally, pick one action to tackle this week and put it on your calendar. By breaking down your big goals into smaller steps and committing them to specific timing, you transform abstract ambitions into actionable plans.

Action Steps for Doing the Right Work

- **Define your goal.** Be as specific as possible. Instead of "grow my business," try "make $500 this month from Etsy sales."
- **Identify key actions.** Break the goal into actionable steps.
- **Schedule the work.** Block time in your calendar for each step.
- **Track your progress.** Keep a simple list of tasks completed–it's motivating to see how far you've come!
- **Celebrate small wins.** Did you send that pitch e-mail? Treat yourself to a coffee. Little rewards keep you motivated.

The most accomplished artists I know didn't get where they are overnight. They turned up even when the work was boring or uncomfortable. They learned to delay gratification with their dreams. The effort you put in today might not pay off immediately, but over time, it will compound into opportunities and results you can't yet imagine.

So, the next time you're avoiding a task because it feels too small or too boring, remember that these, too, are the building blocks of your dream. It's not fun stuff, but that's the type of work that will be the bedrock for everything else.

GROW WHAT'S YOURS, WHEN IT'S TIME

When I started my business, there was another artist I knew who was getting so much bigger than me, when I was working just as hard. I didn't believe she was more talented than I was, but somehow, her story turned into a million-dollar business within six months. It drove me crazy.

Another artist I admired had a lovely storefront studio, and I thought, well, I have to have one too. These two facts burrowed deep into my brain, where they grew on a steady diet of jealousy and insecurity. Ultimately, they contributed to one of my biggest missteps and most valuable lessons: the Storefront Saga.

By all accounts, Gingiber was thriving in 2017. I'd landed features on Martha Stewart Online, was selling in Crate & Kids, and had a lively wholesale business. But I wanted more. Specifically, I wanted a storefront. Other artists I admired had them, and it seemed like the logical next step.

So, I leased a space, poured money into renovations, and spent months decorating it to perfection. But once it opened, I quickly realized something: I didn't actually *enjoy* running a storefront. *At all.* I love designing products and connecting with other artists, not sitting in a shop all day, wondering if anyone would walk through the door.

The financial strain was immense, and I closed the shop less than a year later. I felt like a complete failure, and at first, I didn't even want to tell my audience about the closure. But then I thought about how so many artists out there, just like I had done earlier in my career, base their goals on someone else's picture of social media perfection. So, I decided to be honest. This is what I wrote:

> *There is this constant struggle in my heart about what to share on social media & what to keep private. Things like business failures & financial struggles are not really par for the course here on IG. I share with you my victories, my fun collaborations, & all of the energizing parts of running this colorful business of mine. I've had many people tell me in the past few weeks that I present myself as incredibly confident, which is funny, as I have struggled with a distinct lack of self-confidence my entire life. And, I guess, when I project a certain safe, happy persona, it is hard to let the cracks show through.*
>
> *Truth be told, this has been the year that I have made more financial missteps than ever with Gingiber. I took many risks that didn't pay off. Many highs & lows. But, maybe the thing that I am most confident of is my ability to work hard, not just for my own self-preservation, but for family's well-being. These kids of mine remind me that when I'd rather be down licking my wounds, I have to pull myself up and find a new way forward.*
>
> *I closed my local retail shop last month and moved to a smaller studio. I couldn't stay in the building I was in, & all of the time I was spending at the shop meant I was away from these kids too much. I have fought the idea of feeling like a failure ever since. All the money I poured into the storefront. All the workshops I planned on hosting. The amazing holiday plans I had for the retail shop are gone. I didn't want to tell you all for a fear of embarrassment.*
>
> *But, I was reminded of what Joanna Gaines wrote on her Instagram account about how years ago she closed her own retail shop, mourned the loss of that dream, but today she has far more than she could have ever hoped for. So I'm not gonna stop hoping.*
>
> *Someday I will reopen the retail shop. Timing is important. Sometimes simply trying to push a door open because you want it open will only leave you feeling exhausted. So now what? Gingiber is still selling online. Our wholesale business is thriving, & I have so many licensing opportunities ahead of me. And, I'm doing every craft show possible this season. Because, I'm gonna work hard. It's what I do best.*

It felt like a failure at the time. The shame was real.

But even if it was painful, it also gave me what might have been the best lesson of my life: You can't rush alignment. You can't skip the foundational work and expect to flourish—just like you can't force a flower to bloom before it's ready.

For me, and for the artists I mentor, this is often the case. I've witnessed how acting too hastily—whether because of comparison, fear of missing out, or impatience—can cause burnout and regret. Comparison, as they say, is the thief of joy. And it's especially dangerous if we're only seeing other people's Instagram highlights and not the messy behind-the-scenes work it took to get there.

I remember scrolling through Instagram in those early days, jealous at an artist whose brand had somehow blown up overnight. Her million-dollar business had grown within a few months, while I was at my dining room table, attempting to sew pillow seams without jamming my machine. I'd think: *What is wrong with me? Why is it taking so long?*

Here's the thing about growth: It's very much like gardening. You can't force it or micromanage it. You don't dig up your seeds every day to check their progress. You tend, you trust, and you give it time to take root.

For the longest time, I was obsessed with other people's gardens. *And her hydrangeas are so much bigger than mine,* I'd think. Or: *Why does her lawn look like a magazine spread while mine is patchy and brown?*

Over time, however, I learned to ignore my neighbor's garden and turn to my own little patch of earth. I began asking myself: *What can I do today that will help me grow?* Maybe it was writing one pitch e-mail, sketching out a new design, or cleaning up my workspace. Little, steady actions nourished my business, like water and sunlight.

Here's what I didn't realize at the time: Aligned growth helps your roots go deeper. It buys you time to stake out what you truly desire—neglecting this is what led to my storefront snafu. Comparison is the enemy of happiness! Don't let the vanity metric of what looks good on Instagram fool you into eating crow in your business after trying to force growth when the time isn't yet right.

The truth is that we only ever see the end of someone else's process. We don't witness the entire struggle behind their achievements. Consider Martha Stewart, a model turned stockbroker and then caterer before her writing launched a series of books that finally resulted in her TV show. That was intentional growth that resulted in huge success.

We assume way too many times that if we don't get fast results, we must be doing something wrong. In my 16 years of running my art business, I often look back to see where my slow progress paved the road ahead. I'm so thankful that I've always had this mentality of excitement about the future. Just do your best to maintain enthusiasm (it's hard doing what you love, on top of your day job), and be ready to play the long game!

Now, I embrace aligned growth by savoring the small wins. I do a happy dance when I sell a product that's been collecting dust in my shop for months. When I hit "Send" on a pitch e-mail, I reward myself with a coffee break. Or I wait until I get home and open a special pint of ice cream, just for me, and slowly eat it. It reminds me to enjoy the journey and acknowledge how far I've come—even when I'm not yet where I want to be.

Melissa Charette Laganiere: Growth Is Growth

When Melissa Charette Laganiere picked up a dollar-store watercolor set in 2022, she had no idea that a simple creative experiment would change her life.

At the time, Melissa worked in marketing, spending most of her day on the computer. She craved something different, something tangible. On a whim, she began drawing in the evenings, sharing her work on Facebook. The response surprised her.

Encouraged by the small but enthusiastic reactions, she made a commitment to herself: She would paint every evening. At first, it was just a hobby. But after a year of steady practice, she made her first real investment—buying better supplies and ordering her first round of products to sell at a Christmas craft fair.

That show was a turning point. Customers responded to her work, and she realized she could turn this into something more. She took a business course, refined her branding, and steadily grew her art business over time.

Just two years later, her products were in eight boutiques, and she was participating in multiple trade shows a year. She still paints every evening and now dedicates one or two full days a week to her business—because she knows growth isn't about rushing, but about showing up consistently.

Melissa's journey is a powerful reminder that slow growth is good growth. You don't have to take huge leaps; small, daily actions will get you there.

PUTTING IT ALL TOGETHER

Take a deep breath. You've just done some serious work in the sunlight, and that's no small task. Your side hustle is not built on having all the answers at the start; it's built on doing the work that matters and trusting that each little step you take is taking you somewhere amazing.

You are planting seeds right now—whether that's designing your workspace, establishing a daily ritual, or cobbling together a portable toolkit—and those seeds will bloom in their own time. Not tomorrow, maybe, but someday in the future, you will look back and find much progress. And it will be well worth every minute.

This thing? It's *yours*. It really doesn't matter if someone else seems to be beating you to the finish line or if what they are doing seems a lot shinier. What really matters is that you're creating something to suit your life, your dreams, and your definition of success. And you're doing it the right way—mindfully, deliberately, with soul.

So now, as you go forward, remember these truths:

- **Prioritize the important work.** Your time is limited, so focus on the actions that will move you closer to your goals.
- **Pat yourself on the back.** That e-mail you sent? That five-minute doodle? Those are wins, and they deserve your happy dance.

- **Stay aligned.** Remember your affirmations, your vision board, and the people in your corner.
- **Trust the process.** Progress can feel slow or unspectacular, yet the actions compound over time. Keep putting one foot in front of the other.

You're not only creating a business, but you're also creating a life that reflects who you are and what you care about. You've got the tools. You've got the courage. And you've got this spark that nobody else can replicate.

So, take care of that portable toolkit, blast your hype song (maybe even join me in some Darkness-style falsetto), and take the next small step. Because sometimes the most powerful thing you can do is turn up the volume on your own voice and drown out the doubt.

13

MAKING YOUR SIDE HUSTLE WORK FOR YOU

Years ago, I drew a simple sheep. A black sheep, to be specific. Like you, I was just trying to create something—anything—in the scant few hours a week I had available to devote to my art. If I could somehow sell this piece and maybe pay off a bill or two? Even better.

I had no idea at the time, but that black sheep became so much more than a late-night sketch. It became a lesson that would change everything about how I run my creative business—and how I help other artists build theirs.

That sheep has had quite a journey. It started when my mentor Grace Kang looked at my work and asked a question that would shift my entire perspective: "Why create entirely new designs when you could leverage what you already have?"

She suggested taking that black sheep and creating thoughtful variations. A simple shift in ear position here, a change in expression there, different colors—suddenly one sheep became a collection. What started as a $20 single print could now be sold as a $60 trio, then adapted for greeting cards, tea towels, and other products.

One quiet evening's work, thoughtfully leveraged, blossomed into multiple income streams that are still active today, some 15 years later. That's a pretty good return on investment for one late-night drawing session.

Grace's question led me to the realization that I wasn't just creating art—I was building assets. Each piece could work harder, reach further, and create more opportunities than I'd ever imagined. And the best part was that this approach meant more income without more late nights at my dining room table.

Way back in Chapter 5, we learned about the S.T.A.R. Cycle for growing an art business using five hours a week. Now imagine those hours aren't just productive, but *superproductive*; every piece of art you create has the potential to spawn multiple new income streams.

For example, my Black Sheep design has generated income in multiple ways. It started as an original art print sold in my shop, then evolved into a greeting card design. From there, it became a repeating pattern for fabric, which was later used for pillows and tea towels. Eventually, the entire process of creating and leveraging that design became a teaching example in my workshops, demonstrating how a single piece of art can have a long and profitable life.

That's five income streams for one drawing—not bad for just a few hours on my tablet. This didn't happen because I worked five times harder, but because I learned to think in layers.

This is where your S.T.A.R. Cycle really starts to shine. After consistent practice chipping away at one of your art side hustle goals and seeing stable results in one income stream, you can begin to pivot. Instead of using your five weekly hours to constantly create new work, you're going to use them strategically to multiply what you already have.

Superproductivity does not mean grinding in every spare moment or chugging coffee to stay up all night working. It means using your effort wisely to increase the value it brings without encroaching on the rest of your life.

Over the years I've distilled my thoughts about superproductivity down to what I call the **Three Principles of Side Hustle Leverage**. These principles transformed not just my business but the businesses of countless other artists I've worked with. They aren't just theory; they're a practical framework that will help you build a sustainable creative business even if you only have five hours a week to spare.

- Principle #1: Leverage with Intention
- Principle #2: Build Predictable Income (Even When Life Isn't Predictable)
- Principle #3: Grow at Your Own Pace (Really!)

PRINCIPLE #1: LEVERAGE WITH INTENTION

Let me be clear: You do not have to do *everything*! The key is to find the right mix for you. Some artists start with licensing, then gradually add product sales as they understand their market better. Others begin with weekend workshops, using that steady income to fund their product development. I've seen several variations of this strategy work beautifully.

Some artists start with art licensing, earning royalties before expanding into their own product line. Others build a foundation through monthly teaching while gradually growing their passive product sales. Some mix seasonal market appearances with steady year-round licensing income, while others balance weekend workshops with ongoing royalties from past licenses.

There's no single path, just a mix of opportunities that can be tailored to fit your strengths and goals.

Action Step: Map Your Mix

List the income streams you're currently using (or interested in exploring). Circle the one that feels most aligned with your strengths right now. Then, list one to two complementary streams you might add later to support or grow your business with intention.

PRINCIPLE #2: BUILD PREDICTABLE INCOME (EVEN WHEN LIFE ISN'T PREDICTABLE)

Something I've learned about creative side hustles is that consistency beats quantity every time. When you're building around a day job and family life, you need income you can count on even during those weeks when your toddler gets the flu or your day job has you working late.

In the early days of Gingiber, I'd get so excited about a big holiday market that brought in $2,000—only to face the dreaded January slump when sales dried up completely. My income looked like a roller coaster, and I had the stress levels to match.

But then I started thinking about income differently. Instead of chasing big wins, I focused on creating small, steady streams that could flow together into something reliable. Think of it like building a garden: You don't want just one giant sunflower—you want a mix of plants that bloom throughout the seasons.

Here's what this might look like in practice: That woodland pattern you licensed brings in quarterly royalties. Your digital downloads sell while you sleep, providing passive income. That monthly workshop at the local art supply store creates a steady stream of weekend revenue. And the products you stock in three local boutiques? They generate regular reorder checks, adding another layer of consistency to your income.

Each stream might feel small at first—$50 here, $100 there—but together they create something magical: more predictable monthly income that grows steadily over time. The key is starting small and adding streams gradually as your confidence and capacity grow.

Leveraging your work across multiple income streams has another benefit almost by accident: demand for products will wax and wane, but in my experience, they tend to do so at different times. Spreading your eggs across multiple baskets means that when one stream has a low season, another is there to keep the business going. This helps to even out the dips in income, making your business more sustainable.

Action Step:
Plant Your First Seeds of Predictable Income

Even if you haven't made any money from your art yet, imagine what *steady* income could look like for you. Choose one idea that feels both doable and exciting–like setting up a digital download, offering a mini class, or pitching a design to a licensing platform. Write it down, and list one tiny next step you could take this week to move it forward. This is how you begin turning creativity into consistency.

PRINCIPLE #3: GROW AT YOUR OWN PACE (REALLY!)

When I started Gingiber, I felt immense pressure to grow quickly. Every other creative entrepreneur on Instagram seemed to be quitting their day job and "living the dream." I felt like I was falling behind because I still needed my regular paycheck.

With the benefit of hindsight, I know better now. Some of the most successful artists I know still have their day jobs—by choice! They've built sustainable creative businesses that complement their lives rather than consuming them. They're not "falling behind"; they're leveraging what I call "the side hustler's advantage." When you don't rely on your art for all your income, you gain the freedom to take creative risks without financial pressure, say no to opportunities that don't align with your vision, build genuine connections with your audience, and grow your business organically and sustainably.

Start small and grow slowly. Just like you wouldn't try to run a marathon without training, you shouldn't try to launch multiple income streams without building your entrepreneurial muscles first. I'm not preaching a get-rich-quick scheme—the next time I see one of those that works and can be replicated will be the first time. No, this method is about slow and steady and repeatable growth.

What I want for you is not just success, but sustainable success. The kind that lets you sleep at night, take weekends off when you need them, spend quality time with your family, and still build something meaningful that's all yours.

Action Step:
Define *Your* Version of Success

Write down what a successful art side hustle looks like for *you*—not for Instagram. Is it making your first $100? Having one product you're proud to sell? Spending five peaceful hours a week creating? Be honest and specific. Then circle one element from your list that you can start building toward this month, no hustle required.

OPPORTUNITY OVERLOAD: WHEN AND HOW TO SAY NO

I want to be very clear: Super productivity is not about instant growth. I learned this lesson the hard way. When I first discovered the power of multiple income streams, I tried to do everything at once. I wanted my art on every product, in every store. The result was entirely predictable: complete burnout.

In 2018, my business was booming—my art licensing deals were expanding, my products were selling, and I had just been invited to teach at a dream conference. It should have felt like success, right? Instead, I was drowning. My dining room table was covered in half-finished projects, my to-do lists seemed endless, and my inbox was overflowing with "amazing opportunities" I didn't have the capacity to take on but was increasingly anxious about declining. Rather than feeling accomplished, I was exhausted and wondering how I could possibly keep up. Maybe you've had a season like that too.

Here's what I wish someone had told me then: *You don't have to do everything at once.* I call this predicament *Opportunity Overload*, where you have more (paying!) projects than time. On paper this sounds great! The whole point of running an art business is to get contracts! But . . . is that really true?

Opportunity Overload isn't just about having too much to do—it also means you might be losing sight of what really matters to you. It's the creative equivalent of trying to eat everything at a buffet just because it's there. Sure, everything looks delicious, but your plate (and stomach) can only hold so much. Saying *yes* to everything is not sustainable and will eventually lead to burnout. (Ask me how I know!)

There's a twisted cruelty to burnout. When we work too hard, and care too much, for too long, it's usually because we want to maximize our productivity. But nothing destroys productivity like deep, sustained exhaustion. There's nothing to be gained by pushing yourself to that point, and everything to lose.

The good news is that burnout tends to announce its arrival in advance, and if we pay attention, we can take action to prevent it before it's too late. If you experience any of these warning signs, you might be on the verge of Opportunity Overload.

The Warning Signs of Burnout (Opportunity Overload)

- **The joy is gone.** Creating feels like a chore instead of a calling. You dread opening your e-mail every day, and your art practice has started to feel more like a prison than a passion. It becomes difficult to experience joy in your art because when something brings more pain than pleasure, our brains learn to avoid it.
- **The numbers don't add up.** You find yourself working twice as hard but making the same money and you can't remember the last time you checked your profit margins. Your income is spread too thin across too many projects.

If a business runs a deficit every month, it will eventually cease to exist. Similarly, you have an emotional and energy budget that needs to remain at least balanced in order to be sustainable.

- **The pressure is mounting.** You've started creating from a place of panic instead of purpose. Every social media post feels like life or death, and you've forgotten what it feels like to create for fun. Simple decisions feel overwhelming. You're constantly tired but can't sleep because your mind won't stop racing. The stress of work has started encroaching on your personal and family life.

Even knowing the warning signs in advance, I expect that you will hit this stage at some point. You almost have to go through it to learn from it. I warn artists about this so often, because when there is an opportunity, it is so hard to say no. I understand now that the root cause of Opportunity Overload tends to be fear. The Chaos Goblin sits on your shoulder whispering, *You have to say yes to this; you might never get this chance again!*

But you will pay for saying yes to too many things, in one way or another. And usually, it will not be at the expense of your business because you want the art side hustle to succeed, especially once people start paying attention to you online. No, what will suffer is your health and your relationships. Oh, the irony, because you probably started your art journey so that you would have more time for your self-care and to be with your loved ones.

However, until you are faced with the consequences of too much forward momentum, it's hard to truly understand the self-discipline required to keep your margins healthy. If it sounds like I know what I'm talking about, it's because I do.

The Wake-Up Call I Didn't See Coming

In 2013, I was on an upward trajectory. My illustration and product-based business had gained local recognition, and I had finally moved my studio out of our spare bedroom and into a real workspace—just 10 minutes from home. My husband had finally graduated with his PhD in mathematics. We had two healthy children.

And then came the dream moment: A local magazine wanted to feature me. A photoshoot and a full story about how I had turned my side hustle into a full-fledged career. I was ecstatic.

The shoot was scheduled, and I threw myself into preparation. Between fulfilling Gingiber orders, completing licensing jobs, and getting my house picture-perfect for the magazine spread, I barely had time to breathe.

Then, one morning, I felt a small pain in my side.

I brushed it off. There was too much to do. I spent the day moving furniture, lifting heavy wholesale orders into my van, running on pure adrenaline. But by the next morning, the pain had sharpened into something deeper—side-splitting, to the point where I couldn't stand upright. Still, I ignored it. I had to push through.

Then came the morning when the pain became unbearable. Nathan suggested I call my OBGYN, but I waved him off. *I don't have time for this,* I thought. *I have to hang the last of the art. I have to prepare for this shoot. This is my big moment.* He kissed me good-bye, told me he loved me, and left for work.

Minutes later, the pain crippled me. I couldn't walk. I couldn't lift my daughter. Then—I started bleeding.

Something was wrong.

I fumbled for my phone and called a friend who lived around the corner. *I need help. Can you drive me to the hospital?*

The next hours were a blur.

The doctors told me I was pregnant. But it wasn't just any pregnancy; it was an ectopic pregnancy, meaning the baby had implanted in my fallopian tube instead of my uterus. That bleeding? It was my tube rupturing.

I was lucky to be alive.

"If you had waited even another day," the doctor told me, "You would have bled out."

I had woken up that morning preparing for one of the biggest achievements of my career—ready to step into the spotlight. By the end of the day, I had lost what would have been my third child. A baby I never had a moment to celebrate.

And I went through it alone. Nathan was teaching classes, unreachable. By the time he checked his phone, I had already been admitted. He rushed to my side just as they gave me the medicine that saved my life.

I had pushed too hard. I had ignored the warning signs. I had been so afraid of missing my one shot at that magazine feature that I had put my own life at risk. It was a wake-up call.

And here's the thing—two weeks later, the magazine editor heard my story and rescheduled the shoot.

Because you don't get just one shot at a dream.

The S.T.A.R. Cycle is not just a framework for getting things done. It's a blueprint for ensuring that opportunities will keep coming back to you. They aren't like Halley's Comet, circling back to earth once in a lifetime—they're more like the Perseid meteor shower, streaming across the sky in bursts (plural) every year. If you miss it this time, you'll still have another chance. But forcing yourself to keep going when you're already breaking? That doesn't benefit your business, and it certainly doesn't benefit your life.

You have to believe that your dreams are not a one-time event. That they are not fragile. That opportunities will return. That pushing yourself over the edge isn't worth it, because there will always be more chances.

And when they come? You need—you *deserve*—to be here to see them.

THE ONLY ANTIDOTE TO SAY YES SYNDROME

After that experience, I had to face a hard truth: I was my own biggest risk factor. My inability to say no, my fear of missing opportunities, my belief that I had to do everything all at once—those things weren't just making me exhausted. They had nearly cost me everything.

Maybe you've felt this too. The pressure to keep going. To say yes because you should. To take on more, even when your plate is already overflowing. But when we're stretched too thin, when we refuse to slow down, we risk breaking in ways we can't always see until it's too late.

The only antidote I know to Say Yes Syndrome is—you guessed it—getting better at saying no.

Instead of trying to do everything at once, imagine building your creative business like you're making a layer cake. (Again, with the baking metaphors!) You need a solid foundation before adding the next layer. If you pile on too much too soon, the whole thing collapses. That's why I have a few strategies for staying grounded while growing.

Set Your Nonnegotiables First

What truly matters to you? What are the most important ways you can respect those priorities? Make these your nonnegotiables and guard them fiercely. This might mean blocking out family time in your calendar before anything else or protecting your creative hours like they're made of gold. And one thing I highly recommend for all artists? Schedule regular breaks. (Yes, actually schedule them.) Rest isn't a reward; it's a necessity.

When a new opportunity comes your way, ask yourself: Does this make me say *Hell Yeah!*? If it's just a *maybe* or an *I should*, it's a no. I learned this the hard way after saying yes to a licensing deal that looked good on paper but felt wrong in my gut. It was draining, uninspiring, and ultimately not worth my time. Trust your instincts; they're rarely wrong.

You do not need to be running at full speed 100 percent of the time. It's not worth pushing yourself to the point of burnout just to keep up. I encourage leaving gaps in your schedule for unexpected opportunities and building in buffer time between projects. Give yourself permission to work at 80 percent capacity instead of 100 percent—because when you're constantly maxed out, you have nothing left for the things that truly matter.

Before committing to a new opportunity, project, or income stream, I run it through a three-part filter to gauge whether it's worth my time:

The Smart Yes Filter

- **Strategic Fit.** Does this align with where I want to be in a year? In three years? Will this complement my existing work, or will it compete with it? Does it actually move me closer to my definition of success?

- **Time Reality Check.** Do I realistically have the energy and resources to do this well? Does it fit into my existing margins? (Be honest.) Is this sustainable with my current life commitments?
- **Energy Investment vs. Return.** Can I say yes to this without sacrificing something more important? Will this help me work smarter, or is it just keeping me busy? Could this energy be better spent improving something that's already working? Most importantly—does this excite me, or does it just sound good on paper?

If a project doesn't pass this filter, I must decline or postpone it.

Just because you *can* do something doesn't mean you *should*. In a marathon, your time and energy are your most precious resources. Protect them fiercely.

Action Step: Busy or Aligned?

Take 10 minutes to audit your current commitments. Make a list of the tasks, projects, or responsibilities taking up your time each week. For each one, ask yourself:

- Is this moving me closer to my bigger vision?
- Am I working smarter–or just staying busy?

Circle the aligned tasks, and place a star next to the ones you might need to pause, delegate, or let go of. Let this list guide your next steps.

THE POWER OF INTENTIONAL CHOICES

The idea that growth means having to say *no* is a little counterintuitive. What makes it work is keeping capacity to say *yes* to high-leverage projects that take concrete steps toward your big goals. Slowing down helps you get there faster.

Remember that Rome wasn't built in a day! When I first started mixing art business frameworks, I made sure each one was stable before adding another. I started with selected products made in small batches, well tested. Later I added licensing, focusing on that until I got six months of consistent royalties. Then I incorporated teaching only when I had systems in place for the other two.

I tell my students all the time that *slow growth is good growth*. Consider this your official permission slip to start small, grow slowly, and take breaks without guilt. You don't need to feel bad about saying no to "good" opportunities when you're saving that energy for great ones.

This isn't a race; you're not competing for the title of Best Artist. Build at a pace that feels sustainable for *your* life.

Creative businesses that succeed over the long term aren't built on relentless hustle and burnout. They're built on intentional choices, sustainable practices, and the courage to say "not right now" to opportunities that don't serve your bigger vision.

Layer these frameworks in a way that energizes rather than exhausts you. This will feed the artist squirrel within, knowing that at some point, no matter what, you will have the chance to shake things up. Knowing that there are always opportunities just around the corner means there is always something to look forward to.

Sometimes the best opportunity isn't a new one; it's maximizing what's already working. One of my students, Jessica, was about to launch a new product line when she realized her existing art prints could be licensed for greeting cards—doubling her income without adding to her workload. That's the kind of strategic thinking we're after.

I want you to write yourself a Slow Growth Permission Slip. Yes, really write it down on a piece of paper! Mine looks like this:

> *I, Stacie, give myself permission to start small and grow slowly, to learn from what doesn't work, to celebrate every victory, and to value my art enough to give it every chance to succeed.*

Visit **staciebloomfield.com/bookbonus** to download your printable Slow Growth Permission Slip—perfect for filling out, framing, and keeping your goals front and center.

Your creative future doesn't depend on you doing everything at once. It's far more valuable to take intentional steps that honor both your art and your life's realities. Remember what we learned about those precious five hours: They're enough when you use them wisely.

EPILOGUE

When I sat down to write this book, I wanted to create the art business blueprint I wish I'd had when I was starting out—not just about the mechanics of running an art business, but about the inner journey of becoming the person who could run that business.

Looking back through these chapters, I realize we've covered so much more than just how to make money from your art. We've explored how to transform yourself from someone who sometimes makes art into someone who can truly step into the role of and own the title of artist.

Remember where we started? That first chapter about the world not always being kind to artists, and how we must learn to be kinder to ourselves in response? That wasn't just about feeling better; it was building the foundation for everything that followed.

You've learned how to carve out time in the margins of life, how to choose your framework (passive, products, or teaching), and how to handle the practical aspects of running a business.

Now you have the tools to work strategically in those margins, to stretch a single piece of art into multiple income streams, and to build a business that supports both your creativity and your lifestyle. Whether you're sketching on the backs of receipts or dreaming of turning this side hustle into your full-time thing—you now have a blueprint. Not just theory, but real-world, battle-tested strategies from artists who started exactly where you are.

But here's what I want you to know as we close this journey together: **I don't have it all figured out**. Even now, years after starting Gingiber, there are days when I struggle to make time for my art. There are seasons when I feel like a hypocrite for writing this book while simultaneously wrestling with the very challenges I'm helping you navigate.

In fact, writing this book itself became an object lesson in everything I've tried to teach you. I pushed myself incredibly hard to meet deadlines, afraid of losing this opportunity if I asked for more time. I took on too much simultaneously. I stepped right into the trap I'm warning you about—trying to do too much at once without letting anything go.

And that's exactly the point.

The promise of this book was never about achieving some perfect artist's life in three years or generating a full-time income in just five hours a week. The promise was—and is—about learning to bootstrap a creative business even when you only have those few precious hours and continuing to show up for yourself and your art even when it gets hard. *Especially* when it gets hard.

It's like running with a kite, trying to maintain a steady stream of air while simultaneously wanting that kite to soar as high as possible. It is both keeping things moving and reaching new heights. Both sustainable and ambitious.

What each artist profiled in these pages has in common—me included—isn't that we've reached some magical state of artistic nirvana. It's that when the difficult moments came, whether we were fully prepared for them or not, **we kept going**. We chose to continue making art despite the inner critic, despite the naysayers, despite the exhaustion.

The truth is, it's always going to be easier to project an image of perfection on social media than it is to do the actual transformative work of building an art business. The person with the seemingly perfect Instagram life, frolicking in linen dresses through sunlit fields, probably isn't spending much time making art, packing shipments, or speaking with actual customers.

Real art businesses require real work. And the only people who ultimately succeed are those who make mistakes and keep going—who miss a day, or a week, or even a month, but get back up without self-loathing and simply continue where they left off.

So, as you close this book and continue on your own creative journey, I hope you'll carry this with you: You don't need to have everything figured out. Your art can be significant and profitable, even if the path isn't always clear or easy. You're closer to that reality than you probably realize.

There's a whole community of artists who've walked this path before you, making mistakes, learning, growing, and ultimately creating something beautiful that belongs only to them. Just as you're doing now.

This is the blueprint. Not for perfection, but for a journey worth taking.

Remember the permission slip exercise from the last chapter? I want to offer you one more:

> *I give myself permission to build an art business that honors both my creativity and my humanity, to invest in community, to balance my life, and to rest when I need it.*

But now you have something I wish I'd had when I started—a blueprint not just for making art that sells, but for becoming the kind of artist who can weather criticism, overcome obstacles, and still find joy in creation.

The world may not always be kind to artists. But you can be kind to yourself while still committing to the work. You can both rest when you need to and persist when it matters most.

And in those quiet early mornings, when doubt creeps in and those unkind voices start their chorus in your brain, you can remember that you're not alone. That kindness isn't weakness—it's the foundation that will sustain you through moments of uncertainty and long creative nights.

This is just the last page of the book—not the last step of your journey. You're just getting started.

Now go make your art. The world needs what only you can create.

SELECTED BIBLIOGRAPHY

Chapter 2

Lieberman, M. D., et al. "Putting Feelings into Words: Affect Labeling Disrupts Amygdala Activity in Response to Affective Stimuli." *Psychological Science* 18, no. 5 (May 2007): 421–428. https://doi.org/10.1111/j.1467-9280.2007.01916.x.

Matthews, Gail. "The Impact of Commitment, Accountability, and Written Goals on Goal Achievement." Dominican University of California faculty podium presentation for the 87th Convention of the Western Psychological Association (2007). https://scholar.dominican.edu/psychology-faculty-conference-presentations/3.

Chapter 4

Marshall, Lisa. "Your Brain on Imagination: It's a Lot Like the Real Thing, Study Shows." *CU Boulder Today*, December 6, 2018. https://www.colorado.edu/today/node/31511.

Reddan, M. C., Wager, T. D., and Schiller, D. "Attenuating Neural Threat Expression with Imagination." *Neuron* 100, no. 4 (2018): 994–1005.e4. https://doi.org/10.1016/j.neuron.2018.10.047.

Rhodes, Jonathan. "Using Science to 'Manifest' Success." *Psychology Today*, January 10, 2024. www.psychologytoday.com/us/blog/imagery-coaching/202401/using-science-to-manifest-success.

Chapter 5

Amabile, T., and Kramer, S. *The Progress Principle: Using Small Wins to Ignite Joy, Engagement, and Creativity at Work.* Boston, MA: Harvard Business Review Press, 2011.

Csikszentmihalyi, Mihaly. *Flow: The Psychology of Optimal Experience.* New York: Harper & Row, 1990.

"2023 Work Trend Index: Annual Report: Will AI Fix Work?" Microsoft. 2023. https://www.microsoft.com/en-us/worklab/work-trend-index/will-ai-fix-work.

"Global Social Media Statistics Research Summary," Smart Insights. 2025. https://www.smartinsights.com/social-media-marketing/social-media-strategy/new-global-social-media-research/.

Rubinstein, J. S., Meyer, D. E., and Evans, J. E. "Executive Control of Cognitive Processes in Task Switching." *Journal of Experimental Psychology: Human Perception and Performance* 27, no. 4 (2001): 763–797. https://doi.org/10.1037//0096-1523.27.4.763.

Pasteur, Louis. "Chance Favors the Prepared Mind." Lecture at the University of Lille, 1854.

Chapter 8

McNab, Shannon. Surface Design Industry Survey, 2024. https://sketchdesignrepeat.com/surface-design-industry-survey/.

Chapter 9

United States Copyright Office. "Copyright in General." Copyright.gov. 2003. https://www.copyright.gov/help/faq/faq-general.html.

Chapter 12

Holiday, R. "Tell Me Who You Spend Time With, and I Will Tell You Who You Are." *Medium*, December 9, 2017. https://ryanholiday.medium.com/tell-me-who-you-spend-time-with-and-i-will-tell-you-who-you-are-2b4865358e19.

ACKNOWLEDGMENTS

To **Nathan**, my first and most constant supporter, who believed in my dreams even when I couldn't see them clearly myself. Your encouragement made this journey possible, and your painstaking attention to detail saved my business more times than I care to admit. Though you've been an unofficial full-time employee at times, you've never been threatened by my ambition. You don't love me for what I accomplish. You simply love me. I treasure you.

To my children—**Violet**, **Lucy**, and **Dexter**—who've grown up watching their mom chase her creative dreams (and occasionally hide in the bathroom to answer e-mails). You are my daily inspiration to keep building something meaningful, stable, and secure. I can't wait to watch you forge your own beautiful paths in life.

To my big sister, **Angie**, who traded her own career to help make my dreams reality. You stepped into my world as my right hand at Gingiber, but you've always been my best friend (and forever puppy mentor). You're the only person I trust with both my deepest fears and wildest ambitions, celebrating every milestone as if it were your own. While I'm off drawing or leading courses, you're quietly architecting our product-based success, proving that sometimes the greatest visionaries work behind the scenes. Having you by my side has made this journey not just better, but possible. You're an unsung hero to Gingiber's success.

To my **dad**, **Dennis (Buzz)**, whose constant refrain of "You're a winner!" became the voice that drowns out self-doubt. Your words still echo when I need them most.

To my **mom, Pam**, who drove me three hours (both ways) each week when I was little just so I could learn how to draw portraits from a real dog portrait artist (and who never once suggested I get a "real job").

To my **mother-in-law, Lynn**, who bought nearly every product I made in those early craft show days. Your quiet encouragement and belief in my work gave me the confidence to keep going when I needed it most. Thank you for always being in my corner.

To my **stepmother, Donna**. I so appreciate how the first time you came to visit me with my dad and I was on bedrest, you jumped right in and offered to cook and clean and fold tea towels. Thank you for being so supportive.

To my **father-in-law, Conway**, who joined our family right after Violet was born, and chose to surprise me by purchasing me my first computer. You believed in me when there wasn't much proof that I could make it happen. I'm so lucky to have you all in my life.

To my **father-in-law, Ed**, thank you for setting up Gingiber's LLC back when I had no idea what I was doing (especially when it came to staying legal as a small business!). Your help in those early days meant the world. And thank you for always being so generous with us, especially during those uncertain years when our jobs were shaky and we had little ones at home. Your support gave us stability when we needed it most.

To **Hay House**, for championing this book and helping it find its home in the world. And to Allison Janice, the acquisitions editor who reached out after being a member of my Tea Towel Club—what are the odds?! Your belief in this project gave it wings, and I'm so grateful our paths crossed.

To **Lisa Cheng**, my editor at Hay House, thank you for helping me shape this book into something clear and focused. Your thoughtful feedback and guidance kept the project moving forward.

To every friend, student, and colleague who generously allowed me to share your stories in these pages: Thank you for trusting me. Your courage, creativity, and honesty are the heartbeat of this book.

And to **Mike Scholars**, who stepped in at the eleventh hour with clarity, kindness, and surgical precision to help edit this book—thank you. Your calm presence, insightful notes, and relentless focus on elevating every paragraph were exactly what I needed. Your edits were thoughtful, empowering, and always anchored in the heart of the message. This book is stronger because of you.

To my incredible product and education teams: While I disappeared into writing mode, you kept the wheels turning—and not just turning, but accelerating. You shipped orders, supported students, answered every question, and kept both sides of this business growing and thriving. Because of you, I was able to step away and pour myself into these pages without worry. You didn't just hold things together—you elevated them. I owe you more than thanks (and yes, still the best almond croissants in town—I haven't forgotten).

ABOUT THE AUTHOR

Stacie Bloomfield is a creative force—a loving mother, illustrator, entrepreneur, and educator with a lifelong passion for art and dogs (in that order—on most days). After earning her degree in graphic design from Drury University and managing a coffee shop for several years, she founded her illustration company, Gingiber, from her kitchen table. With an Etsy account and a leap-of-faith printer purchase, Gingiber was born.

What started as a small creative venture has grown into a thriving brand with a tight-knit team, hundreds of products ranging from stickers to tea towels, and a loyal customer base from around the world. In 2020, Stacie expanded her impact by launching her first online course, Leverage Your Art, sharing her creative business strategies that she used to build Gingiber, with thousands of students, many of whom have gone on to secure licensing deals and grow successful product-based businesses of their own.

Stacie lives in Arkansas with her three children, three dogs, and one very supportive husband. She's happiest sipping coffee with her close-knit group of friends (fondly known as the Coffee Gals) or wandering the streets of Edinburgh, her favorite city away from home.

staciebloomfield.com

NOTES

NOTES

NOTES

NOTES

NOTES

NOTES

NOTES

NOTES

Hay House Titles of Related Interest

THE SHIFT, the movie, starring Dr. Wayne W. Dyer
(available as an online streaming video)
www.hayhouse.com/the-shift-movie

HIGH PERFORMANCE HABITS: How Extraordinary People Become That Way by Brendon Burchard

LAUNCH (UPDATED & EXPANDED): How to Sell Almost Anything Online, Build a Business You Love, and Live the Life of Your Dreams by Jeff Walker

ONE BOX AT A TIME: How to Build and Grow a Thriving Subscription Box Business by Sarah Williams

PREDICTABLE PROFITS: Transform Your Business from One-Off Sales to Recurring Revenue with Memberships and Subscriptions by Stu McLaren

TWO WEEKS NOTICE: Find the Courage to Quit Your Job, Make More Money, Work Where You Want, and Change the World by Amy Porterfield

All of the above are available at your local bookstore or may be ordered by visiting:

Hay House USA: www.hayhouse.com®
Hay House Australia: www.hayhouse.com.au
Hay House UK: www.hayhouse.co.uk
Hay House India: www.hayhouse.co.in

All of the above are available at your local bookstore,
or may be ordered by contacting Hay House (see next page).

We hope you enjoyed this Hay House book. If you'd like to receive our online catalog featuring additional information on Hay House books and products, or if you'd like to find out more about the Hay Foundation, please contact:

HAY HOUSE

Hay House Publishers (India) Pvt Ltd
Muskaan Complex, Plot No. 3,
B-2, Vasant Kunj, New Delhi 110 070
Phone: +91 11 41761620
www.hayhouse.co.in

—

Published in the United States by:
Hay House LLC, P.O. Box 5100, Carlsbad, CA 92018-5100
(760) 31-7695 or (800) 654-5126
www.hayhouse.com® • www.hayfoundation.org

Published in Australia by:
Hay House Australia Publishing Pty Ltd
18/36 Ralph St., Alexandria NSW 2015
Phone: +61 (02) 9669 4299
www.hayhouse.com.au

Published in the United Kingdom by:
Hay House UK Ltd
1st Floor, Crawford Corner,
91–93 Baker Street, London W1U 6QQ
Phone: +44 (0)20 3927 7290
www.hayhouse.co.uk

—

CONNECT WITH

HAY HOUSE

ONLINE

hayhouse.co.in

@hayhouseindia

@hayhouseindia

@hayhouseindia

Join the conversation about latest products, events, exclusive offers, contests, giveaways and more.

'The gateways to wisdom and knowledge are always open.'

Louise Hay